Margit's STORY

An Autobiography by
Margit Meissner

To Kayla
with best wishes

Margit Meissner

May 2006

Margit's Story
By Margit Meissner

Published by Schreiber Publishing
Post Office Box 4193
Rockville, MD 20849 USA

First Printing

ISBN 1-887563-82-2

Library of Congress Control Number: 2003105401

Printed in the United States of America

CONTENTS

DEDICATION v

ACKNOWLEDGMENTS vii

PROLOGUE ix

INTRODUCTION xi

PART 1
PRIVILEGED CHILDHOOD

1. AUSTRIAN ORIGINS 3

2. LIFE IN PRAGUE 23

3. TURBULENT TIMES 53

PART 2
REFUGEE

4. PARIS AND BEYOND 85

5. ESCAPE 99

PART 3
A NEW LIFE

6. AMERICA 129

7. EUROPE AND BEVERLY HILLS AFTER THE WAR. 163

8. FOREIGN SERVICE 181

9. A NEW BEGINNING 205

10. BERKELEY AND PALO ALTO 225

11. ARGENTINA 241

PART 4
KALEIDOSCOPIC VIEW OF THE YEARS SINCE 1968

12. WHITE PLAINS 261

13. BETHESDA. 275

14. FRANK'S LAST YEARS AND DEATH 295

15. ANOTHER BEGINNING 303

EPILOGUE 317

DEDICATION

For my mother's great-grandchildren:

Jono, Rebecca, Deborah, Ben, Simon, Lia and Itai in Australia

*Chris, Mitch, Graham, Jenn, Laura, Clark, Nicholas, Sarah,
Stewart and Jamie in Canada*

Lynn and Rita in the U.S.

Xandro and Adrian in Spain

ACKNOWLEDGMENTS

I WOULD LIKE TO acknowledge the help I received while writing this book and thank a few individuals specifically. I am indebted to Bette Hanson, who used her fabled interviewing skills to get me to focus on the story of my life; to Sue Shoenberg, who, while editing my writing, insisted that I add details to make incidents come to life; to John Wykert, the childhood friend who knew my family and edited early chapters, adding important information on Vienna; and to my loyal friend and skilled editor Sally Carson, who read this manuscript twice and gave me precious advice and encouragement. A special thank you to Chuong Pham, who saved me from desperation and retrieved "unbacked-up" parts of this manuscript when lightning "fried" my computer. Friends and relatives too numerous to mention were willing to answer my SOS calls when I was not able to dominate my computer. I am especially grateful to Adam Singerman, John Diamond, Jonathan Engler, David Shinar and Ivan Ponomarev, who stood out among those willing to come to my rescue. I trust that without mentioning them by name, the family members and friends who kept urging me to complete this project know that I would not have been able to do it without their support. I thank them all.

With special gratitude to Jeffrey Kibler, Judy Gibson, Brenda Waugh, and Winslow Tuttle at The Magazine Group who designed and produced this book.

1

PROLOGUE

ON FEBRUARY 26, 1922, as the story of my birth goes, a stork flew high above the snow-covered Alps that surround the medieval city of Innsbruck, Austria, and delivered its special bundle to the home of Dr. Gottlieb Morawetz and his wife, Lilly. When the stork arrived, Lilly cried out, alarming her three young sons—Paul, Felix and Bruno—in the next room.

My brothers were unaware that a baby was coming. Such knowledge might have caused them to ask embarrassing questions. Sex was not discussed in our family; not then, nor later as we grew up. So when my father accounted for my mother's cries by telling his sons that "the stork bit Mummy in the leg and brought you a baby sister," Paul, age eight at the time, recalls that he was satisfied with Father's explanation.

My life began in Innsbruck as a result of my father's rising career in banking. He had been sent to Innsbruck, capital of the western province of Tyrol, in 1912 as the representative of the Oesterreichische Kreditanstalt, the most important bank of the Austro-Hungarian Empire. In December 1913 he married my Viennese mother, Lilly Tritsch, settling her in the modern and elegant city apartment at Claudiaplatz 4, where my brothers and I were born.

World War I began less than a year later. Despite the turbulent economic situation, my father was able to maintain a relatively affluent lifestyle for his young wife, who raised their three sons—and now a much-desired baby girl—with the help of a cook, a maid and a young governess.

Like every other aspect of her life, my mother had definite ideas about baby care. Just as she had done with my brothers, Lilly insisted on nursing me every four hours by the clock without picking me up between feedings. To train me to sleep though the night, she placed me in the room farthest from her bedroom and kept the doors closed so no one could hear my screams. Eventually I would go back to sleep, exhausted from crying, until it was time for the next feeding. My mother related that story with great pride, adding, "After six weeks, Margit learned to sleep through the night like a good girl."

Being a "good girl" and becoming resilient were lessons I learned early. Having been born into an affluent family and living a privileged life into my teens is part of what makes me who I am. These early years gave me the confidence to confront the hardships that followed and equipped me to make the most of the adventures that have defined my life.

Mother with Margit

(The "Cast of Characters" as depicted on page xii sorts out graphically both Mother's and Father's families mentioned in this book.)

INTRODUCTION

I HAVE TO THANK my children and my nieces and nephews for having urged me, then pleaded with me, to write our family's story. They nudged me for years about sorting out the boxes with family letters in the basement. Above all, they wanted me to organize and annotate the many photographs that cluttered my closet. I am now grateful for their insistence. Though writing this tome has been difficult, completing it has been a satisfying labor of love.

I had put the children's request on the back burner when both the Holocaust Museum and the Spielberg Foundation came to interview me for their archives. I hoped that these extensive audiotapes would satisfy the children. But they did not. The interviews covered only my early years and did not incorporate anything about the rest of the family nor did they include any photographs.

When I retired in 1992, both family and friends kept telling me that now was the time to devote myself to chronicling my life. Promising to try but initially not getting very far, I at least started to look through the boxes. I found that my mother had kept all the letters her children had sent her from the time of her arrival in the United States in 1940 until her death in 1981. A more surprising find was a batch of moving letters that my father had written to my mother during their engagement in 1913. I did not know they existed. In addition, the boxes contained revealing and saddening letters that my husband Frank's parents wrote to him starting in 1938, just after he left Czechoslovakia on a children's transport to Denmark. The letters continued until 1942, when his entire family was deported to Auschwitz, where they perished. Although finding these treasures awakened my interest in the past, I continued to procrastinate about starting to write my own story.

At about that time a serendipitous event turned the tide. Bette Lee Hanson, a television journalist friend from visits to Birmingham, Alabama, moved to Washington. At our first reunion she exclaimed, "You've had such an interesting life. I'd love to interview you!" She did not realize that I needed just such an inspiration to overcome my lethargy and begin the memoirs you are about to read.

Bette's extensive interviews, which I had transcribed, helped me to get started and form the basis of this book. I tried to answer her questions as completely and truthfully as I could. Often I looked for clues in the letters, but I could not find what I was seeking. Frequently I wished that my mother were still alive to answer questions about the past; I now longed for information that had never interested me previously.

I became fascinated by my lack of recollection of my emotions in my early childhood. If psychoanalytic theories deal with such a void, they have not influenced me, because I was not sufficiently interested to study them. Similarly, I was shocked that I recognized nothing when I returned eight years ago for the first time to the village in Southern France to which I escaped after the Germans entered Paris. Yet in my memory I clearly see the village square where the gendarmes led me to the police station. Though I have been in France frequently over the past fifty years, never once had I wanted to retrace my escape. Even if some buried pain blocks my ability to retrieve the feelings of these years, I have not let it stop me in making the most of the adventures that define my life.

You will find in this book the story of my eighty years of living in Europe, South America and the United States. Interwoven throughout are the lives of my peripatetic mother and my brothers: Paul in Australia and Israel, Felix in Spain and Bruno in Canada. You will meet my first husband, Otmar, my second husband, Frank, and my present companion, Ervin, who became important in my life in the last few years.

If readers find a lack of balance between the length of the account of my young years and my later years, the discrepancy is somewhat intentional. I believe that the family wanted me to write about my life mainly to tell them about their family background and about our escape from Europe during World War II. Originally, I was going to end this memoir in the 1940s.

However, when I reflected upon my whole life, I decided that the events of the last thirty years were as formative for me as the early years. Thus I decided to include them, albeit with brief and less detailed descriptions.

Although my recollections diverge sometimes from what I wrote to my mother, I opted to write here about what I remembered. Clearly, my memory may at times be unreliable, but it is real to me and I decided to stick with it. Readers are welcome to look through the original letters, which are still in boxes in the basement and now filed by date.

For some of the contextual background, I used much of what I know from various readings and from what I heard from people I met. I added bits of history beyond my own because I believe that for many of the younger readers, World War II is as ancient a history as the Persian Wars in the sixth century B.C. are to me. To understand my life's story, the readers must appreciate what political events shaped my universe. For those who are interested in more history, I will gladly point out an array of sources. Responding to questions and requests for further information would give me the pleasure of discussing this book with those for whom it was written.

Good reading!

Margit Meissner
Bethesda, Maryland
2002

Descendants of David Tritsch

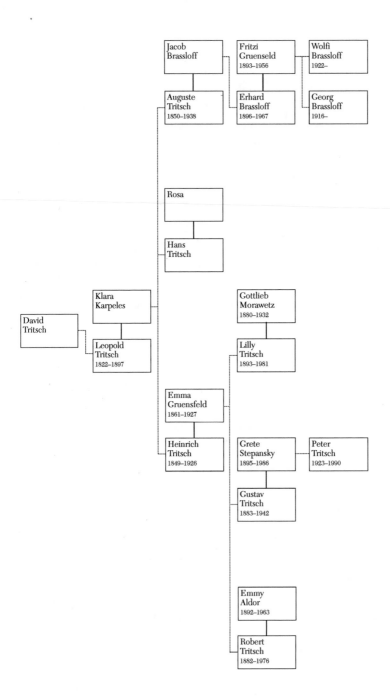

Descendants of Heinrich Gruensfeld

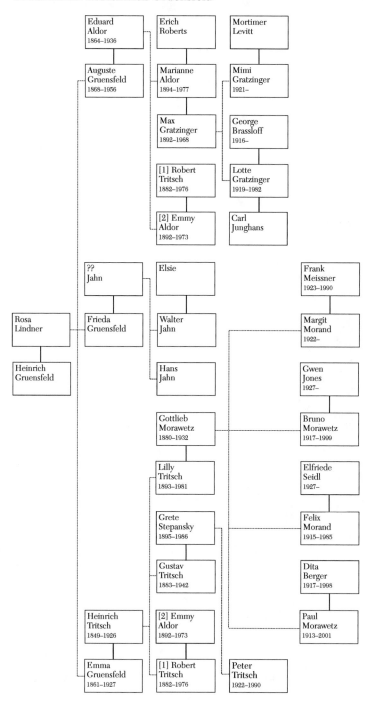

Descendants of Isaac Morawetz

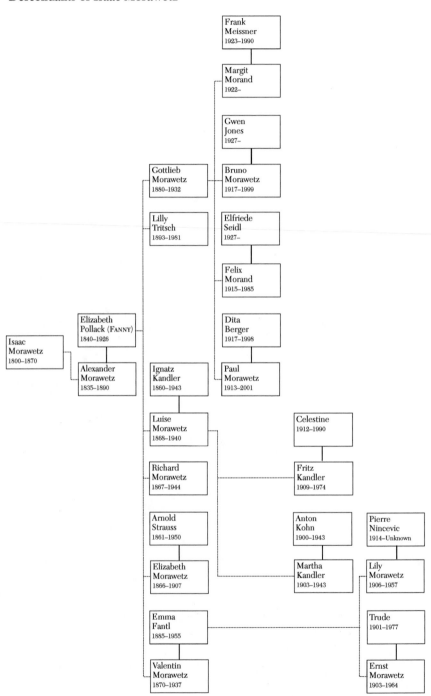

Descendants of Gottlieb Morawetz

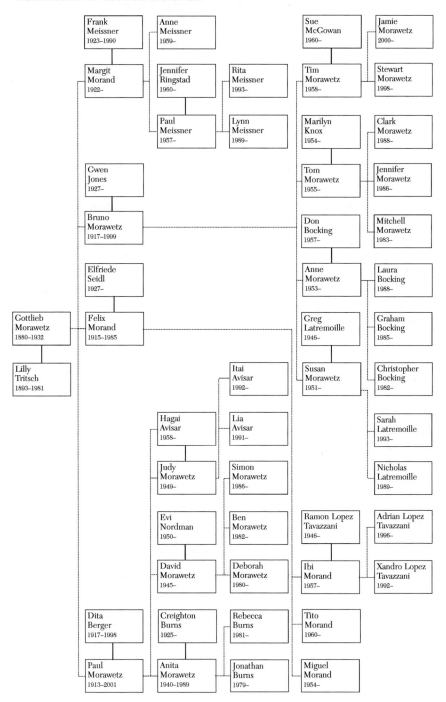

PART 1

PRIVILEGED CHILDHOOD

1

AUSTRIAN ORIGINS

My Father, Gottlieb Morawetz, and His Family

MY FATHER WAS born on May 3, 1880, in the small village of Dobrá Voda (Good Water) in southern Bohemia, then part of the Austro-Hungarian Empire. Gottlieb was the youngest by many years of Grandfather Alexander Morawetz's five children. Grandfather was a tenant farmer, a most unusual occupation for a Jew of that time. He died a few years after Gottlieb was born and left his wife, Fanny, barely able to support her children. Two of them, Elizabeth and Richard, immigrated to the United States in the 1890s. Louise married Ignatz Kandler and eventually moved to Moravia. Fanny sent 11-year-old Gottlieb to Vienna to live with his brother Valentin to continue his education. It was the custom to send young children away from home for further study when there was no high school in their native village.

If Gottlieb's early years in Vienna were lonely or if he felt alienated in that grand and demanding city, it must have been reassuring to share in the life of Valentin's family, which included Valentin's wife, Emma, and their two young children, Ernest and Lily. Gottlieb realized that he was privileged to be among the small number of village youths to have access to an education, but he also knew that he had to help support himself. A very good student, he was soon able to earn money by tutoring other boys in subjects required in the gymnasium, including Greek and Latin. The gym-

3

Vienna Before World War I

During his gymnasium years, just before the beginning of the 20th century, Gottlieb became aware of the Viennese social and cultural scene. Existing side by side with the flowering of the Viennese intellectual elite, the pomp of the empire with its ceremonial occasions inspired the citizens' loyalty. Titled families with historic names had their boxes at the opera, but their interest in that or the other arts frequently appeared superficial. The aristocracy-by-birth and the intellectual aristocracy rarely mixed in turn-of-the-century Vienna. The lives of the wealthy and landed aristocrats were inextricably bound to the imperial court and frequently revolved around their country estates. The upper bourgeoisie emulated them, preferring hunting and fishing to active participation in the tumultuous cultural life of Vienna. Behavior was carefully polite. French was the language of culture, and Britain set the standards for behavior and manners. Among the well-educated in Vienna, English and French were spoken interchangeably with the native German. Social status was rigidly fixed. Proper behavior and dress, acceptable manners and intellectual conversation helped open doors, allowing a young man such as Gottlieb to enter into educated society.

In Gottlieb's early-20th-century Vienna—before World War I put an end to the Austro-Hungarian Empire—men of genius initiated scientific, philosophical, artistic and political movements that would prove influential throughout the world. Modern thought departing from the past arose triumphantly here with Sigmund Freud and psychoanalysis, which proved to be a new way of contemplating human conduct and delving into the secrets of human motivation. New views of philosophy were expounded: Ludwig Wittgenstein, one of the most influential thinkers of the 20th century, contributed to the system of analytic and linguistic philosophy; Edmund Husserl posited that things did not exist independently unless they were constructed by the mind; and physicist-philosopher Ernst Mach developed the theory that sensations were the source of all knowledge. Adolf Loos, pioneer of the modern functional style in Europe, and Otto Wagner, leader of the Viennese architectural revival of the late 19th century, originated modern architecture. Robert Musil, who wrote about the disintegration of Austrian hierarchical society; Arthur Schnitzler, author of psychological dramas of contemporary Viennese life; and Franz Werfel, novelist, poet and dramatist who later became successful in the United States, created new literature. New music flowed from world-renowned composers: Arnold Schoenberg originated the 12-tone harmonic system; Gustav Mahler experimented with infusing folk music into composition; and Alban Berg made emotionally intense use of the 12-tone system and championed an intellectual approach to music. Visual artists such as Gustav Klimt, who painted landscapes and portraits with exotic and erotic sensibilities, and Oskar Kokoschka, best known for expressionist portraits and landscapes, invigorated the cultural scene. During that period, Hitler, Stalin and Trotsky spent time in Vienna developing their totalitarian ideas. Hitler later wrote: "Vienna gave me the harshest but also the most thorough education of my life. In that city I acquired a point of view, and a political approach which...has never left me."

Vienna was also the birthplace of another visionary, Theodor Herzl, father of Zionism, who characterized the city's importance in the following way: "In this city of Vienna one day I tore myself loose from the whole circle in which I lived, from all my friends and acquaintances, and, as a lonely man, devoted myself to that which I considered right." In 1896, Herzl published *Der Judenstaat* (The Jewish State), which would become the most important political document in the 2,000-year history of the Jewish Diaspora and eventually the blueprint for the state of Israel. Jewish Vienna was shocked and surprised by, but not supportive of, that revolutionary idea.

Viennese Jews contributed to the extraordinary cultural flowering well beyond their small number in the population. These cultural accomplishments did not occur in a vacuum; they coincided with ominous political undercurrents in which restive ethnic minorities—Czechs, Slovaks, Ruthenians, Hungarians, Bosnians and others—sought self-determination and national independence. Loyalty to the authority of the ancient emperor Franz Joseph kept these factions precariously together.

nasium curriculum was designed for boys who were hard-working and able students preparing to enter the university.

In addition to his native Czech and German as well as the Latin and Greek of his schooling, Gottlieb learned English, French and Italian. To these pursuits he added the study of law and economics at the prestigious Vienna University, from which he graduated in 1903 summa cum laude, then as now a great distinction. Extremely good-looking, he was fun-loving and always interested in "wine, women and song," but without neglecting his studies.

Upon graduation, the Oesterreichische Kreditanstalt recruited him. Early on, his superiors recognized his outstanding intellect and sent him first to Pola, then to Trieste—parts of Italy that then belonged to the Austro-Hungarian monarchy. In 1912 the bank offered him the important position in Innsbruck, which made him eligible as a suitor who would ask for my mother's hand.

My Mother, Lilly Tritsch, and Her Family

Mother's parents were Heinrich Tritsch and his wife, Emma, neé Gruensfeld. The Tritsch family originally came from Bohemia, where my grandfather's grandfather, David Tritsch, had been a restaurant owner in the Prague ghetto. David's son Leopold married Klara Karpeles from Hungary. Leopold and Klara went to the United States with the intention of settling there before Heinrich was born to them in Metuchen, New Jersey, in 1849. Because they did not like the United States, they returned to Austria when Heinrich was just a baby. Little is known about Klara's Hungarian background, although the Karpeles family was prominent in Vienna. "Portrait of Mrs. K.," a family portrait painted by Oskar Kokoschka, hangs in Washington's Hirshhorn Museum.

Emma's father, Samuel Gruensfeld, a wealthy merchant in Vienna, was married to Rosa Lindner from Hungary, who bore him seven children. Emma was the third, born in 1861. Mother remembered Grandmother Gruensfeld as an impeccably groomed, elegantly dressed, carefully coiffed, autocratic old lady. Heavy-set and paralyzed in old age, Grandmother had to be carried by attendants wherever she went in her spacious apartment. Emma insisted that little Lilly go along on her frequent visits to Grandmother Gruensfeld. Lilly hated those visits.

The Gruensfelds were austere and old-school, formal yet elegant, even stylish. Dressed in rich silk, with embroidered lace inserts in her fitted gowns and adorned by precious baubles, Grandmother Emma's pearl and diamond jewelry was indicative of her social status. The family's wealth gave them access to Vienna's cultural elite. Although their intellectual interests were limited, they knew who was writing and composing.

Like the families of their brothers and sisters, Heinrich and Emma Tritsch followed the rules of the upper bourgeoisie. They hired governesses to care for their children. The governesses who raised Mother and her two older brothers, Gustav and Robert, Grandmother's favorite child, monitored their behavior carefully so as to make it acceptable to adults. Children knew their place as clearly as servants knew theirs. Parents were not close to their children by today's standards; families of means and culture accepted such emotional remoteness as the norm. They loved their children but seldom included them in their lives.

As enormously wealthy assimilated Jews, Heinrich and Emma took their social cues from the Christian nobility. They rejected all forms of what they considered "Jewish" behavior. They accepted the anti-Semitic prejudices of the dominant culture and looked down on the Jews from the Eastern provinces, who dressed medieval-style in caftans, wore black hats and grew side curls. The more assimilated Jews viewed the visible Orthodox Jewish customs as an embarrassment. Further distancing themselves, some of the assimilated Jews even chose to baptize their children. My grandparents did not stray that far, although their boys neither were circumcised nor had bar mitzvahs.

Work and social life were intermingled for my Tritsch grandparents. Heinrich and Emma each followed their own interests; Heinrich's were fishing and his career, Emma's her social life. Heinrich was the director of an important sugar mill in southern Moravia, the headquarters of which were in Vienna, where his offices were located. With clients throughout Europe and beyond, Heinrich's position at the sugar mill enabled him to increase his international social and political connections while furthering the ambitions of the sugar refinery. In return for his effectiveness, his employers allowed him the leisure to pursue his avocation.

A handsome man, tall and muscular, always well-tailored and good company, Heinrich lived in the world of leisure of the haute bourgeoisie, where hunting and fishing were valued pastimes and men of well-honed sporting skills received admiration and rewards. Heinrich specialized in catching brook trout, and amateur fishermen from all over Europe, especially from England and Scotland, came to fish with him. An abbot of the famous Melk Monastery had bestowed on him the cherished right to fish in the Danube

River and its tributary, the Melk. To make the most of this right, Heinrich hired assistants throughout the year who kept track of the trout population. That he was a fishing partner of certain members of the royal family was also well-known. Such connections added to his prestige and his reputation throughout Europe.

According to a family friend, Heinrich Tritsch was much admired in Vienna for his close relationship to the reigning prince of Liechtenstein. The Liechtensteins had an enormous palace in Vienna, with a world-class collection of old masters that they later moved to the country of Liechtenstein. Friendship with them provided entree to the highest levels of European society. That Heinrich and the prince were friends was not so unusual, even in these virulently anti-Semitic circles. For generations, princely families had relied on Jewish bankers for financial guidance. If my grandfather was thought the prince's "house Jew," a trusted financial advisor, he was also a friend and frequent companion of the hunt. The following anecdote proves the social intimacy between these two men:

The prince and Heinrich had made a killing on the market and, to reward his friend for his good advice, the prince urged Heinrich to choose five paintings from his collection. Heinrich came home with paintings of trout jumping out of the water and enormous hunting scenes featuring frightened stags. Grandmother Emma was appalled. She made him take them all back and exchange them for some small Dutch and Austrian paintings. One of these handsome sketches, by the great Austrian painter Waldmueller, was still in my Uncle Robert's possession after World War II, when he sold it for a lot of money.

According to my mother, in addition to his fishing prowess, her father was also an experienced hunter. In the elegant family apartment, the antlers of bucks he had shot were proudly displayed on the walls. Guests and family were frequently treated to fish and venison supplied by Grandfather and expertly prepared by a well-trained cook. Mother adored her father; to her he was a *grand seigneur*, one of a rare breed that no longer exists. She never spoke this glowingly about her mother.

Emma was famous for the musical soirees she held in their well-appointed Viennese apartment. She also attended and gave regularly scheduled tea parties for her large circle of interesting friends. An invitation to the Tritsch afternoon tea or evening parties, often held at a fancy hotel, was highly coveted and something of a social prize.

I learned more about my grandmother from Mother's friends than from Mother herself. They spoke about Emma in glowing terms, saying that she was exceptionally elegant, very attractive, charming and witty. She also had the reputation of being a great matchmaker. Some of the offspring of these matches are still my good friends. While nobody of my mother's generation of friends is still alive, Grandmother's role in their lives has remained a bond in several of my friendships. One of Mother's lifelong friends adored Emma Tritsch, preferring her presence and wise counsel to that of her own mother. She admired Emma for her unruffled sophistication and for her social aplomb. Emma's parties had attracted the young and the interesting of both sexes.

This friend understood that Emma met all these nice young men by dropping a handkerchief whenever she spied someone "suitable." When the well-dressed young man retrieved the dropped item, Emma would smile her thanks, hand him her calling card, and then invite him to one of her hotel soirees. One could easily identify desirable guests in pre–World War I Vienna, assuming a great deal by their appearance, clothing and demeanor. These evening parties would come to an end when Heinrich arrived to escort his wife home. I heard that although they stayed firmly married, they mostly went their own ways. Or, as they sing in the operetta *Die Fledermaus* (The Bat), *chacun à son goût*. Such was the sophisticated *fin de siècle* Viennese way of life and love.

If no social obligation kept them in the city, Heinrich and Emma would visit their mountain cabin, where my grandfather kept his sporting gear. Before the advent of the motorcar, hiking was a national passion and popular in Austria, so my grandparents often took the special sport train early in the morning to go hiking, taking Lilly along. She loved these outings. Already, as a young child, Mother shared her parents' interest in individual sports. They regularly rode a tandem bicycle in the Vienna Prater, the large amusement park, and my grandmother was one of the first women tennis players in Vienna. The leisure to enjoy sports was a privilege of the upper classes. Vigorous sport was not something usually associated with Jewish life, and my grandparents' delight in the rigors of sports fit with their rejection of all things Jewish.

The relationship between Mother and her mother started out on the wrong foot. My grandmother had not expected another child, and Lilly's birth was an unwelcome surprise. Lilly's two brothers, Robert and Gustav, were ten and nine when Lilly was born. Both boys were sent to boarding school when mother was only a toddler, and they left Vienna for good in their late teens. In effect Mother grew up as an only child, with a governess but with little attention from her mother. Emma, a chic and socially active lady, seemed to have resented this little girl, whose presence may have interfered with her social life.

Little Lilly would be particularly unruly at home when guests arrived. Mischievous and high-spirited, she would hide under tables and pinch the legs of guests, whose squeals would gain her her mother's notice. Mother used to boast about how out-of-control she had been as a child. At the time, people did not understand the connection between this acting-out behavior and her need for attention. She was most likely a lonely child in a setting where children's feelings were neither taken into account nor supposed to be shown. Whatever positive attention she had received had come from her father, who clearly loved her. He spent time with Lilly when he was in Vienna instead of attending Emma's social events.

Despite her father's affection and all the accoutrements of class and wealth, I believe that Lilly grew up quite neglected. She never felt really loved or wanted, and the feeling of being neglected helped fashion her adult personality. To protect herself from this vulnerability, she developed a certain toughness that influenced the way she raised her own children and that she maintained until the end of her life. She became the equivalent of a sabra, the Israeli cactus that has become the symbol of the Israeli character: hard outside, soft inside. However, I am not sure that Mother would have appreciated that analogy given her lifelong ambivalence about being Jewish.

Mother in England and France

At age 15, Lilly's parents sent her to a boarding school in England. The environment of the Beachcourt School was austere and cold and meant to tame her. At the request of her oldest grandson, Paul's son David, she described her experiences there in a letter she wrote to him a year before her death. Portions of her letter follow with minor edits by me:

"...my parents saw fit to get me out of the house. I was sent with a lady to London, where she put me on the train to Newton-Abbott in Devonshire. I was met by the headmistress, who recognized me because I was wearing a sailor dress and a little white straw hat called a Girardi.

In England I encountered class differences for the first time. I was shocked to see that girls from my elite school who took dancing lessons were permitted to make up missed dancing lessons, whereas the daughters of the tradesmen were not permitted to do that.

From Devonshire, I moved to the Beechcourt School in Walmer, Kent. The school was located near the Downs, where one could hear the foghorns constantly. Many ships were wrecked there. My stay was very eventful. It was a small school with very good teachers, and learning was fairly individual. I was the only Jewish girl there. We had morning prayers every day and went to church every Sunday. I became very involved with the Anglican religion and wrote to my parents that I wanted to convert. Although they were not at all religious, they were the typical assimilated Jews of Vienna who never went to the synagogue or observed Jewish rituals, they refused my request. We had an excellent clergyman, whose sermons impressed me deeply. I felt moved by the church rituals and I believed that I had found a spiritual home that I didn't have in Vienna. That is why even now [at age 86, in 1979] I don't feel in the least Jewish, although I am very interested in all things Jewish.

To this day I am very grateful that my parents sent me there. At home I was a very spoiled brat, in England I was just a number. We had to get up at 6 every morning, take a cold dip in winter in the bathtub and in summer in the cold sea. It made us tough. Sports were very important. We played hockey, basketball and tennis. Every afternoon we were outdoors for two hours, in uniforms so that there was no distinction between the rich and the poor girls. After sports, with our outdoors shoes deposited in lockers, we dressed for dinner.

Our French mistress was also our sewing teacher. She was very demanding. If things weren't perfectly mended, she would put her finger through the mend so that we had to do it all over again. I learned the hard way, but it stood me in good stead, as later, when I had maids, I was able to teach them how to sew.

I only saw my parents once during the three years that I was away. They spent the summer with me in Folkstone. During other vacations I was invited by people in Cornwall, which was very beautiful, and in London.

After two years in England, I spent an outstanding year in France. I lived with Madame LeBreton in a little house in Bourg la Reine, twenty minutes outside of Paris. Madame was a widow who supported herself by taking in boarders. There I met my first Americans. Two American girls came to stay with us. For the first time I heard that people had cars and what the distances were. There were also English and Danish girls, but the most important person was Madame's older son, Didier. He was my first love. He was killed in the war.

In addition to the French lessons by Madame, I went to the local lycée and attended some classes at the Sorbonne. Madame knew a lot about art and took us to museums and on trips to Versailles and Chantilly. I got to know Paris well. We also went to the student performances at the Comédie Française and the Odeon theatres. I knew Paris so well I could have made an excellent tourist guide. We spent a few weeks during the summer in Normandie, and I was greatly impressed by the beauty of the landscape.

My mother was very ambitious for me. She wanted me to learn a lot of different things in addition to French. I took classes in embroidery and metal craft.

When it came time to leave, I was extremely sad. My heart had been in Paris. I took the famous Orient Express, which went from Paris to Istanbul, and my parents picked me up in Vienna.

Back in Vienna in 1912 I went to sewing classes, cooking school and language classes. At that time, girls from my bourgeois background were not meant to have a profession; they were trained to become efficient housewives.

My mother had a large circle of friends and had weekly open-house gatherings. There I met a number of interesting young men, lawyers, medical doctors, all highly interested in the cultural life of Vienna, the arts, music, opera. We went to lectures and avant-garde plays, and I had a gay time."

Even in later years, Mother commented frequently on how profoundly she had been changed by her stay in England and France. The more egalitarian political environment in both countries sharpened her distaste for the class distinctions in imperial Austria. The harshness of the English school taught her to put up with hardships without complaining. She considered learning self-control a lifelong asset. As her children were growing up, she remembered how valuable the English experience had been for her, and she primed them for becoming similarly resilient. She expected them to leave home at an early age and find their way on their own in a different and demanding world.

Engagement and Marriage

My mother met my father in the summer of 1913 after she returned from France. Lilly was 19 and Gottlieb was 32. With his good looks, charm and important position, Father was a very eligible bachelor. He was not like the other young men Mother had been seeing in Vienna, who were rich, fun-loving, aimless and decadent; he was more mature and serious. Significantly, he was able to support a family in the lifestyle the Tritsch family had imagined for their only daughter. For Gottlieb, as a lifelong friend of Mother's suggested, meeting Lilly was his good fortune. Lilly was perhaps more of a catch than her betrothed. With her attractive face and appealing personality, she could have had her pick among the Jewish men in their circle; she was cultivated and educated, lively and interested in everything. Even more important, she had a large dowry. In the pre-war days, it was customary for up-and-coming professionals to expect a dowry when they got married.

The couple's first meeting, prearranged by one of Mother's cousins, took place at the railroad station in Innsbruck. Lilly and her parents were traveling from Vienna to their summer fishing vacation in the Austrian Alps. Though no record exists of what Lilly and Gottlieb thought of one another at that encounter, they must have liked each other. After that meeting, Gottlieb visited the family every weekend in the mountains. By the end of the summer they were engaged and had set the wedding date for later that winter.

Gottlieb and Lilly were fortunate. Theirs turned out to be a love match. That came as a surprise to me. I had always thought that my parents had a strictly arranged marriage. I found out differently quite recently, when my sister-in-law Friedl in Spain discovered and sent me a batch of letters that my father had written to his fiancée. These precious letters likely survived because Mother gave them to Felix when he left Prague for the United States in 1936. I was amazed when I read the loving letters Father wrote to her, largely about the daily events of his life, each day during their short engagement. He addressed her as his "darling girl" and by other pet names, told her how much he loved her, and emphasized how eager he was to get married and start their life together. Though my father's letters were deeply affectionate, they were also stern and demanding. When he chided her for poor handwriting, he added, "But I am gratified to see that you are beginning to realize that I only want your best." If she did not do exactly as he had expected, he would scold her to do better. In a letter of December 2, three weeks before their wedding, he wrote:

13

"I have the fervent hope that we will understand each other. Unpleasantness could be avoided if you were willing, as I have asked you repeatedly, to rein in your youthful temperament. Your intentions are surely the best, but you must also keep a clear head and not be governed exclusively by the flashes of your youthful blood. Believe me, I am not asking too much of you. If you really care for me too, you can't possibly find it too difficult to accede to my wishes."

Reading these letters, I began to understand why Mother was never really at ease with my father and always feared his criticism.

After finding an apartment for them in Innsbruck, Father sought the advice of Emma, his future mother-in-law, before having it renovated. Together, and without always consulting Lilly, they ordered all the furniture and supervised the changes necessary to accommodate the anticipated lifestyle of the young couple. The dowry came in handy.

I found it interesting that Father never asked for Mother's opinion concerning the apartment. His main advisor and final arbiter in all decisions about furnishings was my grandmother! He treated Mother, the woman he intended to marry, as a girl who was not yet ready to make serious decisions. Lilly's mother and husband-to-be carefully groomed her for her role as a proper wife. I never heard Mother question this arrangement. If she had doubts or resentments about her life with him, she never expressed them. Hers was not to question his way of life.

Father's letters did not touch upon any religious issues, which may have emphasized differences between him and his fiancée. He must have known of the Tritsch family's negative views of Orthodox Jewry to which his own family belonged, views he did not share. When he moved to Vienna, he left his family's traditions behind and found his own way of living as a Jew in a secular environment. The wedding plans exemplified both parties' willingness to accept each other's customs. Out of respect for the religious sensitivities of Father's immediate family, the wedding ceremony, performed by a rabbi, took place in the anteroom of a local Viennese synagogue. A small wedding lunch at a kosher restaurant followed the service.

After the wedding, the couple went on an extended honeymoon to the French Riviera planned by my father. Mother described it in her letter to her grandson David:

"Our first stop was Beaulieu, at the time a very fashionable place, where my husband had arranged for a wonderful hotel. We had breakfast on the balcony, overlooking the Mediterranean, and tried out all the best restaurants. From there we went to Monte Carlo because my husband enjoyed the casino. There were many members of the Russian nobility there, and I admired the beauty and elegance of the women.

My husband set himself a limit as to what he could lose. The *jetons* at the casino were Louis d'Or gold coins. I can still vividly see the distorted faces of the gambler when they lost. There were many suicides, since people lost whole fortunes in one night."

When my parents arrived in Innsbruck after their honeymoon, they moved into the apartment set up by my grandmother. She had carefully organized the household so that the young bride could devote herself exclusively to the demands of her husband. Two servants, a cook and a parlor maid took care of the daily chores. At first Mother found it difficult to gain the respect of these older women servants, but as time went on she learned to manage her responsibilities. Wanting to have four children, she became happily pregnant almost immediately.

World War I

By the time Paul was born in November 1914, the world was undergoing profound changes. World War I had broken out in August 1914 after Archduke Franz Ferdinand, the Austrian kaiser's nephew, was assassinated in Sarajevo. Quickly the Austrians, supported by the Germans, declared war on Serbia. One week later the major European powers expanded the conflict, and suddenly most of Europe was at war: France, Britain and Russia, the Allies, on one side; Germany, Austria-Hungary and Turkey, the Central Powers, on the other. Believing that France was unprepared to fight, the Central Powers sent troop trains quickly to the French front. In Innsbruck, jubilant crowds were on hand to wave them off. With superior tanks and troops, the Austrians were convinced that the war would be short. Victory would be theirs with very few casualties. The Allies, however, put up a strong resistance, and soon the Austrian mood turned somber. The short war dragged on. Large numbers of Austrian men were drafted, and many were killed. As his work was considered essential to the war effort, my father was not drafted, but both my uncles were directly affected by the war.

Mother knew nothing of the wartime adventures of her brothers while she was having babies in Innsbruck. Father was thrilled with Paul, his first-born, but for some reason Mother was not as overjoyed as her husband. She resented the attention he showered on the new baby. Then she had to cope with the arrival 13 months later—and a month premature—of my second brother, Felix. He was born with severe health problems that required Mother's full attention. She described the anxiety of the time in the letter she wrote to David:

"It took Paul 24 hours to see the light of the world, and the cut that was performed hurt more than the whole delivery. Felix was born 13

Gustav and Robert Tritsch

Mother's younger brother, Gustav, called Gustl, served as an officer in the Austrian army. The Russians captured and held him in a prisoner-of-war camp. There he contracted a particularly virulent strain of syphilis for which there seemed to be no effective treatment. He carried the disease with him when he returned to Vienna after the war. Symptoms of the disease plagued him intermittently for the rest of his life.

Robert, Mother's older brother, spent the war in an internment camp in Australia. Robert's Australian adventure and subsequent acquisition of British citizenship enabled him to come to our rescue several times in later years.

A friend who knew Robert well shared what he knew about how Robert happened to go to Australia following boarding school in Austria. Around 1909, Heinrich, his father, had a long talk with Robert. He told his son that their world would not last and that war seemed imminent; he believed that great upheavals would follow and that Austria-Hungary would not long outlive the old emperor. Heinrich feared that under these changing circumstances, his position and his ability to retain his fortune would be uncertain and that his children might not end up with much money. Troubled by his son's poor record as a student, Heinrich suggested that Robert take his "inheritance" right away and use it to prepare himself for making a living. To get Robert the necessary business experience, Heinrich activated his worldwide contacts by arranging months later, in December 1915, one month premature. He came out buttocks first, didn't have any fingernails and his testicles had not descended. His head was far too big for his body and the doctor feared he would be a moron; he told my husband, who had to go back to the office preoccupied that he might have an abnormal child whose heartbeat could hardly be detected."

Alarmed, my father had nonetheless returned to his office soon after the delivery, leaving Mother alone with the fear of having had an abnormal baby. Even then, Father's work seemed to take precedence over his family.

apprentice jobs in Constantinople, Berlin, London, New York and, finally, in Sidney, Australia. He seemed to want his son to become an investment broker. But Robert had other ideas. When Robert returned to Vienna three years later, the Austrian government was interested in setting up trade relations with Australia. Few Austrians had worked in Australia, so with his experience there, it was not a great feat for Robert to be named Austrian consul in Sydney. Before leaving again for Sydney in 1913, he converted to Catholicism to hide his Jewish origins.

Back in Sydney, Robert quickly established himself as the Austrian trade consul. He also became a star polo player. At the start of the war in 1914, he was interned as a de facto enemy alien. Because of his polo skill, he was allowed out of the internment compound to continue to play on a local team. He was reasonably well-treated in detention and afterwards remembered mainly how bored he had been.

Before his repatriation after the end of the war, Robert managed the usually unattainable: his Australian teammates arranged for him to obtain British citizenship. Hurrah for polo! From then on, Robert was proudly British at a time when Great Britain ruled the world. With his impeccable British accent, new friends never suspected his Austrian origin. For as long as the group met, he faithfully attended the small yearly gathering of his fellow internees in Australia during World War I, an exclusive and slowly dwindling men's club. Robert greatly appreciated the formality of these occasions.

Mother became totally devoted to Felix and made no secret of preferring him to Paul, who was born cross-eyed and physically clumsy, traits mother found not to her liking. Felix charmed her with his long, blond curls and winning personality. My father clearly doted on his firstborn son, and though he was aware of Lilly's inability to nurture Paul, he did not interfere in the children's upbringing. I have always believed that it was Mother's early neglect of Paul that contributed to the turbulence of his childhood and adolescence.

Soon after Felix's birth, Mother was pregnant again. Even though she had said she wanted four children, I doubt that she would have chosen to have them so close together in age, especially during the war. Effective birth control did not exist, and I do not believe that my parents would have considered an abortion. Bruno arrived on March 30, 1917, when Paul was three and Felix was 16 months old. Though Father was extremely pleased with Bruno's birth, Mother apparently was very unhappy that the third child was again a boy. The stage was set for my longed-for arrival five years later.

The war years were years of severe shortages and great psychological upheaval throughout Europe. Even though my parents were well-off, money could not shield them from the ravages of war. Food was both scarce and rationed. Throughout her life, Mother was convinced that Felix was premature and sickly because she had not had enough to eat when she was pregnant with him. The rough war years in Innsbruck, when she had to care for three small children, were indelibly etched in Mother's mind. She told stories of how she would walk several miles after dusk to the farm of a doorman at the bank to ask for milk and then swear him to secrecy. Or she would walk deep into the countryside to get much-needed milk and butter from the local peasants. Mother was enterprising and quickly learned to bargain. She would dress in a large, full skirt with deep pockets where she could hide the vile-tasting bread—made of a little flour mixed with saccharin and sawdust—that she brought from the city. That was what she bartered for the indispensable milk and butter. Before filling her pockets for the long walk home, she would sweeten the deal by sitting down to eat with the country folks. She used this devious way to circumvent my father's refusal to buy on the black market. Food was strictly rationed, and if the left-leaning cook had seen the food Mother had brought home, she would have reported Mother to the local authorities. A possible arrest, or worse, could have caused terrible embarrassment for my father. With money most things that were available could be purchased, but the markets had little to offer—even for the privileged.

Life was easier in Vienna. Mother's parents had most of what they needed, and Father's relatives in rural Bohemia at least had enough food. Trying to get food parcels to Innsbruck would have been impossible, even if the relatives had been aware of the hardships facing my parents. Mother never told her relatives of her difficulty in caring for the children. Complaining about things that could not be fixed was not in her nature, especially since the relatives were not able to help. Mother saw her parents only once in the four years of war. Travel was hazardous; few trains for civilians ran, and those that did run were without heat and light.

When the war finally came to an end in November 1918, great misery spread throughout Austria. Innsbruck was occupied in succession by French, Italian and British troops, who raided available food supplies and left little for the local population. According to Mother, freed Russian prisoners—former enemies—roamed the streets, going from door to door begging for food. The local population would be enraged if anyone tried to help. Even after the occupying troops left, food was still in short supply. Mother told the story of an Austrian army officer who came to their rescue and gave them food in exchange for the privilege of eating meals with them.

Mother always felt that World War I held the worst experiences of her life. She often said that only those who had lived through it could understand the trauma. I feel certain that the war must have brought up other conflicting issues. After her long stays in England and France and in spite of her daily struggles to survive, Mother must have had divided loyalties during the war. My father, too, must have felt some ambivalence. He was keenly aware of his Jewishness, and I am sure that he would have been uneasy about the anti-Semitic nature of Austrian society. Also, as a native of southern Bohemia, an area that supported the efforts of Czech politicians in exile, he must have known that these exiles were mounting efforts to create an independent Czech republic. The chances of their succeeding would be greatly enhanced if Austria were to lose the war. Whatever solidarity my father felt with the Czechs, their independence movement must have touched him. His education had all been in German and he was a loyal subject of the Austro-Hungarian monarchy; but his understanding of the political situation would have told him that a new era had arrived, requiring a new orientation.

Following the collapse of the empire, my father's job now included the development of monetary relationships with the emerging countries and their new currencies. Mother was busy with the children and with trying to fashion a new normality in the changed conditions. Their situation changed even more when my father decided to accept a new position and move the family to Prague. The move from provincial Innsbruck to Prague, the cap-

After the War

Chaos followed the end of the war. England, France and the United States had defeated Germany as well as the Austro-Hungarian and Ottoman empires. Russia, originally an ally of the West, had undergone a violent revolution that overthrew the czar. The new rulers, the Communists, opted out of the war to build the Soviet Union and create a new world order. The armistice signed November 11, 1918, in Versailles sealed the fate of post-war Europe. The Allies carved up the once-proud empires and created several new countries, among them Czechoslovakia and Yugoslavia.

After Austria lost World War I, it became a tiny, truncated republic, with Vienna—the late monarchy's important capital—tucked in its eastern-most corner. Vienna became a large head on a small body. For Austria as well as for the newly independent countries, peace proved to be almost as hazardous as war.

Austria's defeat also intensified difficulties for the Jewish population. Before the turn of the century, a great number of Jews had moved to Vienna from the provinces to improve their economic conditions. In time they blended into their new environment. In contrast, the Jews who crowded into Vienna during and after the war did not adapt as easily. Having fled the pogroms of the Eastern territories as well as the advancing armies of the Russian czar, thousands of Eastern European Orthodox Jews sought the safety and relatively greater tolerance of Vienna. But once there, they competed for scarce food, housing and jobs. Many spoke German badly, some only Yiddish. Their dress and customs seemed strange and unfamiliar to

ital of a new state, required considerable adjustments and presented Mother with exciting challenges. I wish I had been able to learn more of the details about my parents' lives during that difficult post-war period.

the local population. Amid the grave post-war economic problems, all Jews, but especially the recent arrivals, soon became convenient targets for the increasing anti-Semitism.

Even assimilated Viennese Jews were ambivalent about these new arrivals. Some were embarrassed by the behavior of their "foreign" brethren. Others felt threatened in their own security, social standing and professional positions; they were unwilling to admit to themselves that anti-Semitism had been there before the sudden increased appearance of the *Ostjuden,* the Eastern Jews. The longer-established Jews continued to believe that their length of residence, their local familiar accent and their service to the nation would protect them from the more virulent strains of anti-Semitism.

Another factor that triggered increased anti-Semitism was the prominent role the Jews were playing in virtually every field of intellectual endeavor. While acknowledging that Vienna's cultural life owed much to Jewish writers, artists and musicians, many Austrians were grumbling about too much Jewish presence and influence in society. Many Austrians also grumbled about politics.

From the beginning of the republic in 1918, the new Austria was deeply divided politically. The Social Democratic Party with its interest in social justice and the Christian-Social Party with its focus on religion opposed each other bitterly. None of the politicians in power possessed the intellectual stature and the spirit of reconciliation that would have bridged the gap between these two hostile blocs.

2

LIFE IN PRAGUE

I WAS ONLY FIVE months old in 1922 when we moved from Innsbruck to Prague, the capital of the new Republic of Czechoslovakia. Father had been offered an important position at the Vienna home office of the Kreditanstalt. However, on the advice of Grandfather Tritsch, he accepted an equally good offer to become managing director of the new Ceská Banka Union, the Bohemian Union bank—or Boehmische Union Bank, as we called it in our customary German.

Father's decision remains an enigma to me. Why did he take the position in Prague when he might have had an excellent career in Vienna? I can only speculate that the volatile post-war politics in Austria had influenced him.

In contrast to Austria, Czechoslovakia was enjoying days of great hope. After 400 years of gradually increasing subjugation, the Czechs and Slovaks were intoxicated by their newfound independence and by a mood of heady aspirations. Unfortunately, these aspirations were tempered when at the Versailles peace conference the new republic was not created as a natural entity. The new country now consisted of three distinct units: Slovakia; Carpathian Russia; and the historical Crown Lands of Bohemia, Moravia and Silesia. Shaped like a boomerang, with very long borders, Czechoslovakia had 13 million inhabitants. Five million were non-Czech minorities, including Poles and Hungarians. There were 3.5 million Germans, most of whom lived in the border regions along the Sudeten mountains. The

Orthodox Jewish minority numbered 350,000 and lived mostly in Carparthian Russia. The makeup of the new country made its governance difficult.

As in Vienna, many of the assimilated Jews of Prague felt uneasy about the presence of the Eastern Jews, who settled there in large numbers after the Eastern province became part of the new state. Eager to belong to the mainstream, longtime Jewish residents resented the newcomers, whose appearance was ridiculed by the local population. The newly independent Czechs had their own prejudices. As could be expected, they harbored a great deal of animosity against anything Austrian or German, against devotees of the monarchy and against black marketers who grew rich on the profits of war. Bolsheviks, the Leninist communists, and German-speaking Jews also were suspect. The Czech intelligentsia saw Jews as natural allies of the hated former monarchy and mistrusted their commitment to the new state.

Many upper-class Jews chose to continue speaking German. German-speaking Jews financed the Prague German theater and the respected daily German-language newspaper, the *Prager Tagblatt*. German predominated in Prague cafes frequented by Jews. Hearing German spoken rankled the Czechs, who, after 300 years of virtual exile in their own country, were trying to eradicate any German influence while re-establishing their own roots. Many of the German-speaking Jews underestimated the stubborn competition for linguistic and cultural control of Prague.

Fortunately, between the masses and their desire for revenge stood the powerful figure of Tomáš Garrigue Masaryk, the first president and patriarchal head of the new, multinational Czechoslovak Republic. All the ethnic groups in the republic admired the tall, aristocratic, white-goateed 68-year-old professor. Widely held in high esteem, his many special qualities included his realistic humanism, his faith in justice and the triumph of truth, his belief that citizens must strive toward self-improvement and assume social responsibility, and his concept of democracy with the inherent right to differ. I like to believe that one of the reasons why my father chose to go to Prague instead of Vienna was because Masaryk's cause had inspired him to want to ally with the potential of the new republic.

Insufficient political strength unfortunately did not allow Masaryk to realize his goals. He strove to help minority communities become autonomous in matters of religion, culture, education and welfare. But he lacked the necessary support of the middle classes. Without it, his policies fell short of their goal. Most of the middle class was conservative; they did not want their world to change. They wanted life to remain comfortably the same, their children well-educated, well-married and well-fed; they liked being able to sit in cafes talking with their friends or visiting the theater occasionally. When Masaryk died in 1937, he left the country in the less capable hands of his Socialist deputy, Edvard Beneš.

For Mother as well as Father, the move to Prague was a milestone. She was leaving a provincial town in Austria for the capital of a new and vibrant state. When we first arrived in Prague, we lived in an apartment while waiting for the completion of the house that the bank proposed to build for the family. The bank had offered Mother the opportunity to specify the interior design of the imposing structure. Mother worked with the architect to design not only a comfortable family home but one well-suited to the new and extensive social obligations that came with my father's position in the banking and business community.

My first memories are associated with that big house, which the family referred to as "the villa." The house had four floors. The main floor combined reception rooms and the kitchen wing. The second floor featured family living quarters and bedrooms, while the third floor held guest rooms and a gymnasium. Rooms for most of the help and the laundry were in the basement.

Unlike most of the homes of the wealthy, the imposing house was not located in one of the residential suburbs. Atop the capital's main railroad station and close to the city center, our house had a panoramic view of the city. From the gate to the house, a cement walk lined with rose bushes led to the main entrance. That entrance was reserved for guests. The family entered through the kitchen wing, which included a very large kitchen where a cook and a kitchen helper produced the family meals. Our food arrived upstairs in the family dining room via dumbwaiter.

The main entrance doors opened onto a shining, white, marble-floored foyer with a garderobe, a walk-in closet where the maids hung the guests' overcoats. One of the great and forbidden diversions for us as children was to sneak into the coat closets during receptions and try to guess who owned the expensive fur coats and wraps.

Off the foyer were reception rooms furnished with antiques bought in Vienna. A large, elegant hall that doubled as a music room was covered by rare Persian carpets and furnished with heavy, richly carved antique chests and a Boesendorfer grand piano used for home recitals. The bronze reliefs of sitting figures on the wall were the work of a famous Austrian artist. At one end of the music room, a red-carpeted staircase led upstairs to the family living quarters. Although it was strictly forbidden, I used to sit at the top of the stairs trying to get a glimpse of the grown-ups when my parents entertained. I still remember the awe I felt when I peeked down the staircase.

On one side of the music room was the formal dining room with a table that seated 24 when fully extended. The chairs were covered with maroon velvet that matched the drapes. A built-in glass cupboard held the "good" china used on special occasions. The silver tea and coffee sets and the many silver trays and serving bowls were stored in a huge sideboard. Since I was never included in adult dinners, I never knew the full extent of Mother's silver collection.

On the other side of the music room was a formal *Rauchzimmer*, a smoking room to which the men retired after dinner to smoke their cigars. The wall bookcases contained beautifully bound leather classics in several languages, richly illustrated art books as well as numerous volumes of modern fiction. The walls were lined in purple velvet. The furniture was green velvet, and the table was covered with a richly embroidered tapestry-like table cover with green fringe. The paintings that adorned the walls were by renowned artists.

When I first returned to Prague after World War II, I found that the house had become the training center for the young Communist elite. I was amused that the purple velvet wall cover and the sideboard were still there. The sideboard was too big to be moved out through the doors, so the Nazis just left it there, although they stole everything else. The Communists did not move it either.

Coming up the red-carpeted stairs to the second floor, one entered a large hall, richly furnished with Biedermeier period furniture, leading to our rather formal family dining room.

Off to one side of the hall was my parents' bedroom. Their furniture was custom-made light oak, hand-carved and hand-painted. The bed was covered with a light-colored embroidered silk spread. We were forbidden to sit on or place anything on top of the bed. So that Father, too, could avoid disturbing the carefully covered bed, he took his nap after lunch every day on a corner sofa with a specially designated day blanket. The "children's room" was next to my parents' bedroom. Bruno, my governess and I shared that very large room.

Off another end of the hall, the living room for the children had an upright piano on which the children practiced. We regularly ate dinner there with Yeya and whoever was looking after Paul and Felix, but never with our parents. Either they were out or they had guests. Beyond the living room were two bathrooms and five or six bedrooms, including Paul's and Felix's and their mentors'.

On the third floor, the extensive gymnasium that Mother had insisted on held Swedish wall equipment, horses, rings and parallel bars that we used. Her English boarding school days had convinced her that physical exercise was an indispensable part of a child's development, a rather revolutionary concept at the time. We had regularly scheduled gymnastics lessons taught by a qualified instructor who came to give lessons to me and other little girls, to my brothers and their age-mates as well as to Mother and her friends. I used to watch the ladies doing calisthenics with great interest, feeling privileged just to be near them. Also on the third floor, the maids had their quarters, next to elegant guest rooms for visiting family and famous musicians whom Mother liked to invite when they visited Prague.

In the basement, the butler, whose wife was the family seamstress, used one apartment. The housekeeper, who oversaw the smooth functioning of the house while her husband did odd jobs, used the other one. The chauffeur, who spent most of his down time waiting in the kitchen, did not live on the premises. The wine cellar, the size of a walk-in closet, was next to the laundry, which held two big tubs, a sink, two large tables for sorting and a mangle to iron sheets. The woman who came to iron every week worked in a specially designated ironing room near the laundry.

The house was basically my world, and I became fully aware of what it took to run such an organization in a dusty city with coal used for all heating purposes. Our house, situated just above the Prague railroad station, was always sooty from the coal-powered trains going by. The maids were constantly dusting the furniture, especially the windowsills. Keeping the house and the laundry clean was a complicated procedure. The customary "airing out" of the bedding every morning took considerable effort; the process required first lining the windowsills with protective sheets and then spreading the sheets and comforters on the sills. If soot from the windowsills got onto the sheets, they would have to be laundered before the normal washing cycle. I was in awe of the laundresses who came every other week to do the family wash. Washing sheets was a major job, with the laundresses heating water in huge kettles in the basement. They used washboards to scrub the linens and then carried them, wet and heavy, up to the attic to dry. The kitchen staff prepared special food for laundry days, more substantial dishes suitable for people performing heavy physical labor.

Eager to minimize the need for washing, Mother constantly admonished us not to get our clothes dirty, not to make spots when eating and not to create more laundry. Despite our family's affluence, the maids only infrequently changed the bed linens; Mother was mindful of the immense physical effort needed to do our laundry.

Mother was fully occupied supervising the staff, including those who cared for the children. She had the reputation of being a good employer who treated her help fairly and compassionately. Planning the extensive social life my father's position demanded took up much of her time. She was becoming a gracious and knowledgeable hostess, determined to satisfy Father's high standards. From remarks she made in later life, she apparently was afraid of Father's judgment and frequently worried that her way of running the house or entertaining would somehow displease him. His penchant for criticizing Mother started before they were married, as expressed in his letters to her during their engagement. Mother learned to accept her resulting apprehensiveness early in her marriage.

When talking about her marriage, Mother said that she saw herself as the wife who pleased her husband; she subordinated the children and the role of parenting to that of perfect wife. Putting her husband in first place struck me as odd, but considering the complexity of the household and her extensive social obligations, how Mother managed her life and her relationship to her children has become more plausible.

In other ways she was always a free spirit, at times breaking loose from the constraining mold of her social position. Although customary among the ladies whom she invited to tea, the traditional gossip about the help and the children did not interest Mother. She sought out struggling artists whose careers she was in a position to further by giving them money and by connecting them with potential patrons among her acquaintances. In appreciation, the artists invited her into their intellectual circles, adding to her stimulating cultural education. Her interest in people and her eagerness to learn remained lifelong characteristics.

Under Yeya's Wing

My governess, Yeya, with whom Bruno and I shared a very large room, managed my world. Bruno, who was five years older than I, had started school by the time we moved into the big house. I had little contact with my two older brothers, Paul and Felix. They lived in a different part of the house, had their own activities and were supervised by a live-in tutor. Yeya I remember as an old lady who wore long, dark skirts and an apron, her hair on top of her head in a bun. She probably was not old at all. A spinster who moved to Prague from a small town in the Sudentenland, the German-speaking part of Czechoslovakia, she fitted right into our German-speaking family. We learned Czech from the maids. Yeya must have been intelligent; otherwise, Mother would have not entrusted her two younger children to her. She was very kind and loving and had a hairy face that I liked to stroke.

I remember one special incident when Yeya appealed to Mother for permission to discipline me. Bruno, a chubby little boy with tousled dark hair who was usually in short pants and knee socks, was sitting at a student desk in one corner of our spacious room doing his homework. He had the habit of putting his head to one side and directly onto his work, probably because he could not see well, though nobody realized that. To improve his posture, Mother had gotten him a restraint that he was obliged to put on, something like garters to keep his head upright and away from the page. Yeya, who usually supervised him when he did homework, left the room one time and I saw him putting his head down again. I admonished him, but he paid no attention to me. So I went over to the desk and tried to pull his head up with my teeth, biting into the nape of his neck. I drew blood and there was a great to-do. Yeya spanked me! It is the only time I remember being spanked.

Bruno was in trouble more frequently, primarily about picky eating. He hated the porridge that was supposed to be healthy and that we frequently had for dinner. Because lunch was the main meal of three courses, the evening meal for the children was light. We were always expected to finish what was on our plate. Yeya usually dished out Bruno's portion, but he refused to eat it. Whenever Yeya lost her patience and took the dish away, she would bring it back the next morning for breakfast as punishment instead of serving the customary rolls with butter and jam. That a child might not be cowed by an adult was totally unthinkable!

I did not see much of Mother, who felt she could spend her time on her wifely duties and her cultural activities so long as she had competent help and was there to supervise when necessary. I hardly ever saw Father. Sometimes I was permitted to keep him company at breakfast, which was served in the glassed-in alcove of our upstairs dining room. As a special treat I was allowed to scrape out the pan in which the butler served him scrambled eggs. Father liked to eat the eggs out of the pan, a great deviation from the usual formally served meals. At other times Father would call me to keep him company when he was getting dressed. He let me sit on the unmade bed and put the cufflinks into his shirt. I felt greatly honored and was proud when I accomplished that difficult task. Such were the rare but warm and loving moments with my father. I hardly remember him, since he did not play an active role in my life such as fathers do today, reading or playing with their children.

He loved to kiss me with big, wet smooches that I hated. The boys imitated him and used to negotiate with me for kisses. Bruno especially wanted to give me the wettest, most disgusting kisses. When I fought him, he would hit my upper arm with his knuckles so that I seemed to have a permanent black-and-blue spot there. I despised Bruno's cruelty, but I got little sympathy from anybody about it. My antipathy toward kisses persisted into adolescence. I did not want to be kissed by any boy for a long time.

Everybody used to call me "Puppe," German for "dolly," because I was cute. I found it distressing. I wanted to be big and a boy; Puppe meant that I was little and a girl. I wanted to be taken seriously, not seen as a toy. Being the youngest was an ordeal.

My only playmate before starting school was Anička, the valet's daughter, who was about my age and lived in the basement. We sometimes played hopscotch in the garden and took my dolls for an outing. Mostly I see myself in the park near our house walking with Yeya on the manicured paths, with Yeya holding my white-gloved hands so that I would not get dirty. I still associate playing in the sand only with the beach.

Paul's Troubles

Even as a young child I knew that I had to respect and admire Father. Yet some less pleasant memories stayed with me. I must have been about four years old when I saw Father meting out punishment to Paul. Paul had to kneel for a long time in the big, elegant front hall, where everybody could see him, as penalty for some crime that Mother had reported to Father. Another time I remember seeing Father strike Paul with his riding crop. Paul was crying and I was terrified. Of course I did not know that Paul had been sent away when he was eight to be "reformed" in the home of Dr. Pohl, a country teacher in northern Bohemia. Paul stayed there for 12 months. The banishment came about because Mother was so exasperated with him that she threatened Father by saying, "Either Paul goes or I go." Apparently he was not sufficiently reformed during that year.

According to Paul's biography, *What a Life*, he and Felix had climbed onto one of the second-story balconies of the house to drill peepholes in the jalousies, the wooden blinds of the maids' rooms. They wanted to peek at the women as they undressed. Father accidentally found them on the second-story ledge and was aghast at the dangerous position they were in. Whenever the boys did something wrong, Paul seemed to be the one who got punished.

Much later when Bruno and I talked about this incident, Bruno, who had been old enough to understand what was going on, said that Father was always fair. Even though it hurt, Bruno recalls that he was willing to accept the pain of his rare punishment when he felt that he deserved it. When the boys were chastised for a minor crime, Father would ask the culprit to offer up his palm and would give him a good whack with the riding crop. Bruno respected Father enormously and was greatly influenced by his values, especially his commitment to honesty, a characteristic that Bruno maintained.

According to Paul, Mother manipulated Father to act as her disciplinarian without regard to fairness. Physical punishment was an accepted disciplinary method at that time. Unruly boys were expected to learn from the painful experience. The premise did not work in Paul's case; his troubles were just beginning. When Paul was 13 and I was five, my parents sent him to a reform school in Switzerland. According to his biography, his crime was stealing a 100-crown note from his father's wallet.

Paul never had either enough money or enough sweets. Mother was so eager to ensure that her children would not be "spoiled rich brats" that the pocket money the boys got was less than was customary for their friends. The children had no sweet treats except when guests brought some. Then Mother would carefully divide the pieces into four so that each child would get exactly the same number, regardless of what kind of sweets they favored. Paul was very fond of a special chocolate, called Kofila, which caused the major uproar. In his biography Paul says:

"One fine day my dad was having a nap after lunch as was his usual custom. He also had a habit of putting his very small, elegant purse with its neatly folded bills on his bedside table while he napped. On this particular day I sneaked into his room, opened his purse and pulled out a 100-crown note, equivalent to a $100 today. This was a huge amount of money then. One Kofila, for example, cost one crown, so I could have bought a hundred Kofilas with this money if I'd wanted to. I pocketed the 100-crown note, took myself off to the chocolate shop and bought two Kofilas. I then went to another shop and bought myself a watercolors paint set. This cost about five or six crowns, so I had a little over 90 crowns left. I saw a taxi and I hailed him and told him to drive me home. This was only a minute's drive, and I have no idea why I decided to take a taxi. Perhaps it was my way of saying to my parents, to hell with you. I gave the driver all the money I had left over, so I came home with two Kofilas, a paint set and no money."

Unfortunately for Paul, one of the servants saw him step out of the taxi and reported him to his parents. He had to confess and told them everything. His parents retired to the bathroom to have a big discussion. Listening by the door, Paul overheard Father reprimanding Mother, "You're going to ruin that boy by the way you treat him." After hearing Father's comments, Paul felt much better about himself, knowing that Father did not think as negatively about him as Mother. Nevertheless, they sent him away.

He was not happy exiled in Switzerland at a school known for disciplining difficult boys. His stay there came to an end when he got injured and Mother had to go to pick him up and bring him home. The school was happy to be rid of him. I was too little to understand any of this at the time, knowing only that the incident was serious. By then Paul was 14. Upon his return, he entered a four-year commercial academy in Prague, finishing the course a few weeks after Father died.

The effect of Paul's troubles on Bruno was lasting. Twenty years later, when Bruno started Camp Ponacka in 1947, he said that he wanted to be in a position to influence young boys and prevent the kind of troubles Paul had had growing up. He remembered Dr. Pohl and wanted to see whether he could help boys grow up without the negative consequences of mischievous adolescent behavior and become productive adults.

My Grandparents' Deaths

When I was about three years old, Father's mother, Fanny Morawetz, came to live with us. My only recollection is of a rather fat lady in a big, long, black skirt and white lace cap who walked on the arm of an attendant. Grandmother had been ill and Father wanted her to be cared for in our house. She was Orthodox and kept kosher. Her attendant cooked for her, and I have often wondered how she was able to carry out kosher requirements in our decidedly secular household. I wish I had asked Mother how she had handled her mother-in-law's living in, and then dying in, our home in 1925.

Mother told me that she did not cope very well when her own parents died a few years later, feeling bereft even though she had little contact with them. Grandfather Tritsch died the next summer, in 1926, while he was vacationing with us in Velden, a resort in southern Austria. I learned much later that he had become one of the founders of the new Jewish Cremation League, and his body was transferred to Vienna to be cremated there. This surprising fact did not fit with the view I had of my grandparents, who supposedly rejected anything Jewish.

Mother's mother died a year later, also while we were on vacation. After dental surgery she contracted an infection and, before penicillin, had died horribly of blood poisoning in a sanatorium in Vienna. Mother left for Vienna immediately upon learning about the illness but arrived too late to say goodbye to her mother. Mother wore only black for months after each parent's death. I remember her returning to the vacationing family all dressed in black with a black veil covering her face. Wanting to run to her, I was afraid to approach her. I only knew that something terrible had happened. Nobody told me that my grandmother had died. One did not talk about death to children.

Special Occasions

Shortly after her mother's death, Mother came down with a dangerous middle-ear infection that required trepanation, cutting through the bone in the ear. I remember it clearly because Father assigned me a special role in the welcome-home ceremony that he had orchestrated. Mother was very weak and had to be half carried up the walk to the house. I was to walk ahead of her sprinkling rose petals as she approached the house from the car. I was very proud that I could welcome her back that way and remember feeling a great sense of tenderness for her. It took a long time before she was able to resume her normal social activities.

When Mother had one of her frequent ladies' teas at home, I had to put on a Sunday dress, wash my hands, comb my hair and put a bow on the barrette that held my hair out of my face so that I would look presentable. Then Yeya would bring me into the dining room to curtsy to the ladies. I never stayed there for more than a few moments. I remember the beautifully arranged silver trays of sandwiches and cookies that were passed around by one of the uniformed maids. On one of these occasions I looked at the cookie tray not with admiration but with apprehension. Just the day before, Bruno had been caught stealing cookies from a cookie tin in the pantry next to the kitchen. Though the cook always prepared a large supply of cookies for the tea party guests, the children were permitted only one cookie per occasion, if that. Bruno's favorite cookies had just been baked and stored in the padlocked cookie tin. With daring and desire, he unscrewed the lock, helped himself to lots of cookies and replaced the lock so that nobody would know that the cookies were gone. The next day, the cook saw that the cookies were missing and alerted Mother. They were both mystified to find a whole tray of cookies missing. I cannot recall how Bruno was found out, but I do remember the hubbub that ensued.

When I was very young, Yeya and I ate in our room. The chambermaid brought meals to us on a tray. When I was big enough to have reasonable table manners, hold a knife and fork properly, keep my hands on the table next to the plate when I was not eating and my mouth shut, I was permitted to have lunch with the grown-ups. I felt very honored to be included. Lunch was a formal affair. Josef, our white-gloved butler dressed in a gray uniform with gold buttons and his hair slicked down, served the meal. When my parents had a guest, the uniformed chambermaid helped serve. The butler came around with the meat, and the maid—in her white gloves and lace-trimmed headband—immediately followed with the vegetables so that the meat would not get cold before you had filled your plate. You had to wait until everybody was served and Mother had started eating. The children understood that they had to eat everything that was on their plate, whether they liked it or not. We were never allowed to participate in the table conversation unless we were specifically recognized. I do not recall ever raising my hand and asking to speak; I was too intimidated. The great catastrophe that I remember was my spilling a glass of water on the tablecloth. I was mortified. The housekeeper would remind us that even with a heavy felt pad under the tablecloth, the water would mar the highly polished wood beneath.

Discussions at the table never included politics or money, I later learned, because these topics were considered *mauvais ton* (not genteel). And of course sex was not discussed either, even if the sexual mores of my parents' crowd were quite liberal. Men of this crowd, including my father, had affairs openly or covertly; in several *mariages a trois*, an additional man or woman was an accepted member of a triad. I think the loosening of convention kept people from getting divorced. The upper classes must have felt entitled to such a lifestyle.

Father's Habits

My father was a handsome man, impeccably dressed in suits made to order by Prague's best tailor. He also wore custom-made shirts because he had a weight problem and was trying to minimize his *embonpoint* (plumpness). He would go to a spa in Germany near Dresden to lose weight and return home trying to follow the diet he had followed there. It did not do much good. Looking at his pictures, one could assume that he was an austere person, though people who knew him said that he was witty and outgoing. I did not have a chance to experience him that way. I thought that our formal family relations were normal. Later I learned that many families in circumstances similar to ours were even more formal, others less so. In many families the father was primarily feared; yet in others, fathers played an important and active role in the lives of their children.

After lunch, when my father would take a short nap before returning to the bank, doors were shut tightly so that nothing would disturb him. Everybody at home and in the community treated Father with great respect. Bruno recalled that Father sometimes walked to school with him, crossing the Wenzelsplatz (Václavské Námestí), Prague's large main square. Many people on the street would recognize and greet our father. The public acclaim added to the awe that Bruno already felt for this highly educated and accomplished man.

Immediately upon moving to Prague, Father realized that he had to learn more Czech. All of his education had been in German, and it was imperative that he be fluent in Czech in his new position. He engaged a tutor, who came to the house early in the morning to give him lessons. Mother also took Czech lessons.

With his language facility, intellect and experience, Father quickly rose to a leading position in the financial world. In addition to being on the board of many important enterprises, he also acted as examiner at the law faculty of the Charles University in Prague, a prestigious post that added to his already extensive duties. He traveled to Paris and London frequently, representing his bank in international monetary dealings.

When he was home, Father liked to take the children to visit his mother's grave on Sunday mornings. In the car, he and the boys played word games, such as naming all the world capitals starting with B or all the composers starting with M. I was too little to participate, but I learned a lot from listening to these games. These outings were among the few occasions when I was together with my three brothers and my father. On Sunday afternoons, Father frequently played tarot (cards) with a group of friends. Through the glass door in the upstairs dining room, I used to watch them smoking their long Virginia cigars. They seemed to be men of authority who anticipated being respected and whose paths one had better not cross. I remember that I did not choose to linger. They all seemed old, fat and intimidating!

Vacations

We spent the summer of 1927 on the Lido, the beach island near Venice, at the Grand Hotel des Bains. My much older cousin Erni, my Uncle Vali's son, came with us. Uncle Vali was the brother with whom Father had lived while studying in Vienna. Erni was a highly gifted musician, but Father discouraged him from pursuing a musical career. Instead, he suggested that Erni study law. Father's advice was taken very seriously, since he was the only financially successful person in his family. Father not only supported Erni in his law studies in Vienna, but he also invited him to vacation with us.

The first hotel I ever visited, the Grand Hotel des Bains was a huge structure with manicured gardens and walks, overlooking the lagoon and a private beach. We had a beach hut assigned to our family and space for deck chairs. The hotel had a very large children's dining room where I always ate with Yeya. I still remember that elegant dining room, with its white tablecloths and large white napkins, so clearly I could draw a map of it. On one side, the walls were all windows that were kept open while we ate. On the other wall, the swing doors opened to reveal waiters who balanced heavy trays. I had never been to a restaurant, and I could not explain to myself how the waiters always knew what Yeya had ordered. Children occupied most of the tables with their governesses, who made sure that the room was quiet and orderly.

When I went to Venice a few years ago, I suddenly had a great urge after more than seventy years to try to find this hotel. I walked along the beach, instinctively, as though I knew where I was going. When I finally asked a passerby whether he knew the hotel, he said that I was almost there. Sure enough, I came upon the colorful beach huts looking just as I remembered them. Then I walked into the hotel. There was no children's dining room anymore and nothing inside seemed familiar. Still, seeing the hotel, now the site of the Venice Film Festival, brought back a happy memory of a privileged childhood.

Alt Aussee

In 1928, when I was six, my parents bought a summer house so that the family would have a place to spend vacations. After an intensive two-year search, they bought a villa in Alt Aussee with a magnificent view of the renowned Dachstein Glacier. Alt Aussee is a resort village in the Salzkammergut, a part of Styria, a mountainous province in central Austria. The area has been well-known for at least a thousand years because of its important salt mines (*Salzkammer* means "salt storage"), which gave the region its income.

Another draw of this spot was the people it attracted. In the 19th century and the first half of the 20th, Alt Aussee had become a favorite vacation spot for artists, writers and musicians as well as for the Jewish upper-class bourgeoisie from Vienna and Prague. The composer Gustav Mahler, the writers Franz Werfel, Franz Kafka, Stefan Zweig, Jakob Wasserman and others came regularly. They either owned homes or returned every summer to their favorite rented rooms.

Three miles from the railroad or a major road, the village of Alt Aussee is nestled among meadows with a lake surrounded by mountains—one of the most picturesque places in the area. Standing all by itself in a unique location at the top of a meadow surrounded by a grove of pine trees, our house had a spectacular view of the village, the lake and the surrounding mountains.

When my parents bought the house, it included some valuable 16th- and 17th-century peasant furniture and well-preserved *Kacheloefen*, handmade tiled stoves used for heating. As the house had no indoor plumbing and no useful electricity, Mother spent more than a year modernizing it before we moved in.

The main entrance to the house led to a foyer with the kitchen off to one side. On the other side of the hall was the salon, the only room in the house that seemed not to fit into the rustic setting. Because we did not feel comfortable in the elegantly furnished salon, it was later turned into a pingpong room. All the food was prepared on a wood-burning stove in the modestly equipped kitchen. Next to the kitchen was the largest room in the house, the dining room, with a beautiful dark red *Kachelofen* and a large, carved wooden table where we ate our meals. In one corner of the room, a square table with benches along the wall became our living area. Without central heating, the wood-burning *Kachelofen* heated the dining room on cold summer days. With the door left open, some of the heat would waft upstairs. Eventually Mother put a coal-burning stove in the entrance hall that made the upstairs bedrooms livable in the winter when we arrived for Christmas.

On the second floor, my parents had a magnificent large bedroom with a door to the balcony that surrounded the house. It was the best spot for a view of the panoramic scenery, provided it was not raining. Two other bedrooms, used mainly for guests, and a bathroom completed the second floor.

The next level up had six bedrooms and a bathroom for the children and the help. Some of the rooms were tiny, with sloping walls under the mansard roof. Throughout most of the house, the carpets were *Fleckerl-teppiche*, rugs made from fabric remnants that fit with the rustic feel of the house.

With mixed success, the vegetable garden on one side of the house produced a few carrots and some parsley. On the other side, Mother had a tennis court built next to the house, hoping that Father would get some exercise and play tennis if it was right there. Lacking Mother's affinity for sports and an appetite for good food, he battled constantly with his weight.

At the bottom of the hill were cows belonging to the farmer who cut our grass with a scythe. Frequently I was sent down the hill with a pail to pick up the unpasteurized milk to be boiled. I was very proud that I had been trusted to fetch the milk and even prouder when I brought it home without spilling it.

To get up to the house by car, we had to drive up a steep, unpaved stretch of road to a narrow, level path that led through our property from the road to the house. It was always touch-and-go whether our large car would negotiate the turn into our gate. Walking, we used to come up the meadow from the front because that was a much quicker way to get home from the village.

I remember the excitement of the first summer trip to Alt Aussee. The family and Yeya traveled by car. We had a white Austro-Daimler convertible, a large, fancy car. Father sat next to the chauffeur; Mother, Yeya and I were in the back seat, and the three boys sat on jump seats. I always became carsick, although the fresh air was helpful. All of us wore white car coats and white caps to protect us from the dusty, unpaved roads. As the convertible had no room for luggage, the maids were sent ahead on the train with the family's luggage to ready the house for our arrival. With heightened anticipation I had watched the luggage preparation in Prague.

Traveling in white coats with the whole family was an elegant adventure. When not carsick, I admired the landscape, especially as we neared the mountains. These forests ringed by high mountains combined with lake, meadows, a glacier and the peaceful church steeple surrounded by typically Austrian peasant houses defined a beautiful landscape for me. To this day, whenever I go to the mountains I compare the scenery to Alt Aussee. I have seen many more majestic sights, but nothing can ever live up to my memories of the unspoiled beauty of Alt Aussee.

During the first car trip to Alt Aussee, in 1928, we barely avoided a major accident. We were traveling down a steep hill in that heavily loaded car when suddenly I noticed my father bracing himself against his seat. He grabbed the hand brake and pulled it up with all his might. The car's brakes had failed! With the chauffeur steadying the wheel and my father pulling on the brake, we somehow made it. Father was ashen when we stopped at the bottom of the hill. I will never forget the frightened look on his face.

While my father was alive, we always spent Easter and Christmas school vacations in Alt Aussee. In winter we traveled by train. To get to our house in winter we had to use sleighs, as taxis could not navigate the unplowed roads. We needed two sleighs to carry the family and all our luggage. On the hill leading to the house, we had to get out of the sleighs and walk up because the horses could not pull the load. Getting there was part of the excitement.

A major thrill was learning to ski on the hill in back of the house. At the time we had no ski lifts; even tow ropes did not exist. Skiing was a pretty rigorous sport, but we loved everything in Aussee.

Our Christmas celebration was even more moving in the winter landscape of the countryside than in the city in Prague. Without cars the village was completely quiet, the only sounds coming from sleigh bells and from footsteps in the snow. I imagine that it was the kind of setting that had inspired the Austrian composer of "Silent Night." In later years we used to go to midnight mass in the little village church through the crunching snow with only the stars and the moon to light the way. There the idea of Peace on Earth was conceivable.

During summer vacations these early years, I was still too young to participate in my brothers' activities, but I was able to tag along frequently. The house had many attractions for all the vacationing youngsters. The tennis court next to the house, a rarity at the time, and the former salon, now dedicated to the children with a pingpong table, kept us occupied during many a rainy day. Alt Aussee was well-known for its special kind of rain, *Schnuerlregen* (string rain). When the valley became socked in, it could rain for a week without letup. We got used to walking in the rain, in watertight boots with our loden capes and umbrellas.

In good weather a crowd of teenagers frequently came to play ball, tennis or other games. We went on hikes and went swimming in the lake. We all had bicycles. Among our constant companions were Georg and Wolfi Brassloff, whose grandmother was my Tritsch grandfather's sister Gusti. We used to go berry and mushroom picking with Mother, who was an expert in recognizing the difference between edible and poisonous mushrooms. These early summer vacations were idyllic, but the fondly remembered days were not to last.

Mother and I continued to go to Alt Aussee for summer vacations. Though our lifestyle there changed after my father's death, the pleasure of being there was undiminished. We did not have a car anymore. The Prague maids did not come, and we had local people clean and cook for us. Mother used to invite needy German Jewish refugees who had lost everything or elderly widows to come and stay. Although my brothers visited only sporadically, the house was always full.

One summer when I was 11 or 12, I had a rather frightening experience going to Alt Aussee. Mother and I were going to take the train together, but for some reason the train started to move while Mother was still on the platform in Prague. She waved frantically, but to no avail. There I was by myself! Following by car, Mother tried without success to catch the train at the next station. She did manage to call the stationmaster at the next stop and asked him to reassure me that she was coming on the next train. After I got over the shock of being by myself, I felt proud that Mother had trusted me to go on by myself. I think it was the beginning of my emancipation.

I was in a first-class compartment by myself for quite a while until a man entered who I thought did not belong there. He tried to engage me in a conversation, but I felt uneasy. Suddenly he got up, lowered his pants, exposed himself to me and abruptly left. Stunned, I did not know what to make of that incident. I never told Mother or anybody else about it.

In Alt Aussee, many young people mainly from Vienna often came to our house. Sometimes we would get up at the crack of dawn to climb the Loser, the high mountain just behind our house. I felt very grown up the first time I was permitted to come along. Though exhausted on the steep part of the trail, I was determined to keep up with the group. Usually there was a boy I was trying to impress, although he probably did not even realize that I existed. I had a crush on several of the boys, who paid no attention to me. Some of the older girls befriended me only because they wanted invitations to the house to meet my brothers. I buried my chagrin and waited for the day when I would be old enough to belong.

Uli Pulay was among that group. She was a year older than I but not much taller, although she was already developed physically. She read intellectual adults books and impressed us by declaiming classical poems. She became one of my most beloved lifelong friends.

All in all, those summers are among my fondest memories. Some of my most significant relationships were formed during those times. I made friends with whom I am still in contact today. One of them was my second cousin, Mimi Gratzinger (now Levitt). Our Gruensfeld grandmothers were sisters, both gifted pianists. I was amused to learn that when Mimi's grandmother Gusti Gruensfeld fell in love with Eduard Aldor in the 1890s, she was at first not permitted to marry him because he was not sufficiently well-off to warrant the hand of a Gruensfeld daughter. Only after Eduard obtained the sole representation for the sale of Havana cigars in the Austro-Hungarian Empire was the marriage sanctioned. The Gruensfelds had had strict expectations for their daughters' marriages.

The bonds that were created in those adolescent years meant so much to me, especially as most of us were soon scattered around the globe. Miraculously, some of us found each other again as adults.

The last time I spent the whole summer in Alt Aussee was in 1936, four years after my father's death. I was 14. These were the years during which I came into my own. Mother was no longer the only influence in my life. At the time when I was struggling to develop an identity, my love for Alt Aussee influenced my feelings. I concluded that I was really Austrian. I was born in Austria, I had an Austrian passport, I had a Viennese mother, and German was my mother tongue. I felt more at home in Alt Aussee than in Prague. The natural setting, the atmosphere and the people made me feel as though I belonged there. Finally I had decided who I was nationally— at least for the time being.

Upbringing

I started school when I was six. I attended the school that Bruno was just leaving. We had the same teacher, Fräulein Nahlik, who taught us for the entire five years we attended that school. The authorities may have believed that teachers would be better able to follow each child's development if they taught them for more than a year. The spiritual and rigorous anthroposophic Waldorf schools around the world today still consider this approach pedagogically sound. Our class had about forty students, who sat on school benches for two with desks attached to the benches. The teacher stood in front of the class. Children did not move from their seats. We had to get up when the teacher or any other adult entered the classroom. When the teacher was speaking, we had to keep our hands on our desk. Fräulein Nahlik was a kind lady and an excellent teacher. While she took a while to get to know the other children, I was "special," because she had liked Bruno and she had known me from before. I loved going to school.

The winter of 1928, my first school year, was a particularly cold one. Ice covered much of the streets. I remember the freezing wind one morning as I was walking to school with Yeya holding my hand. With my other hand to protect my face from the cold, I put a handkerchief in front of my mouth. It froze to my lips, which started to bleed when I tried to remove it. Although the chauffeur was heating Father's car in front of our house when I left for school, he was not permitted to give me a lift. Mother was adamant about not coddling us. Most children walked to school, so why should not the Morawetz children? Mother's friends who had cars were pleased to have their children driven to school. Not my mother. With few cars in Prague at the time, Mother shunned unnecessary outward signs of affluence.

Mother took a Spartan approach to our upbringing. Although I never heard any direct remarks about her position of wealth, I was aware that Mother disliked the formality of her position in society. Her rebellion came through in the values she tried to instill in us children. A fundamental precept was that of noblesse oblige: that one had to be more generous because one was rich, never boasting or expecting to be treated deferentially. Among other expectations associated with our social position was Mother's conviction that all four of us would know four languages by the age of 16: German, the language of the family; Czech, the language of the servants and the street; French, the language of culture; and English, the language of commerce. The boys had English- and French-speaking governesses and later studied with language tutors.

From early on, Mother's interest in the arts and music was obvious to me. I used to listen to her when she was practicing for her singing lessons, wondering why it was necessary to repeat the same four sounds over and over again. Even at my young age, I knew that she considered self-discipline very important. If something hurt, you were not supposed to complain. You should be stoic and hide your feelings. Much later she would tell me that she knew she had been a spoiled and pampered child because her mother had indulged her rather than loving her enough to correct her behavior. As a result she had a very hard time adjusting when she was sent to England at age 15. She did not want such a fate to befall her children. She insisted that we go out to get fresh air in the greatest cold, that we eat everything and not fuss when things were not going our way—unintended good preparation for surviving the hardships that were to follow.

Mother's approach to Judaism also influenced our upbringing. She was eager to minimize our Jewishness. Even though anti-Semitism was outlawed in the new Czech constitution, feelings against Jews were endemic and she was troubled that she could not protect her children from the prejudice.

Father had strong Jewish roots, although he was not particularly observant, going to the synagogue by himself only on the High Holidays. Mother had wanted to have her children baptized as babies, as had some of her Austrian cousins, but Father would not permit it. Many affluent Jewish families were choosing this method of trying to obliterate their Jewish past and give the children a chance to grow up without the burden of their origins. Little did one know at the time that Hitler would come along with the Nuremberg anti-Semitic laws specifying that you were Jewish if you had Jewish grandparents, regardless of your present religion. Being baptized at birth did not protect one. Mother made it quite clear to us that being Jewish was not something to be proud of. She would admonish us not to speak with our hands, considered a typically Jewish custom, and discouraged the use of Yiddish expressions such as *nebbich* or *shlemiel*, even though many non-Jews used these colorful expressions as well. Most of the family's friends were Jewish.

Lorle was my best friend in elementary school. She used to come to our house after school and we enjoyed playing together. I lost touch with her when I was older. After the war I found out that she had been deported to the Lodz ghetto in Poland. There she was forced to become a prostitute. She did not survive. It still upsets me to think about the fate of such a gentle little girl.

Robert, my now British, polo-playing uncle, visited frequently. After he returned from Australia in 1919, my father helped him to become the world sales representative of Mautner, a large Austrian textile-manufacturing firm. In that position, Uncle Robert traveled the world and would send us postcards from exotic places that helped us learn geography. He was a fascinating storyteller, and I eagerly looked up all the places he described in the atlas. Since he was married only briefly, he considered us his family.

From a trip to Abyssinia (Ethiopia), he brought back with him a live gazelle named Coco as a pet for us children. Mother was horrified but finally agreed to let the gazelle live in our garage. Every afternoon, Uncle Robert and I would spend time trying to get her to come to us. He called, "*Viens ici, Coco*" (Come here, Coco), the first French words I learned. I was fascinated and felt very protective of that gentle and fragile animal. I wanted to pet her and get her to eat out of my hand, but she was too shy. Neither Uncle Robert nor I succeeded, but in any case the presence of Coco was exhilarating. He rose in my esteem because he had gone to the trouble of getting the gazelle and over Mother's objections insisted that we keep her. I felt very fortunate to have in our garage this live creature, the likes of which I had never seen.

On a tragic Sunday afternoon not long after Coco arrived, she died. She apparently had eaten rat poison that was strewn in the garage to kill the rats that had invaded it. She had horrible sores on her thin legs, and the veterinarian could not determine whether she had died of rat poison or of rat bites. But before she died, she had managed to destroy most of the stage sets stored in the garage. That same afternoon, my playmate Anicka died of scarlet fever. I remember that Sunday afternoon as the saddest day of my childhood. Mention of the stage sets brings back mixed memories of that terrible Sunday as well as the excitement of my parents' social life.

My Parents' Social Life

The stage sets in the garage were used in two costume balls that my parents hosted. My mother commissioned stage sets by well-known stage designers for these events. One time, they transformed the entire first floor of the house into a Tyrolean wine cellar; the other time, into an Apache den. The invitations asked the guests to come in costumes and masks for one of the balls.

Because all the food was prepared at home for these parties, the kitchen was also rearranged to accommodate a specially hired chef and several additional people working in the kitchen. On one of these occasions I was privileged to be invited to the normally out-of-bounds kitchen to help prepare orange juice. Orange juice was a special delicacy because the oranges had to be imported from Italy. All juicing was done by hand, and it took a day to prepare enough orange juice for the many guests. My job was to extract whatever juice was left after the first juicing by a kitchen aide. I think I spent most of my time sucking the used rinds dry.

Besides these major events, my parents gave many large dinner parties. When Mother commented on them later, she always said that her greatest concern was whether her husband would be satisfied with her performance as hostess. I found it surprising that she accepted his critical attitude without apparent resentment. She had a specific budget for each of these parties and she kept careful track of the costs. My father expected it, she said. She had a little black book for expenses in which she made entries every day, keeping up the practice until she died. Despite this emphasis on expenditures, Mother never knew how much money my father made or how much money he had. She thought it was not hers to know and did not find it demeaning that she was not privy to financial matters. But when Father died unexpectedly in 1932, she was left with all the decisions and not the slightest idea how to deal with money matters.

Visits to Father's Family

As an adult, Father lived in a very different environment from that of his childhood. Still eager to keep in touch with his family, he established a routine of our yearly visits to his sister, my Tante Luise. These visits are some of my most vivid memories from that time. Tante Luise was 12 years older than my father. Very heavy, her body was hidden under the long skirts and layers of blouses she wore. She always welcomed me with tight embraces and the same sort of wet kisses that I tried to avoid from my father and brothers. I liked hers even less.

In her village of Doeschen (Dešná) in southern Moravia near the Austrian border, village life was primitive. So few cars were seen on the unpaved roads that the village children would gather and wave at our car. Tante Luise's house had no toilet, only an outhouse where newspaper was used instead of toilet paper. Toilet paper was a luxury few people could afford. Obviously appalled by this lack of hygiene, Mother would smuggle in toilet paper for us to use. Only the front part of the house had electric lights. The rest of the house used gas lanterns. As the youngest, surprisingly, I got to sleep alone in the master bedroom, which was lighted by a portable lantern. I hid under a huge mountain of a featherbed to keep snug in the unheated room. However cozy, I was scared in that big bed all by myself.

Tante Luise's husband was Ignatz Kandler. He was a grain and horse trader and had a small farm with horses. A small, gaunt man, very thin in contrast to his wife, he wore heavy boots that he changed to slippers as soon as he entered the house. Onkel Ignatz always wore a gray cap, even inside the house. He smoked a long Virginia cigar and he smelled of garlic. To this day, I associate Doeschen with the smell of the cigar mixed with the smell of garlic.

Onkel Ignatz had two sons from a previous marriage, Julius and Leopold, who also lived in the farmhouse. The sons were in charge of the farm as well as the seed business. I always thought of them as country bumpkins because they ate so sloppily and did not know how to hold a knife and fork according to our standards. Bruno liked them because they let him care for the horses in the stable and took him along on their buggy on trips to sell seed.

Tante Luise did all the cooking on a wood stove. She kept a kosher house. Without knowing what kosher meant, I associated it with the heavy and greasy food that smelled up the house. I disliked most of the dishes she so carefully and lovingly prepared. Because I was her darling, she gave me extra-large portions. As an obedient child, I struggled to finish everything she put on my plate.

The fun part of the visit was getting to ride in Onkel Ignatz's buggy and being allowed to spend time in Tante Luise's dry-goods store. She sold a mix of things—food, dry goods and hardware. I think hers was the only store in the village. I admired her greatly because she was able to make paper cones that she filled with sugar or whatever the customer wanted and weigh the contents on a hand-held scale without spilling anything. I tried to roll the cones (*Stanitzl*) but could not manage it. With so much to see and observe, the visits to the store were a real treat. Buttons and thread were mixed in with pins and needles as well as ribbons and lace. Little wooden boxes held yellow and brown pungent spices that were sold by the spoon. Large jute sacks with flour, rice or macaroni stood on the floors. These staples were also sold in paper cones, but larger ones. The store carried wicks and oil for lamps and all sorts of farm items that did not interest me.

I felt ambivalent about the visits to Tante Luise. Little as I was, I sensed that I did not belong there and that Mother was doing Father a favor by going on these family visits. Although she never said anything derogatory, I thought that she tried to be a good sport who did not quite succeed in feeling comfortable there.

In Doeschen I met my cousins Martha and Fritz, Luise's two adult children. Martha had moved to Prague, where she worked as a secretary. She married Tonda Polak, a non-Jewish professor at Bruno's school. The couple used to come for Christmas Eve dinner to our house; that is the only other contact with them that I recollect. During the war, Martha's Christian husband was not able to protect her; she was deported to a concentration camp, where she perished.

Fritz came to live with us in Prague while attending a business administration course. I was very fond of him. He affectionately called me his little fiancée, *die kleine Blaut* instead of *Braut* (fiancée) because I could not pronounce the *Br* yet. I must have been about four or five. After he finished the business course, he went to work for a Czech firm in Pamplona, Spain. Of course I had not yet heard of Spain, but Pamplona is engraved in my memory because of Fritz. He used to dance the tango with me when he came back to visit! Later he moved to Istanbul, where I visited him as an adult and where we became good friends. Our well-traveled family members kindled my love for exotic places and different languages at a very early age.

Christmas

Among my favorite early memories is Christmas in our villa in Prague, a magical time of the year. The Christmas season began with the arrival of St. Nicholas on December 6. A big man with a long, white beard and a "real" Santa Claus costume, he came to our house with his helper, the *Krampus*, in a devil's outfit with a long tail. He arrived in the late afternoon just after dark. I awaited him eagerly, half in joyous anticipation, half in fear, because I knew that St. Nick brought goodies and fruit for children who had been good; for those who were bad, the *Krampus* rattled his chain and left pieces of coal. I also understood that angels in the sky observed children and reported to St. Nick which ones had been good or bad. For weeks I would plead with Yeya not to pull the shades at dark so that the angels could observe what a good girl I was. I was very scared of the *Krampus*. For years, I did not know that my father played St. Nicholas and our butler the devil.

During the Christmas season the streets of Prague were full of street vendors who lit their small kiosks with candles, making the whole city look festive. The flickering lights, the sparkling candles and the beautiful decorations enchanted me. As a special treat the children were allowed to buy hot roasted chestnuts from the Christmas market. The vendors always wore half gloves with their fingers unprotected from the cold as well as from the hot chestnuts. They used to warm their fingers by blowing on them, which intrigued me. After it snowed, the main streets became slushy and dirty, but in our residential street and in our garden everything was silent and white. To me, Christmas remains associated with snow and quiet.

Although we did not celebrate the religious aspect of Christmas, the festivities required much preparation and engendered much excitement. Mother spent weeks getting presents for all the servants and other helpers, such as the manicurist, massager, hairdresser, piano teacher, gymnastics teacher and various other tutors. As I watched her wrap the presents in colorful papers with elegant bows and name tags for every recipient, I sensed that no effort was too great for her to create a memorable occasion. I had no idea at the time that celebrating Christmas in a Jewish family was unusual. I can only assume that Mother must have used all her powers of persuasion on my father to allow her to celebrate Christmas. Thus it would have been even more important for her to prepare an outstanding occasion.

I always had a new Christmas dress made by the house dressmaker, the wife of the butler. Because Christmas presents were supposed to be a surprise, I had to try the dress on with my eyes blindfolded so that I would not see it. Our family expected the children to make the presents ourselves; bought presents were unacceptable. I would embroider hankies or weave little mats out of colored paper strips.

The anticipation of the presents and of eating with the grown-ups in the downstairs dining room was almost more than I could bear. We had to wait upstairs at the head of the red velvet staircase until the gong invited us to come down. We did not get to see the Christmas tree until Christmas Eve. When we came down, the room was dark; only the wax candles and the sparklers lit the elegant room, as electric candles were unheard of. It was a very solemn moment. I admired the beautiful tree, which reached up to the ceiling with its many ornaments and all my favorite candies hanging from the branches. I will always remember the wonderful pine smell.

When we assembled downstairs, the staff came in and joined us in singing "Silent Night" with Felix at the piano. Then the lights were turned on and every staff member received presents. After they left, it was the children's turn, starting with me as the youngest. Everybody had to watch everybody open his or her presents, and you could not play with your presents until the next day. In spite of the long process, I do not remember being impatient. For once it was an advantage to be the youngest!

Dinner was served in the formal dining room, the only occasion when I ate there. Christmas dinner started with fish soup that I hated, followed by fried carp, the traditional Czech Christmas dish. I do not remember what we usually had for dessert, but we got to taste the edible cookies on the tree. Mother always invited Father's Jewish family. I wonder whether they felt uncomfortable celebrating Christmas. Did they feel privileged or resentful as the poor relatives invited to this exquisite celebration? I'll never know.

Because of my childhood memories, Christmas had become an important tradition for me. Though I follow no religious traditions, I insisted on celebrating Christmas with my own children in our secular way. I knew it was not possible to recreate the atmosphere that I had loved as a child. My husband Frank was not in favor of such celebrations, but in view of my determination he did not interfere with my plans. His parents never celebrated Christmas in their observant Jewish home in Třešt'.

The array of creative holiday celebrations we had when our children were little stopped when we moved to Argentina in 1963. In December it is hot summer in the Southern Hemisphere; we could not recreate the "Silent Night" atmosphere of Prague and Alt Aussee.

We resumed the Christmas celebration custom when Mother came to live with us in Bethesda at age eighty, because this holiday was so important to her. I knew that it reminded her of the best years of her life in Prague. It also reminded her and me of the even more romantic Christmas celebrations in Alt Aussee.

Father's Death

My father died young in 1932 at age 52, when I was just ten years old. He had injured his leg in a fall on a train to Paris or London and as a result developed a blood clot in that leg. Blood-thinning drugs had not yet been invented. Without them, Father's only choice was to lie in bed for six weeks with his leg elevated and motionless. I visited him for a little while every day in his room next to mine, and I still remember the threatened feeling these visits engendered. Although Mother said that he carried on his business from his bedside and was in good spirits, I was distressed. Just as the doctors thought he was getting better, the clot went to his brain and he died suddenly of an embolism.

The moment I found out that Father had died is etched in my memory. My room was close to the central hall on our living floor where the telephone was located. I woke up one morning later than usual and worried about being late for school, when I heard Mother in the hall talking on the phone. I rushed out and saw that she was crying. Stunned, I heard her say that her husband had just died. Mother was busy on the phone; she motioned me away, so I could not run to her. Only later did she come to my room to give me the news. She was in tears. I was even more upset about Mother crying than about Father's dying. The emotional impact came much later. Nobody explained anything to me except that I was to go to the house of friends and stay there for a while.

I did not return home until the funeral and all funeral-related activities were over. Common practice dictated the shielding of children from this type of trauma. I found out that all of Father's family had gone to the funeral and that lots of people had been at the house. I do not remember anybody talking to me about Father's death, even after the funeral. For a long time I kept expecting him to come home any minute; it took months before this feeling of anticipation disappeared. A sculptor was commissioned to make a death mask of him that Mother prominently displayed in our living room.

Over the years I heard a lot of talk about Father and his death, but none at the time he died. Only recently did I find his obituaries in the Prague press. These showed the high esteem of his many colleagues and the owners of companies in which he held important positions.

About twenty years ago I had an interesting experience that finally brought his death home to me. A Jungian psychotherapist friend wanted to demonstrate to me how she worked. She tried to probe how the loss of my father at age ten affected me. After much effort, she managed to make me recall the event, and eventually I started to cry. The release of strong emotion came as a great surprise to me; until then, I had never considered what I had lost when Father died. I can now relate to my own loss only when I think about how greatly deprived my grandchildren or my brothers' grandchildren would feel if they did not have a father.

All our lives—Mother's especially—changed drastically when Father died. She was 39 years old and on her own for the first time, with four children to raise and finances to manage, something she had never done before. She received a large pension from the bank on which we lived comfortably. All other financial matters were to be turned over to a guardian in Vienna whom Father had named in his will. Mother never questioned this arrangement.

Despite the disappointments she must have felt over Father's frequent and poorly concealed skirt-chasing and philandering, she never uttered a negative word about her husband. His affairs seemed not to have seriously damaged their relationship. Given her reticence in discussing sexual matters with her children as well as her rigid moral standards, she demonstrated considerable tolerance about her husband's behavior. To the end of her long life, she repeated what a wonderful and exceptional man he had been and how fortunate she was to have been married to him.

As it turned out, the early years of Mother's widowhood tested her severely. Yet she persevered admirably. Some of the stoic characteristics that made Mother what she was stood her in good stead in the difficult years that followed.

3

TURBULENT TIMES

F ATHER'S DEATH SIGNALED the beginning of many changes in our family in a short time. At age 39, Mother was learning to cope with being a widow with four children. Paul went to England. His leaving added to a certain sense of disintegration within our family. A year later Felix also left, and then Bruno began the transformation from city boy to farmer. I became a teenager. Overshadowing all these milestones was the rise of Hitler in Germany.

Soon after Father's death, we moved out of the spacious villa. Although the villa had been built for us and according to Mother's specifications, the bank retained title to it. I doubt that the bank urged Mother to vacate the house immediately after Father's death. Rather, the precipitate move may have been due to Mother's grave concern about the family's financial situation. Clearly she felt insecure on her own and wanted to curtail living expenses as soon as possible. The move into a temporary apartment in a working-class neighborhood of Prague gave Mother time to look for a suitable home for us.

Even in our much-reduced quarters, we still had a cook and a maid and a "mother's helper" for me. Yeya, my governess for the past ten years, had left before we moved out of the villa. Though it must have been sad to lose my beloved, affectionate caretaker so soon after Father's death, I only remember how pleased I was that I now had a room of my own. No longer sharing a room with anybody was a sign of growing independence. Fortunately, my life soon assumed a new and reassuring routine.

Felix

In the rather dark and dingy apartment, Felix, whose room was next to mine, and I now became close. He was a lanky, handsome, blond and slightly absent-minded 17-year-old. Very thin and anemic, he had to take all sorts of medications and vitamins. As Mother did not believe she could trust him to take the prescribed pills, she deputized me to keep an eye on him. I was to remind him to take his medicine and do his homework. My influence on Felix was minimal.

He did as he pleased. He liked to buy gadgets and spend his time tinkering. When he came home from school, without changing his school clothes and instead of doing his homework, he would examine and test the various chemistry kits he had ordered by mail. Mother disapproved of them because she said they were too messy and could be dangerous. He induced me to be his audience, and I admired his prowess when he performed experiments. Mother's condemnation did not stop him; he just became more circumspect to evade her criticism and her often-expressed exasperation. She had hoped that he would become more mature, pointing out that Felix had been the one who handled all the arrangements at Father's death so efficiently. Although she loved Felix dearly, she was annoyed by what she considered his continuing childish behavior. She remained critical of him for the rest of her life, accusing him of "playing at living." Pointing to his lighthearted attitude, she said that he never took anything seriously. Their love–hate relationship was mutual and lasting.

Mother's nagging of Felix and his ignoring her put me in the middle of their warring relationship. I was proud that Mother had asked me to watch over Felix, but I did not enjoy being pulled in two directions. I was glad that I started having less time at home.

Secondary School

The fall after my father died, I started secondary school with a schedule that filled most of my time. I attended a middle-class, German all-girls academic high school in the center of Prague. To get to school, I now had permission to take the streetcar unaccompanied. Some of my classmates, many of them Jewish, were driven to and picked up from school by their chauffeurs. Passers-by or parents arriving to pick up students frequently whispered anti-Semitic remarks at the sight of those cars waiting after school. The derisive remarks added to my discomfort about being Jewish.

In our social circle, the desire to play down one's Jewishness was not limited to my family. Some of my classmates attended Catholic religious instruction because they had been baptized at birth, although everybody knew that the families were Jewish. In Czechoslovakia, one hour of religious instruction per week was obligatory for all schoolchildren. Pastors, priests or rabbis came to the school to teach the class. Parents could request an exemption for their children, which our parents did for all four of us. Bruno told me much later that Father agreed to the exemption because "he was too religious to want to have his children participate in organized religion." Father also claimed that people only transacted business in the synagogue, even though he alone of our family attended services on the High Holidays. I never considered the significance of the exemption that kept me from learning anything about Judaism. All I understood then was that being Jewish was a definite disadvantage.

My feelings about school were mixed. My teachers liked me because I was conscientious and ambitious, but I was not popular among my contemporaries. My classmates resented me for knowing so much about a wide range of subjects and because I was not shy about showing off my erudition. Smart as I was, I was not happy with myself. Besides the reactions of my classmates, I also internalized Bruno's pronouncements that no boy would ever look at a girl with such an ugly nose and such thin legs. I used to sit in the streetcar with my profile toward the window and my hand covering my face so that nobody would see my loathsome nose, eventually corrected with cosmetic surgery when I was a teenager.

A year later we moved to a much larger, elegant apartment in a central location in Prague. The apartment was light and airy because it was on the fourth floor of the building. The building had an elevator that was free for house occupants with a key, but visitors had to put a coin in the elevator door to use it. We made a game out of keeping the door open when we saw a visitor coming so that he or she would not have to pay.

We had a pingpong room in the apartment. Felix was an excellent player and used me as his "partner," the person who returned the pingpong ball. Felix insisted that he had to beat me 21 to 0. Whenever I made a point, we started the game all over again and did not stop playing until he reached his goal. Sometimes I got mad, but I learned to play pingpong well.

Unwittingly, Felix speeded up my education. He needed my help in studying for the difficult *matura*, the gymnasium's final examination that allowed graduates to attend a university. I enjoyed being his private tutor because I learned as quickly as he. I realized that much of what he studied would be useful to me later. His passing the final exam seemed to me an unheralded feather in my cap.

Besides learning from Felix's schoolbooks, I absorbed a lot of worldly knowledge at home. As the youngest in a fairly intellectual family, I profited for many years from being around adult conversations when we had guests. Also, my far-flung family's visits and stories about their lives and travels inspired my imagination. In those days, travel was still rare and romantic and associated with privilege and danger. I readily soaked up all new and exotic information, especially about Paul's adventures abroad.

Paul

We eagerly awaited news of Paul from England. Paul had not known what to do with himself upon graduating from high school. But he was sure he did not want to stay in Prague, where he felt he would always be seen as the son of the prominent Dr. Morawetz and would never be valued for his own sake. In England he took a short summer course in English language and literature, English history and law at Cambridge University and received a summer course diploma, which proved useful in later years. That summer course was the full extent of his formal college education, sufficing for the rest of his life.

Through Father's connections, Paul found a position as one of two volunteers at the Swiss Bank Corporation in London. The work soon proved extremely tedious. To alleviate the boredom, the 19-year-old Paul started writing for Prague newspapers about soccer and tennis matches in England. Earlier, at age 15 in Prague, he had started covering these sports for Czech newspapers. While Paul was never good at athletics because of his poor eyesight, much to Mother's chagrin, he always interested in them. He even managed to get a much-coveted press card. I remember how proud Mother was showing off his articles from London in the Prague press.

Later that year (1933) Paul was promoting an international soccer game between Czechoslovakia and Ireland. He sent back photographs of himself and Eamon de Valera, the Irish president, and other newspaper clippings full of admiration for the young entrepreneur. But the promising enterprise came to a disastrous end when insufficient funds prevented the Czech team from returning home, and Paul had to go begging to one of his father's contacts in London to make up the shortfall. As a result of this fiasco, Paul lost his job at the bank.

Soon he got another banking job, again because of Father's good connections. Although Paul had left Prague to escape his father's limelight, he was still using the association to his advantage. At this job he became aware that gold mining shares were booming in South Africa and decided to try his luck there. Armed with an ample supply of chutzpah and his press pass, he persuaded both the Cunard Shipping Lines and the South African Railways to give him free passage. Before he left, Paul returned to Prague to tell Mother that he was going to South Africa and to ask her for some money. She was appalled. What was he going to do there? She did not trust him after the soccer debacle but nevertheless gave him 200 British pounds, a sizable amount at the time.

I remember that he sent home articles he wrote about South Africa for both Czech and South African newspapers and that his picture frequently appeared in the press. Mother was very proud of him although occasionally disapproving when she considered his accounts too pretentious. In following his travels throughout Africa, I learned a lot of geography. Author Gloria Frydman describes Paul's South African adventures in detail in his biography, *What a Life* (Wakefield Press, 1995).

Only much later, when Paul returned to Prague at the end of 1935 after an absence of nearly three years, did I find out that he had been in trouble with the law in South Africa. He had gotten involved in a number of unsavory deals, naively relying on untrustworthy business associates. Paul was lucky that he had escaped with only being deported. Upon his return to London from South Africa, which was then a member of the British Commonwealth, he found that his reputation had preceded him. When he got off the boat, the British authorities asked him to leave immediately. Instead of going to Rhodesia (now Zimbabwe) as he had intended, Paul returned to Prague, where Mother greeted him with "I told you so."

Felix Leaves Home

By the time Paul returned to Prague in 1935, Felix was gone. After graduating from high school, to perfect his language skills Felix first went to France for the summer and then to England for a year. These sojourns seemed almost preordained, since Mother had made it clear that she expected us to become fluent in French and English. I added to my knowledge of geography by plotting Felix's travels on the map.

In retrospect, I wonder why neither Paul nor Felix went to a university after high school. I think they both felt what they could learn out there in the big world was more important. Since Mother had gone abroad at a young age and had found that the experience had broadened her horizon, she was all in favor of the boys' leaving. In addition, she believed that Czechoslovakia was too small and insular a country in which to test one's wings. She wanted her children to benefit by seeing the world from different perspectives.

While studying in England, Felix fell in love. After a few blissful months, this lovely young lady left him. Her leaving proved so painful that he decided then and there, at the age of 19, that he would never let himself fall in love again. Basically, I think he kept that promise. Although he had many affairs and eventually married a beautiful young Austrian woman, he never got over the pain of his first rejection and never permitted himself to fall in love with the same abandon.

In the summer of 1935, Felix left for Spain to learn Spanish. The Spanish Civil War had just begun when he arrived in San Sebastian on the Basque coast. He was walking down the street when two men grabbed him and stood him against a wall, intending to shoot him. In that instant, two other men arrived running and shouting, "No, that's not him. You've got the wrong man." The experience was so traumatic for Felix that he decided on the spur of the moment to leave Europe and go to America. He returned to Prague just long enough to prepare to leave for the States.

In 1935, the decision to emigrate was not as daring as it may sound. The anti-Semitic Nuremberg laws had been in existence for several years. These set out Hitler's proposals to severely restrict the life of Jews and included such prohibitions as no longer permitting Jews to own businesses or sit on park benches. Seeing the handwriting on the wall, many smart Jews from Germany and Austria and some from Czechoslovakia were emigrating. The wealthy ones started to smuggle their money out to circumvent the currency exchange restrictions.

Mother's helping Felix with his preparations began with finding a surgeon to fix his fairly hooked nose, which did not fit with his otherwise Aryan blond good looks. Then he acquired a Catholic baptismal certificate. Whether he ever saw a priest I do not know, but I assume one could easily buy such a certificate. Someone must have told him that even in America being Jewish would be disadvantageous. It was easy to believe. We already knew that to be Jewish in Europe was a drawback.

Then Mother gathered up as much cash as she could and gave it to him. She told him to turn the money over to a friend, a prominent Prague banker who was already in the United States, to safeguard it for her. She did not have much money to spare. After Father died, Mother's income had consisted of a sizable pension from the bank. Able to live comfortably on that amount, she still decided to be as parsimonious as possible and save money by instituting some draconian measures. For example, she subscribed to a special low electricity rate that limited the use of wattage during the day. Thus when the maid was ironing or vacuuming and too many lights were on, a fuse would blow and plunge the apartment into darkness. We derided Mother for these clearly unnecessary measures. However, when Felix needed money to go to America, the soundness of saving for an uncertain future became apparent. She was glad to have these savings to give to Felix, eager to avoid any dealings with the Viennese trustee whom Father had appointed in his will and whom she did not particularly like or trust. Certainly he would not have been amenable to Felix's smuggling out money to America!

To get as many valuables as possible out of Czechoslovakia, Mother gave Felix some of her fine jewelry. She also bought a mink cape—a very rare and expensive purchase at the time—having heard that mink was greatly appreciated in America and could be sold at a high price. This Siberian fur was the utmost in luxury at the time. The cape was light brown, waist length, with a rounded collar and with arm loops attached to the lining to keep the fur from slipping off the arms. Felix was supposed to put the mink cape into storage so that the moths would not eat it.

With the money that Mother had accumulated, Felix had enough money to get a "capitalist visa" to the States. One could obtain an immigration visa either as a capitalist or with an affidavit of support from a well-to-do American who guaranteed that you would not become a burden on the state. With a sufficient amount of money, you could take care of emergencies and avoid becoming dependent on government support.

For many families, the idea of emigration was daunting despite the increasing danger inherent in Hitler's well-publicized intentions. For Mother, I think, the decision to let the barely-twenty-year-old Felix go to America was not as difficult as for most families. If Felix's leaving took him out of harm's way, it also reinforced her priority for her children to be out in the big world. After Paul's escapade in South Africa, Mother did not hesitate to let Felix go to America, even though in her mind it was an undesirable destination—a country of skyscrapers and gangsters, with no cultural merit. To me, Felix's departure seemed more like an adventure. I do not know how he felt, but the idea of his leaving forever never entered my mind.

After Felix left, Mother started studying the ship departure announcements to decide on which ship she should send her letters to Felix. Airmail did not exist at the time. If you did not specify a ship, the post office would send your letter to the nearest port and onto a ship that might take two weeks to make the transatlantic journey. I remember Mother carefully considering whether to send a letter via Southampton, Calais or Genoa and precisely calculating how long before the sailing date the letter had to be mailed in Prague.

Felix had an eventful crossing. On the boat, he met a couple of young American socialites, Mary and Peter Cadwallader, who had just started a new business venture. "Supervapor" was supposed to enable people to have a steam bath akin to sauna in their own bathroom and was certain to revolutionize the way people bathed. They talked Felix into investing in their venture and assured him he would make a 100 percent profit in six months. Although Mother had given him specific instructions on how to safeguard the money and had pleaded with him to follow them, he disobeyed. He wanted to be a better son who made a profit for his Mother. In his complete financial inexperience, he gave all his money to the Cadwalladers. Within six months, he had lost it all.

The day the letter came announcing that the money was gone, Mother was as mad as I had ever seen her. She was furious not only because he had lost the money but also because he had failed to follow her instructions. Her response was to accuse him of always doing what suited him best.

With the Depression still on, Felix had trouble finding a job. He pawned some of the jewelry and the fur cape to survive.

Sometime later, Thomas Watson, head of a growing company called International Business Machines (IBM), hired Felix as his personal assistant. I understand that he got the job because he knew English, German and French as well as stenography in all three languages.

The job did not last, and Felix again resorted to pawning Mother's jewelry and the mink cape. Without enough money to retrieve the jewels, he lost some of them. I do not know what happened to the rest. Eventually the mink cape became mine. I wore it many times over the years when I wanted to be particularly elegant. I still have it in one of my storage boxes. Some of the money that Mother had used for that purchase was part of my dowry, she told me much later.

At one point, Mr. Watson had suggested to Felix that learning stenotyping would be useful. Luckily, Felix acted on his advice and studied stenotype, a skill that eventually contributed to a remarkable career in the U.S. Army that changed his life.

Bruno

Bruno remained at home with me. He was a slightly pudgy, dark-haired, serious youngster who was often quite opinionated. With occasional help from a tutor, he did well in the technical gymnasium, which emphasized math and science instead of the humanities that were necessary for acceptance at the university. Like Felix he was a great pingpong player and spent much time at a pingpong club and at a Jewish sport club, Maccabi, where he swam.

Out of keeping with our family's desire to downplay its Jewishness, Bruno became interested in things Jewish and for a while was an ardent Zionist. At that time, The Jewish Agency was collecting money to buy land in Palestine to settle more Jews. The agency distributed little blue and white saving boxes and urged Jews to collect money. Bruno used every occasion to accost people, asking them to throw a coin in his box. I have never managed to ascertain how this surprising interest in Zionism started and stopped.

After graduating from high school, Bruno joined Felix in France for the summer in Saint-Malo in Brittany near the famous Mont-Saint-Michel. He returned with glowing accounts of his stay in France and speaking fluent French. He also recounted that the last few days, spent alone in Paris, he was very homesick. In old age he still remembered that it was the only time in his life when he felt really lonely.

Back home in Prague, Bruno was making career plans. With Paul and Felix gone, Mother became very involved with Bruno's future. At first, she supported his desire to study medicine. He would have to take a full year's course in Latin at the university, since he had had not studied Latin in high school. He started the Latin but soon gave up, saying that he could not manage it. At a loss as to how to help him, Mother took his handwriting to a graphologist, who suggested that Bruno would be well-suited to becoming a landowner or a gentleman farmer. The idea appealed to Bruno, harking back to his visits to Tante Luise in Moravia. Mother next arranged for him to spend the summer on a farm in Slovakia, where he followed the farm manager around. Since the manager walked with a cane and never got his hands dirty, Bruno expected to behave in an equally superior manner, far removed from the soil.

In the fall, Bruno enrolled at the university to study agriculture, but after a few weeks he became disenchanted; he was not interested in the botany or biology that he had to study. He wanted something practical. He transferred to an agricultural school in Kutná Hora, a small town with a beautiful cathedral in Bohemia. At this school, farm boys who had finished the ninth grade could get some further academic education. Bruno was

61

able to finish that two-year school in a year, since he had already studied many of the academic subjects in high school. He then became an apprentice to another farm administrator in Bohemia who also did not get his hands dirty but who was much more involved in the daily activities of the farm. Bruno liked farm life. He could not have anticipated how significant his knowledge of agriculture would become in shaping the rest of his life—in his very survival. As a farmer he was able to gain admission first to England and then to Canada, which was willing to admit farmers as immigrants. Although Canada had no quota, unlike the United States, it was still almost impossible to get a Canadian immigration visa unless you were a farmer.

Bruno used to visit cattle markets with his boss and there observed the judging of animals as well as the beginnings of deals and their consummation. When he would return to Prague on weekends, he would demonstrate to Mother and me and assorted guests how livestock was traded. A talented actor, Bruno took great pleasure in mimicking the coarse language, the hearty handshake and the rough behavior of the cattle dealer. He was funny, but Mother was horrified. He even started to eat salad with his hands because that was what the peasants did, and she frequently sent him away from the table. We stood well back when he showed us how cow manure was used to heal the dry hooves of horses and when he tried to demonstrate how to make blood sausage. Every time Bruno came home with his smelly country boots and pants, the unpleasant odor permeated the kitchen entrance.

His enthusiasm about farming was real. So in 1937, with an incredible lack of foresight in view of the gathering clouds of Hitlerism, Mother used Bruno's share of his inheritance to buy him a farm about 100 kilometers southeast of Prague. The former owner continued to manage the farm, and Bruno became his apprentice.

Programmed Life

Envying Bruno's travels abroad, I continued my highly programmed life. I went to school six days a week from 8 a.m. to 1 p.m., came home for lunch, and then had private lessons: piano and gymnastics, tennis in summer and figure skating in winter, and horseback riding. I studied English, French and Czech as long as I was in the German school, and German when I switched to the Czech school. I even had gardening lessons because Mother believed that learning about nature would round out my upbringing. My lessons also included swimming classes, which consisted of the swimming teacher holding me up in the water by a rope attached to a belt around my waist; he would pull the rope to and fro at the edge of the pool while telling me how to move my arms and legs. I never had to put my head into the water. To this day I cannot make myself open my eyes under water, to the great glee of my grandchildren.

I also went twice a week to Miss Trembath from Bath, England. She was a tiny, well-coiffed, severe-looking, middle-aged lady whose nearby apartment was full of well-cared-for antiques. The setting was fitting for my English lessons. My French teacher was Madame Miagkov, a Russian countess, a refugee from the Bolshevik revolution who came to our house for the lessons because she was ashamed to let me see her modest quarters. From her I heard many stories about Russia, the Russian Revolution and the life and persecution of the Russian aristocracy. I started reading Russian fairy tales in Czech and developed a special affinity for Russian music and literature, the beginning of a lifelong interest in all things Russian.

Of course, many of the private lessons required homework. My talent for learning languages made the studying easy and fun. When walking to my English lessons, I used to speak English to myself on the street, wondering whether passers-by would think me mad. In addition I practiced the piano without supervision every day. I did not have a free minute during the week. But if I felt overburdened, I do not remember it. This regime must have prepared me for adulthood, since to this day I never permit myself any "down time." I had no chores at home and was not expected to make my bed or put my things away. My first role in life was to be a learner. I remain one to this day.

Relaxing Saturday afternoons I spent with my girlfriends. With some of them we played doctor and examined our anatomy, although I believe that none of us knew the facts of life. A scene in a book I read then about the First World War embarrassed me because it described a young man groping a girl's breast. I thought it was not proper for me to read that. I hid the book and read it in bed under my cover with a flashlight so that nobody could see how perverse I was.

Sundays, Mother and I would go to a museum or exhibitions. We often had chamber music concerts on Sunday afternoon at home. To further my musical education, I was allowed twice to skip school and go to dress rehearsals of the Prague Symphony Orchestra. The first time, Nathan Milstein played the Mendelssohn violin concerto; the second time, I watched Bruno Walter conduct Mozart's C-minor Symphony. Those were memorable experiences. The first record I purchased in the United States was the Mozart symphony.

My love for music came from Mother and her very musical family. When I was little, as a special treat Mother would take me along to her singing lessons. After my father died, she stopped singing. She felt it inappropriate for a widow. But she continued to partake of the rich musical scene in Prague.

I got along well with Mother but not so well with Bruno, who took it upon himself to police me and to instruct Mother how to raise me. He was interested in my girlfriends. He invited them out and started necking with them. I do not think they did much of anything else together; but after he had kissed a girl, he urged Mother to forbid me to associate with this girl anymore, saying that she would be a bad influence on me. I lost a couple of friends that way. I was very upset that Mother always let him sway her.

I remember a specific incident when I wanted to go see *The Bengal Lancers,* a movie about the war in India. Bruno persuaded Mother that she should not permit me to go, and she listened to him. I had become so desperate that at that moment I decided to commit suicide. I could not possibly continue living with this kind of injustice.

Hastening to the rear of our apartment, I locked myself in the maid's small bathroom. The room had a tiny sliver of a window opening onto an airshaft over the courtyard. I tried to crawl out of the window to fling myself down the airshaft, but the opening was too narrow for me to slide through. Even now when I think of it, I can still relive the sorrow and abandonment I felt and the loneliness from not having even my mother as my ally. I do not think I ever told her about what I had tried to do.

Without the pressures of her husband's business obligations, Mother followed her own social inclinations. She frequently invited penniless young artists whom she also supported. She liked to think of herself as a patron of the arts. After Hitler's rise to power in Germany in 1932, Prague became a haven for German Jewish intellectuals and artists who had become impoverished refugees. Often Mother invited some of them for lunch. We no longer had a butler, but lunch was still formal, served by a chambermaid in uniform. By then I had internalized Mother's beliefs that breeding and culture and not money were the yardsticks by which one should measure people. Also, I had accepted that good people were expected to be generous and to share their good fortune with the less fortunate.

As part of my high school program, our class went to Monday night performances for students at the German Theater. We listened to concerts, operas or classical plays. If the presentation was an opera or a concert, my piano teacher would prepare me by playing excerpts and explaining the story. Before we went to see a play, the German teacher would ready us by reading part of the play aloud. Everything, even Shakespeare or opera, was performed in German. Of course Prague's Czech theater performed works in Czech, but I never went to it. It is hard to imagine today that we had no radio or television and that records were very scarce. My family was privileged to have a record player with "His Master's Voice" records, the only label in existence then. Live performances were the only way for most people to have access to these arts.

Metamorphosis

I was slowly becoming sufficiently mature to be interested in what was going on in the world. In July 1934, while we were spending the summer in Alt Aussee, Nazi sympathizers assassinated the Austrian chancellor, Dollfuss. My mostly older Austrian friends and I started discussing the precarious political situation. Also, in school in Prague one of my teachers in the gymnasium who was a Communist sympathizer fueled my political interests. This attractive and charismatic man had a group of young girls swooning over him, who attended his after-school discussion groups. The girls from wealthy Jewish families were made to feel guilty about their advantaged position in life. I remember how ashamed I was of being a rich girl and how I vowed to embrace the downtrodden of the earth when I got older. We considered ourselves Communists but of course were too young to join the Party. We were derisively called *Salon Kommunisten,* people who supported the Communist cause without giving up their privileged lives.

While I pondered these arguments, I recalled the first time I ever heard a radio, probably a year or two earlier, when Hitler speaking in Germany was making one of his violent anti-Semitic speeches. I observed Mother fiddling with the primitive crystal radio. Although the background noises made understanding the speaker almost impossible, Mother insisted that the speech was so important she had to hear it. I knew from her face that what he said was frightening.

An atmosphere of crisis was in the air. Discussions during the preparations for Felix's departure reinforced what we had already heard from the many Jewish refugees from Germany who had come to our house. The endless debate ranged over whether Hitler could really be successful in building his "Thousand-Year Reich" or whether he was just a madman whom one should not take seriously. Some insisted that the German people would overthrow him in no time because the Germany of culture and intellectual superiority would never tolerate for long such an uncouth upstart as Hitler. The pessimists said that burying one's head in the sand was foolish and urged those who could to get out of Germany. They also predicted that Austria would be endangered. One thing we all believed for certain: what was happening in Germany could never happen in Czechoslovakia. How wrong we were.

Another Move

In 1937 we moved into a large apartment. The patrician house in which we occupied a whole floor was located on one of old-town Prague's most elegant streets—Pařížská, or Paris Street. We lived on the edge of the Prague ghetto and across the street from the Alt-Neu Schul, Staronová Synagoga. Begun in the second half of the 13th century, the synagogue is the oldest functioning synagogue in Europe and one of Prague's most renowned landmarks. The houses on our street all had elegant facades with turn-of-the-century spikes and turrets. I was not aware at the time that our street was by the old Prague ghetto. More interesting then was Gei's, the little Italian ice cream shop in the same block as the synagogue. I used to stop there in the afternoons to buy Italian lemon ice in a cone and lick it on the way home.

One day I returned home to find a cute little white dog waiting to keep me company. Mother gave him to me as a present. Flippi was likely a wire-haired fox terrier. The only person who could wear him out was Mother. When she took him along on shopping excursions wearing the muzzle obligatory in Prague, he would come home so exhausted that he would flop down on his bed without even waiting to have the muzzle removed. We used to rib her about her stamina. Mother walked so fast on the narrow Prague streets that once, when she ran into a man coming from the other direction, she said, "Excuse me," not even noticing that it was her son Bruno. Although she did not have much of a sense of humor, even she thought that was funny! I used to walk Flippi in a more leisurely fashion along the edge of the river, enjoying the majestic views of Prague from close to home. Contemplating the architectural beauties of the city on these walks, I became interested in the churches and castles of old Prague. Soon I knew enough to guide our frequent out-of-town visitors through the historic parts of the city.

Visitors from Abroad

Among the visitors was my cousin Fritz Kandler, the son of Father's sister Tante Luise. He was now living in Istanbul as a representative of the largest Czech manufacturer of agricultural machines. Always exquisitely dressed, he used a powerful after-shave lotion that had a foreign smell. Fritz became involved with (and eventually married) a beautiful, already married Greek Catholic woman, Celestine. Although born in Istanbul, Celestine considered herself Greek, as was customary among Greeks in Turkey. She had almond-shaped eyes, very dark hair and smooth, light-brown skin. For travel, she carried an extensive and fascinating cosmetics kit. I had never seen anything like her creams, lotions, brushes or eyelash curlers. I enjoyed their visits, feeling a special affinity with Fritz.

When he and Celestine came to visit us in Prague, the hush-hush about their visit also was intriguing. Much later I realized that their sleeping in the same room was considered inappropriate, since they were not yet married. Of course, nobody explained that issue to me.

Another memorable visitor was Tod Catlin, the first American I had ever met. Short, stocky Tod was an outgoing art student from Oberlin College with a Fulbright scholarship to study in Prague. When Mother met him through an artist friend, she "adopted" him and his Oberlin friend Joe Wincenc—a tall, equally outgoing music student with a booming voice and also on scholarship. Both young men were charming, witty and entertaining and stayed in my life.

During that fall of 1937, my second cousin Mimi Gratzinger from Vienna, who was Bruno's great love at the time, came to Prague for a visit. During her stay, she met Tod, whom she married several years later in the United States. Mimi and I have remained close.

The next American I met at our house in Prague was Elsie Jahn, the American wife of Mother's cousin Hans Jahn. Very tall, skinny and loud, she wore a pink outfit that seemed outrageous at the time, because distinguished European ladies never wore bright colors. Her cherry-sized diamond ring was a knockout when she held her cigarette in a golden cigarette holder. Mother considered them the "uncultured nouveau-riches." They were interesting people, though. As a young man, Walter Jahn had accumulated so many gambling debts in Vienna that his family had shipped him off to America. They were sending him to the "wild West," fittingly uncouth, uncivilized and uncultured, the haven for offspring who did not conform to their parents' norm. In this circle, being sent off to America was punishment.

Walter ultimately made a fortune in real estate in Tampa, Florida. He sold out at the right time, moved to California and became involved in industrial plastics. Increasing his fortune considerably was his invention of the plastic hammer used to hammer nails onto metal without leaving a trace on the metal. Once he told me that he popularized chocolate milk, which would have been another lucrative venture.

When Mimi and her family needed an affidavit to immigrate to the United States in 1938, Walter Jahn gave it to them. But when they arrived, according to Mimi, he did not want to have anything to do with them; he was afraid that the family would sponge off him or be "poor Jewish immigrants" who did not fit into his lifestyle.

Robert's Visits

Another frequent visitor was Mother's brother, my uncle Robert. In the mid-1930s, he stopped traveling around the world and settled in Vienna. He and Mother had a unique relationship; they got along fine when they were not together. As soon as they were together, they started quibbling. She disliked his snobbishness and his rigidity, his breakfast egg that had to be exactly three and a half minutes and his shoes that had to be polished a certain way. He wore spats and walked with a cane to emphasize his Britishness. He spent a lot of time monitoring his stock market investments. We knew that he did well, but he never talked about his own finances because that would have been un-British. He counted every penny ten times before spending it, yet he was generous when it mattered. We used to call him "His Highness" behind his back because of his exaggerated sense of decorum.

Uncle Robert disliked Mother's lack of interest in conforming to society's mores, her Bohemian streak and her preference for artists. In spite of his irksome habits and attitudes, he was a good uncle to all of us, and we had a lot to thank him for. Of the many extended family members who visited, he was the only one who truly belonged to the family. Without a family of his own, Uncle Robert reciprocated our feeling. He had briefly been married to his cousin Emmy to please his renowned matchmaker mother, whom he adored. After four weeks Emmy left. She could not stand his rigidity and his miserliness, attributes that he exhibited until his death in Ibiza at age 93. Basically, he was too self-centered to commit himself to a lasting intimate relationship.

Somehow I had to fit the many visitors into my busy school life. In the fall of 1937 and my tenth school year, I transferred to a Czech high school. Bruno had insisted on our being less German. Although the family had retained Austrian citizenship all along, he changed his citizenship to Czech. Mother used to say we remained Austrian so that the boys could avoid military service in the Czech army. Maybe her choice had something to do with her sense that it was superior to be Austrian rather than Czech. She certainly could not foresee that our Austrian citizenship would cause us enormous difficulties during the emigration.

Bruno also urged us to show more solidarity with the Czechs and be more involved with Czech culture. I agreed with him. The Czech school was farther away, but I did not mind the long tram ride every day. The school was more middle class, with fewer rich students and, I believe, very few Jews. Going to the theater every week was not part of the school program as it had been at the German school, but we had more opportunities for sports. Although I did not like the sciences and math, I was still a good student; somehow I managed to do well on the tests but learned nothing in these subjects. To this day I am convinced that my making an effort to try to understand math and science would be pointless.

Summer in England

The summer I was 15, I spent my vacation in England to learn more English, going along with the custom of well-to-do families of sending their children abroad for the summer. Mother had found an English family that took in foreign students as paying guests. The experience proved exciting, and it did not occur to me to be anxious about the trip or about being away from home. The landscape and the new sights were, however, not as interesting as the young men on the dusty train. Toward the end of the trip I started flirting with a nice young man. Like most first experiences, I recall the feeling of excitement more clearly than I remember the young man.

My English family lived in St. Leonhards-on-Sea, just outside Brighton on the south coast, in a large, slightly run-down but still patrician house. As the family's children were all grown and gone, the young paying guests brought some levity into the rather staid environment. Their breakfast arrangement impressed me; I had never seen it before. The food was set out buffet style, where everybody could serve himself or herself. Spread out on silver platters, English breakfasts featured eggs and bacon and porridge, unheard of in Prague, where we ate only rolls with butter and jam.

At the end of the summer I spoke English fairly fluently, the last of Mother's children to speak four languages by age 16. We were all gifted language learners. But my mind was on other matters as well. One of the other paying guests was a tall, sturdily muscular and attractive 18-year-old Swede, whom I thought quite smashing. We liked each other and went on outings together. After the summer I corresponded with him for a while until I left Prague. Although I never saw him again, I learned a lot about Swedish geography and customs from him, another chance encounter that proved culturally instructive.

Skiing in Saalbach

My first real encounter with boys came at Christmas 1937 in Saalbach, a skiing village in Austria where I went with a Viennese ski club to which my cousin Mimi belonged. We stayed at a primitive hut that we reached by climbing a mountain while carrying all our gear. There we slept on communal bunks with straw mats, one dormitory for boys, one for girls. We washed with cold water in an unheated room and used primitive non-flush toilets outside in the bitter cold. The hut had no electricity; whatever light we had came from oil lamps and flashlights.

Ski lifts or tows did not exist at that time. We had to climb the mountain carrying our skis on our shoulders or put sealskins on them so that we would not slip backwards; sometimes we would climb across the mountain back and forth in serpentine patterns. All of these methods were very strenuous exercise. Many of the group were good athletes and managed the strain well. I was always exhausted, but my pride would not let me give in. If we were lucky and it was not sleeting, on any one day we managed one good run downhill, but no more. The days were short.

In the evening we sat around the heated stove and sang and socialized in the day room. After a while, pairs would start disappearing into the bunks, where there was no privacy; but without electricity they felt quite private. I remember a lot of fondling and necking. I first went with one boy, then with another. Since I had not known any of them before, I was not so inhibited as I would have been in Prague; there, I might have felt obliged to safeguard my reputation. Happily absorbed by the new feelings, I was particularly attracted to Peter. But Peter was my cousin's boyfriend, so he was off-limits for me. Two months shy of 16, I was just discovering the other sex and my own sexuality. However, I still did not know the facts of life.

Peter came back into my life twenty years after our original ski trip meeting. I had stayed in loose touch with him, but we had lost contact during the emigration. Mimi had told him to look me up when he came to San Francisco. Instantly, all the unrequited feelings of twenty years earlier reappeared. They led to an unforgettable interlude in my life.

In Saalbach when we were not skiing or flirting, we were thinking about the ominous political situation. Hitler was poised to invade Austria. Premonitions about war made the emotional experiences that much more poignant. Each of us wanted to suck as much sustenance as possible out of each emotional encounter. That last *Skikurs* (ski course) in Saalbach before the Anschluss, Hitler's annexation of Austria, created significant memories for all the participants. Many of them I met again in later years in surprising places all over the world.

Planning My Future

Returning to Prague from Saalbach, I was full of erotic memories. Eager to continue those half-started relationships, I wanted to leave school and study applied arts at the famous Michelbeuern Akademie in Vienna near my new friends. Mother listened to my proposal. My plan fitted in well with the suggestions of the graphologist whom Mother had consulted first for Bruno and then for me. The graphologist had said that I would never be satisfied with a profession that used only my hands or only my head. But he thought that if I wanted to concentrate on anything, I would be well-suited for dressmaking. He could not have known that I had become an expert doll dressmaker. The year before, I spent many days in bed ill with appendicitis. The home dressmaker, who came frequently to do mending or light sewing, took time to teach me to sew doll dresses, a welcome substitute for going to school. So the graphologist's suggestions seemed reasonable to me.

Mother agreed that I could study dress design in Vienna. Dropping out of high school and learning a trade that was not language-bound seemed like a practical plan, for who knew in what country we might wind up if we really had to emigrate. Neither she nor I saw much future in an academic education, considering the uncertainty of the political situation and the apprehension about a terrible upheaval to come. However, a serious threat still seemed remote.

Karel

And then I met and fell in love with Karel. He was slight, dark-haired and dark-complexioned and had an infectious smile. A friend of Bruno's, he was quite a bit older than Bruno and much older than I was. By then, Bruno had given up policing my movements. Karel worked for Intourist in Prague, the Soviet tourist agency. He and Bruno had been on a tour of the Soviet Union together and returned very enthusiastic about communism. With my predilection for things Russian I listened eagerly to their accounts, although they certainly did not accord with my French teacher's views.

When Karel came to the house to visit Bruno, I made a point of being there. He was so attractive! In those days I never would have dared show my feelings; that was absolutely taboo. Fortunately, he started to show some interest in me. Thrilled, I spent a lot of time daydreaming. I wondered how I could be so attracted to Karel after having just been so excited by Peter in Saalbach and the others with whom I enjoyed flirting. I contemplated whether that made me a nymphomaniac, something I had heard of but could not quite define.

Karel and I used to go to the movies in the afternoon. We would sit in the back row and pet and neck, coming out without the slightest idea of what the movie had been about. But we did have long discussions afterwards about the political situations. Karel would spout the Communist line that the Soviet Union would be there to defend Czechoslovakia, with whom it had a mutual defense pact. I doubt that I paid attention.

I went to my first real dance with Karel. After the dance he took me to a bar, the first bar I had ever seen. I found it dark, noisy and smoky, with men standing at the counter drinking beer, wine and liqueurs and the radio blaring. On one side of the large room were booths where couples sat close together, dreamily looking into each other's eyes. The noise of the counter did not reach the booths. Karel steered me to one of the booths and ordered a liqueur for me. Then he put his arms around me and held me tight. Just then the radio played one of the famous love songs from Verdi's opera *La Traviata*. I thought that nothing could ever be more blissful. I did not know then that we were in a sort of bordello and that behind the booths were bedrooms. Karel took me home long before anything serious ensued. Not that I really knew what was possible.

To this day, hearing the *Traviata* song often reminds me of that unforgettable moment and makes me smile inside. The bar, now a restaurant, still exists. Every time I visit Prague, I make a point of passing by to relive that miraculous awakening of a 16-year-old.

Mother's Affair

While I was overwhelmed by my nascent feelings, Mother had her own emotional upheavals. Around this time, she had a serious relationship with a radiologist who was younger than she. He was demanding and jealous. I did not like him; I thought he took too much of Mother's time. Without understanding the issues, I remember overhearing scenes in Mother's bedroom that left her crying. I know that this doctor wanted to marry her and that she refused. Later, Mother told me that Bruno had said he would never forgive her if she remarried, especially someone who was not of his father's caliber. When I much later checked with Bruno, he did not remember having said that. The radiologist threatened suicide if she did not marry him. This stormy relationship must have weighed on Mother as she contemplated future actions. Hitler and the dissolution of our lives resolved the dilemma. Mother left for Paris to join me, and the radiologist eventually immigrated to the United States. He became a well-known specialist in his field and married an American woman. Soon thereafter he died of leukemia, a victim of his profession.

Paul Back in Czechoslovakia

The realization that we might someday become refugees was still far from Mother's mind when Paul returned from South Africa in 1936. Soon after, he got a job with the Bata Shoe Company, one of the largest firms in Czechoslovakia. Bata used American mass production methods to produce inexpensive shoes. Paul first went to Zlin, a company town in Moravia, where the factory was located. There he met Dita Berger, his future wife, who lived in a neighboring town. Bata was one of the first multinationals, with factories all over the world and a rubber plantation in Malaysia. The company had a policy that everybody who worked there had to start out by selling shoes, regardless of what position the person was slated for later. I remember Paul selling shoes on the street in Prague outside one of the Bata stores, not far from our apartment. He came home with hilarious stories about how he motivated old ladies to buy more shoes than they had planned to buy, or how all the shoeboxes crashed to the floor when he was searching for a pair of shoes he could not locate.

Excitement always surrounded Paul during the few months he lived at home. One night there was a great commotion when he invited Mother's manicurist to his room. Our apartment was made up of two connected apartments, each with its own entrance from the staircase. Paul had smuggled her in through the servants' entrance. I was 14 years old and did not understand what all the fuss was about.

In 1937 the Skoda Works, Czechoslovakia's largest and most important industrial complex, offered Paul a promising post in its export division. Skoda wanted to send him to India to negotiate an important sale there. After much discussion, he convinced Dita to marry him and go to India with him. They were married on February 27, 1938, in Dita's home in Moravia. I went to the wedding, which overshadowed my 16th birthday the day before. Theirs was the first Jewish wedding I had attended, and I remember being quite stunned by the custom of deliberately stepping on a glass to break it. I still thought that breaking a glass was a sin!

Immediately after the wedding, not quite three weeks before Hitler marched into Austria, Paul and Dita left Czechoslovakia. I went back to Prague with Dita's younger brother, Hardy, whom I had not met before. Knowing Hardy became significant much later, when he arranged for an extremely important introduction.

Drastic Changes in Our World

At the wedding, the guests had been in a somber mood. The news from Austria was ominous. Hitler seemed poised to annex Austria. On March 9 the Austrian chancellor, Schuschnigg, announced a plebiscite, giving the Austrian voters an opportunity to choose between an independent Austria and one incorporated into Germany. The next day, Austrian Nazis demonstrated openly in the center of Vienna. Viennese Jews behaved like ostriches and put their heads in the sand, although they should have been forewarned by what had happened in Germany. The postponed plebiscite did not happen; Shuschnigg resigned, and on March 13, 1938, Austria became part of the German Reich. The Austrian population jubilantly welcomed the German troops. Overnight, Vienna became a foreign city. Huge flags with swastikas hung from every rooftop. Brownshirts patrolled the streets, and hundreds of ecstatic Austrians strolled toward the center of the city enthusiastically waving small flags with swastikas.

During the first days of the Nazi regime, violence took over the streets of Vienna. The Gestapo, the Nazi police, rounded up Jews, forcing them to scrub the sidewalk in front of their stores. They looted Jewish shops and mistreated and beat the shop owners, foreshadowing Kristallnacht in November 1938, when the Nazis organized the worst anti-Jewish pogrom of the war. After a few days, that particular terror subsided and the streets became less dangerous. During these first few days many Jews could have left, but only a few did. Thereafter, Jews could obtain exit permits only by leaving practically all their belongings behind. It is difficult to know whether their continuing and astonishing indecision amid increasing adversity was simple shortsightedness or disbelief in the reality of the Nazi threat. Vienna's lifestyle must have had redeeming features that were hard to leave. In Prague we worried about friends and relatives in Vienna, urging them to get out as fast as they could.

Many people in Prague still believed that what had happened in Austria could not happen in Czechoslovakia. Mother was not among them. She thought it would be best if I left Prague as quickly as possible. She could not motivate Bruno to consider leaving. Planning to start managing his newly acquired farm after finishing agriculture school, he believed in the inviolability of Czechoslovakia.

Of course my plan to go to Vienna was now out of the question. Anyway, my original goal to be with my new friends had lost its appeal when I met Karel. The graphologist's suggestions, combined with my interest in learning dressmaking and finding an occupation with which I could support myself anywhere, led Mother to suggest I go to Paris, the center of haute couture. Although I was now very aware of the worsening political situation, I was still preoccupied with myself and my romance. Paris held no particular attraction for me. I did not really want to go anywhere. Fortunately, I recognized the necessity for leaving. It did not occur to me that I would be gone forever.

Heinrich Gruensfeld and Rosa Lindner
Grandmother Emma Tritsch's parents

Leopold Tritsch and Clara
Karpeles, ca. 1880
Grandfather Heinrich Tritsch's
parents

Tritsch family, 1905
Robert, Lilly, Emma, Gustav, Heinrich

Emma, ca. 1920

Heinrich Tritsch, 1913
Fishing near Stift Melk

Tritsch family hike, 1908
Lilly, Emma and Emma's brother

*Innsbruck: We were all born on the third floor of
this stately building*

Emma playing tennis, 1901

Only existing photo of Father's family, 1919
back row, from left: Ignaz Kandler, Fini Kandler, Fritz Kandler,
Marta Kandler, Gottlieb Morawetz
seated, from left: Father's sister Luise Kandler, Father's mother
Fanny Morawetz, Lilly Morawetz
front row, from left: Paul, Bruno, Felix

"Prague villa Rauchzimmer" drawing room, velvet wall covers survived the Nazis and the Communists

Stage sets for house ball

Parents in costume for ball, Lilly seated on floor, Gottlieb at right

Guest dining room with sideboard that was too large to be stolen by the Nazis

Villa staff
from left: cook; valet; chambermaid; Yeya, my
governess; house seamstress; housekeeper;
her husband/handyman

Gottlieb, age 52, just before he died, with
Margit, age 10, 1932

Prague villa, 1995

Villa in Alt Aussee

View of Alt Aussee with lake and Loser

Father in Austrian dress, shortly before he died

Alt Aussee, 1933
Margit with cousin Lily Morawetz, Emma Morawetz,Georg Brassloff, Vali Morawetz

Family on the Lido, 1926
from left: Felix, cousin Erni Morawetz, Bruno, Lilly, Gottlieb,
Margit, Yeya, Paul

Paul, Margit, Felix, Mother, Bruno in
our garden, 1927

Uncle Robert with Flippi, Prague, 1937

Uncle Gustl and Tante Grete Tritsch, 1930s

81

Karel

Bruno (second from left) with Zionist friends in Prague, 1935

Margit before nose surgery, 1938

Margit with Flippi, just before leaving Prague, 1938

Margit's first year in the gymnasium, 1932/33. I am in the 4th row, center, right behind the girl with blond tresses

PART 2

REFUGEE

4

PARIS AND BEYOND

ONCE WE HAD decided that I would go to Paris and become a dressmaker, Uncle Robert with his international connections helped Mother find me a place to live. He located a French family on the outskirts of Paris that was taking in paying guests. By the end of March, I was off to Paris by plane. I only felt sad about leaving Karel. A friend of Mother's who was flying to Paris on business agreed to take me along and deliver me to the Dubourguez family in suburban Chatou-Croissy, not far from Versailles.

What an adventure, my first flight! In 1938, flying was still very exclusive, expensive and chic, and I was thrilled that I would go by plane. The DC 3 had two rows of seats, two persons per row, and was unpressurized and very noisy. My seat was not by a window, so I could not look out. At first I was upset that I could not see anything, but not for long. As soon as we reached cruising altitude, all I could think of was that my ears were going to pop out of my head, the air-pressure pain was so awful. The pain overshadowed any other memories I may have had of this momentous first experience with air travel. The flight seemed endless. I was so glad to land that I stopped wondering what living away from home would feel like.

The Dubourguez family lived in a dilapidated but still grand castle, Le Château de la Pièce d'Eau, named after the small pond next to the house. The majestic, dark gray, three-story stone house with turrets was much larger than our house in Prague. Some of the spacious rooms were dark

85

because only a little daylight came in through the small windows. These rooms were hardly ever used and had a musty smell. The house was surrounded by a large, neglected garden, the design of which still showed traces of the grandeur of previous generations.

I soon fit into this household. Two daughters close to my age and an older son were very welcoming. Madame Dubourguez, a thin, tall and distinguished-looking middle-aged woman, was a trained French teacher who took me under her wing. I knew enough French from my lessons in Prague not to feel lost whenever someone spoke to me, although I found it hard at first to follow the dinner table conversation. Meals were in the rather formal dining room. Without servants, Madame's sister-in-law, who also lived in the château, did the cooking and the daughters assisted with the meals. I also learned to help.

So that I would be able to study in France, Mother had somehow arranged for official permission to send me a monthly sum from Prague despite currency restrictions. The amount was just enough for me to pay Madame and cover incidental expenses. For the first time, I was going to be responsible for myself. At age 16 that felt good.

Before arriving in Paris I had obtained a student visa, but because I was an Austrian citizen and Austria was now part of Germany, I was in a special "enemy alien" category. France was not yet at war with Germany, but the atmosphere was charged and very uncomfortable. The fact that I was Jewish was immaterial to the French bureaucrats. They automatically assumed that anybody with a German or Austrian passport could be a spy, whether Jewish nor not. I had to go to the central *préfecture de police* (police commissariat) every couple of weeks to have my residence permit stamped. In long queues, sometimes in the rain and the cold, foreigners from all over the world were waiting for a few grumpy officials who made them feel unwanted, unwelcome and superfluous. With only a few wooden benches for the waiting public, the crowd struggled to obtain seats. Across the hallway, a special waiting room for English and American foreigners had carpeted floors and upholstered benches. Whether the officials were friendlier there I did not know, but at least the atmosphere looked more welcoming. The obligatory biweekly trips to the prefecture kept reminding me of my precarious situation in France. I do not remember being scared, only apprehensive about the obnoxious behavior of the French officials.

Some of my Alt Aussee friends from Vienna with whom I had corresponded appeared in Paris, all of them frightened by the suddenness of their departure from Austria, many unsure of their future. A few lucky ones had English or American visas and were waiting for ships to take them across the water. Most of them had left family members behind and were desperately trying to find ways to help them leave Austria. The mood was tense and the outlook seemed bleak for them.

I felt secure with the Dubourguezes, who treated me like a member of the family. Madame immediately started giving me French lessons. With a total-immersion routine, I spent three hours in the morning with Madame, then had lunch, then worked another two hours with her. After that I did homework, which included standing in front of a mirror, checking the way I pursed my lips to make the right sounds and correcting my pronunciation. After three months of this schedule, I spoke fluent French with hardly a trace of a foreign accent, profiting from my talent for learning languages!

Three times a week I commuted from Chatou to Paris to attend a course at the Sorbonne in French civilization, including French literature, history, philosophy and geography. I took notes as best I could and then went over them with Madame. Very motivated to study, I paid close attention to the lecturers, eager not to miss a single word of what they said. Realizing I was progressing fast, I enjoyed making the effort.

Although my life in Paris was busy, I kept writing to Karel about how much I missed him. He left Prague soon after I did and went to Yugoslavia to join clandestine Communist activities. To protect me from any unpleasantness his activities could cause me, he felt it wise to stop writing to me. We soon lost all contact. After the war I felt terrible hearing that in 1941 the Nazis had caught and executed him in Belgrade.

My life at the château was very different from my life in Prague, where I had never drawn my own bath or washed out my own hose. Quite paradoxically, I who had been so sheltered in Prague now had so much independence in Paris. On Sundays, before spending the day with the Dubouguez young folks bicycling, hiking or playing tennis, I attended Lutheran church services with the family. What felt comforting about their service was having someone to pray to and to protect me.

Religious Conversions

Mother found another kind of spiritual pathway. I knew that she had joined the Anthroposophical Society in Prague before I left. A German pastor, Father Lenz, had stimulated her interest in the society and had inducted her into that nondenominational Christian religious community. Anthroposophy is a spiritual movement based on the early-20th-century worldview of Rudolf Steiner, an Austrian scientist who asserted the unity of body, mind and spirit. The movement encompasses Far Eastern as well as Christian ethics, emphasizing the importance of life after death. Steiner also developed an educational philosophy that led to his worldwide Waldorf School movement. In addition, he initiated the international Camp Hill movement, which established effective rural communities for people with mental retardation. I believe that Mother's joining the anthroposophical community filled her need to belong somewhere other than the upper-class bourgeois environment from which she was trying to escape.

I wrote Mother that I had found true faith and wanted to convert to Lutheranism. She did not object. So after studying with the local pastor for a few weeks, he officially baptized me a Lutheran. At that time we still had illusions that being baptized—having left the Jewish faith—would protect us from Hitler's anti-Jewish laws. Conversion for me meant a combination of adopting a belief and staying alive. To escape private doubts about my real motivation for converting, I convinced myself that this conversion was about my valuing Lutheranism, not the pure opportunism it felt like later. I never really participated in the Lutheran religion. In any case, I lost the belief quickly. Any certificate of baptism I may have had was lost with all the other documents that disappeared during the escape. I never told anybody then that I was no longer Jewish until many years later when I met Frank Meissner, who had undergone a similar baptism.

The political situation was becoming more and more worrisome through 1938. Hundreds of Jews left Czechoslovakia and Austria. A few were still able to leave Germany. Many more tried to leave but had neither the money nor the connections needed for emigration. France was a common transit point for those who searched for a destination overseas. With America's and Australia's severely restricted immigration laws, emigrants in Paris explored access to other countries on all continents. Inexplicably now, as I sift through my letters to Mother that she preserved, though I was aware of the pre-war turmoil, I hardly mentioned it. I wrote mainly about my studies and reported on my daily life with just a few mentions of the worsening crisis.

During the summer I spent a few weeks with German refugee friends at the beach in Normandy. Life there seemed pleasantly normal to me. Mother was able to visit Paris at the end of August to help me select a dressmaking school. I had completed the Sorbonne course and was now ready to learn my future trade. We stayed in Chatou for a few weeks before moving into Paris to live together in a series of rented rooms.

Munich and the Betrayal of Czechoslovakia

The political situation kept growing more grim. Hitler ranted on and on about his goal of incorporating into his thousand-year Reich the three and a quarter million Germans of Czechoslovakia who lived in the Sudeten mountains bordering Germany. By 1938 the majority of these German-speaking citizens of Czechoslovakia were supporting Hitler. Their Sudeten German Party, led by a gymnastics teacher named Konrad Henlein, had become the largest political party in Czechoslovakia's parliament, larger than any of the Czech or Slovak parties in the coalition government. Wanting to be part of Germany, this party now adopted the swastika emblem that had previously been banned in Czechoslovakia.

The Henlein party at first pretended to be independent of Hitler, but in September 1938, encouraged by Hitler, Henlein openly demanded that the Sudetenland become part of the German Reich. Too weak to act, the Czech government put its trust for protection in its alliance with France and the *Petite Entente,* the mutual defense treaty of Czechoslovakia, Rumania and Yugoslavia. But nobody came to the aid of Czechoslovakia, since both France and England were not ready to back up their commitments. The Soviet Union, another guarantor of Czechoslovakia, was preoccupied with its own goals of spreading world communism. Eager to appease the feared German despot, British Prime Minister Neville Chamberlain traveled on his own ill-conceived initiative to Berchtesgaden near Munich in southern Germany. There he handed the Sudetenland to Germany in return for a promise from Hitler not to make any more territorial demands anywhere. Then on September 30, 1938, in one of the most treacherous and self-interested acts of modern European diplomacy, France and Great Britain co-signed the Munich Pact with Hitler and Mussolini. Without consulting the Czechoslovak government, they agreed to Hitler's insistence on annexing the Sudetenland. When he returned to Britain, Chamberlain assured the British public that he had negotiated "peace in our time." The French and British publics were genuinely relieved that they would not have to go to war for, in Chamberlain's words, "a quarrel in a faraway country between people of whom we know nothing."

Betrayed by its allies and fearing bloodshed, the Czechoslovak government capitulated. This action was prelude to Hitler's occupying all of Czechoslovakia on March 16, 1939. The republic's outraged citizens, so proud of their twenty-year-old unique experiment in democracy in Central Europe, felt undervalued and expendable. Mother and I followed these developments, feeling both anxious and indignant, beginning to comprehend the extent of the threat.

Mother had left her Prague apartment as if she had gone on a vacation. She had not prepared for emigration. Now, after Munich, she kept saying that she had to return to Prague to dismantle the apartment and fill the much-vaunted "lift" with her furniture for shipment overseas.

Commonly used by people who intended to leave and take their belongings along, the lift was a large wooden container that would fit on a railroad flatcar. Emigrants had to obtain many complicated permits from the government for such shipments. Mother intended to fill a lift with her belongings and send it to Rotterdam, a neutral port; but still in partial denial, she foolishly procrastinated. Instead of going back to Prague, she went to the French Riviera to be with her brother Robert, while I continued with my studies in Paris.

Sewing School

Having gathered information about dressmaking schools, I enrolled in the public École de la Chambre Syndicale de la Couture Parisienne. The *école* was a vocational school for girls with no high school education who were training to become *petites mains* (little hands)—garment finishers and seamstress assistants. I did not realize that this prestigious school for the trade would lead only to the status of a helper. We mainly learned to make very small, very even stitches, to work painstakingly and patiently, and to execute orders. Most of the girls had just finished middle school and had had sewing lessons in school. I was the only one who was totally inexperienced and therefore the thorn in the teacher's eye. She put me in the first row so that she could keep an eye on me, and she kept admonishing me to be more *minutieuse*, more painstaking. I did not think I would ever be able to please her, nor did I relish the idea of becoming a *petite main*.

So I quickly transferred to the private Académie de Coupe et Couture, where I learned to make patterns. The intensive course, which progressed rapidly, seemed to meet my needs. In addition to my pattern-making studies, I enrolled at the Académie de la Grande Chaumière, an art school with live models where people went to learn to draw. Drawing models and sketching clothes would be necessary skills if I wanted to become a dress designer.

At Madame Paul-Boncour's

When Mother left for the Riviera, I went to live with Madame Paul-Boncour, the widow of a former French finance minister who was willing to take me in as a paying guest. Madame Paul-Boncour was an intelligent, well-educated, elderly lady who was heavy-set and quite immobilized by arthritis. She seemed to enjoy our lively mealtime discussions as much as I did. I learned a lot about France and life in general from her. She was a wise woman with a good sense of humor hidden beneath her authoritarian demeanor. Her equally arthritic old cook/maid, Georgette, in addition to preparing the meals and keeping house, also looked after me. She cared for me affectionately after I had cosmetic surgery on my nose.

Plastic surgery to alter my nose had been my great wish from the time that Bruno convinced me in Prague that no man would ever look at a girl with such an ugly nose. Plastic surgery, almost unheard of in Prague, was more frequently practiced and more advanced in France. The procedure was not pleasant. I had to go to a private clinic where I stayed overnight with lots of ice packs on my face to lessen the swelling. I kept telling myself, *"Pour être belle il faut souffrir"* (to be beautiful, you have to suffer). After a few days of unsightly swelling, my face was close enough to normal so that I could return to school. The surgery had to be repeated, as the first time it was not completely successful. Fortunately, the second surgery was less painful. I was proud that I had managed the process on my own without Mother's help, though she knew that I was going to get my nose fixed. The experience added to my self-confidence about both my appearance and my coping skills.

At Madame Paul-Boncour's I had a sewing machine in my room so that I could do my homework. I felt at home there, generally oblivious to the gathering war clouds. One of the bonuses of that period was meeting Jean Pierre, Madame's step-grandson. Eleven years older than I, he was tall, blond and handsome with an infectious smile. On Friday nights we went to the movies or walked hand in hand along the banks of the Seine. I was in love. It was all very romantic; I knew he liked me from his sentimental

91

comments and clearly reciprocated my feelings. But I was baffled because he did not take any overt action. Unaware of the facts of life and with strong sexual feelings that I did not yet comprehend, I often felt quite frustrated. I learned only much later that he had wanted to make love to me but been afraid to "corrupt a minor."

Farewell to Prague

Mother, surprisingly, did not leave France to return to Prague from the Riviera until January 1939. There she dismantled her household and tried to get the necessary legal permissions for expediting the lift. The documents were slow in coming, but she still seemed in no great hurry to leave the familiar surroundings. Thus she was still in Prague, and still without a lift, when German troops marched into the city on March 15 and annexed Czechoslovakia. There went "peace in our time"!

It was Bruno who ended up enabling Mother to leave Czechoslovakia. Having trusted the Czech alliance with France, not until the Munich agreement did Bruno start contemplating emigration. A couple of months after the agreement he had helped father's sister, Tante Luise, and her husband move to safety by installing them in the house on his farm. As a result of the Munich agreement, the part of Czechoslovakia where they lived was now under German domination and no longer safe for Jews. As it turned out, they did not stay on the farm for very long. Tante Luise died a few months later, and her husband, Ignatz Kandler, was deported two years later to the Terezín concentration camp, where he perished.

Incredibly, Bruno and his circle of friends did not view the Munich agreement with the alarm it deserved. Instead of preparing to emigrate, Bruno went to see his great love Mimi in Nice, France, and stayed there for two weeks in February 1939. Mimi and her family were waiting for their American visas. He returned home just two weeks before Hitler's army entered Prague. After watching the tanks roll in supported by German bombers, he finally comprehended that he had to leave as soon as possible. Mother was still in Prague and she, too, had to leave at once. Both now needed a Gestapo exit permit.

Fortunately, Mother had earlier obtained the required French document, the much-desired *titre de voyage*, that permitted her to re-enter France. I awaited her impatiently, not knowing when she would arrive. Telephone connections were almost unobtainable; one had to go through an operator and the lines were continuously busy. Anxiously I went to the train station every afternoon to see whether she had come. What a relief when she finally alighted from the train on March 29, 1939!

Bruno as Emigré

Bruno now wanted to go to England, which was still admitting Czech citizens without visas until the end of March. As a result of the Munich agreement, England decided to install a visa requirement after that date to avoid a flood of refugees. He had no time to lose. The day after the German invasion, Bruno tried to leave by train without the now-mandatory Gestapo exit permit. Border guards turned him back. Returning to Prague, in desperation he entrusted his Czech passport and Mother's Austrian passport to an unsavory man who promised to get him the exit permits for a large sum of money. None of Bruno's friends were willing to hand their passports to this character. After several frightening delays, the man did get the exit permits for Bruno and Mother. On March 29, the day before the British would begin requiring visas for Czechs wanting to enter England, they left—Mother for Paris, where I was anxiously waiting for her, and Bruno for England. They started out, I believe, on the same train.

Luckily for Bruno, Uncle Robert, the British citizen, was then in England and came to Bruno's aid at the Dutch-German border, where the British had set up an immigration service center. The Dutch wanted to make sure that the refugees would keep going and not remain in Holland. Had Uncle Robert not vouched for his nephew, the Dutch might not have let Bruno in.

When Bruno arrived in England, he had to find work immediately. He had not been able to take any money out of Czechoslovakia. He found a job as a cowhand on an English farm, and although the now-expatriate "gentleman farmer" had never milked a cow before, he knew how to do it. Bruno spent a little more than a year working on different farms in England. Although the farm families treated him well and considered him part of the family, he did not relish the idea of milking cows for the remainder of the war.

Bruno's chance to leave came when he found out that Canada was issuing visas to refugees who committed themselves to work in agriculture. Mother was able to send him $1,000 to use as a required guarantee that he would not do any other work. He arrived in Canada on May 16, 1940, and, as expected, immediately had to turn over his $1,000 to the Canadian immigration officials, leaving $12 in his pocket.

Very soon after his arrival, he found work on a farm in the Niagara Peninsula close to the U.S. border on Lake Ontario. Needing a vehicle to get around, he bought a '29 Nash for $75. The ten-year-old Nash was a temperamental car that occasionally would not start. The creative Bruno devised a remedy: he would hitch a team of farm horses to a rope on his front bumper and, shaking the reins out of the window, get the horses to run and thus start the car. The danger was that the car would bump the horses, but fortunately it never did.

In September, Bruno found a dilapidated fruit farm in Beamsville overlooking Lake Ontario. The farm had no running water, only a well and an outhouse. The price was $4,500 and the down payment $500. The Immigration Department agreed to return his $1,000, and Bruno bought the farm. A kind neighbor gave him a dog to keep him company and so began his tough and lonely life as a poor independent farmer in Canada. Several good neighbors made the adjustment easier. With their help, he learned about fruit farming on the Niagara Peninsula. In addition to learning to farm, Bruno worked in various factories to support himself while waiting for the farm to produce.

Wartime France

After Mother arrived, I left Madame Paul-Boncour's and we again lived in a series of rented rooms. I never questioned whether we had enough money to live in the modestly comfortable way we did. We somehow had enough money. Despite the signs that war was approaching, during the summer vacation in August 1939 Mother and I spent a relaxing month in Pras de Chamonix, an alpine resort next to the famous resort village Chamonix. Hard as it is to believe as I look back, we went hiking, gathered wildflowers and enjoyed the beautiful mountain landscape as though we had not a care in the world. On September 3 we were on a bus returning from the Alps to Paris when we heard that Germany had invaded Poland and France had declared war on Germany. This was it!

Besides no longer receiving money from Prague, we now felt truly endangered. Upon our return from the mountains, we moved into a rented furnished apartment in the middle of Paris near the Place de la Concorde. The apartment, which belonged to an American painter who must have given us a good deal on the rent before he returned to the States, was left in the care of his trusted housekeeper. Maria was a tiny, thin, middle-aged woman with a shrill voice and a heart of gold. Loyal to her American employer, she became as loyal to us. Here we also finally had a kitchen.

In this prestigious neighborhood our windows on the top floor looked directly into the courtyard of the Élysée Palace, the residence of the French president. We felt almost as if we belonged in these upper-class French surroundings. As we watched limousines coming and going, we would guess who was advising President Daladier. Mainly we spent our time wondering how we were going to survive the war.

Although France was officially at war, the shooting had not started. While the Germans were busy in Eastern Europe, the French were fortifying their positions, relying on the Maginot Line. The French army considered this series of fortifications along the French–German border impenetrable. I remember large maps posted on the walls of Paris showing the Allied world in red as a huge expanse across the globe with a small black blob indicating Germany. The Maginot Line was prominently etched across the French–German border with the slogan *"Ils ne passeront pas!"* (They shall not pass!) I believed in that slogan along with most of the French population. How could little Germany stand up successfully to the huge rest of the world?

For a while the limited *drôle de guerre,* the phony war that did not include shooting, was deceivingly reassuring. Nevertheless, we were certain now that we had to leave Europe—but to go where? The U.S. immigration quota for Austrians was closed and had a waiting list of many years. Anyway, we were not so eager to go to the United States; Mother still thought of it as the land of skyscrapers and Dillinger, and decadent music with "no culture." Australia seemed more appealing culturally but equally difficult to reach. Some of our friends had gone to England, which seemed safer than France. We did not pursue that alternative seriously. Uncle Robert had gone to New York, Felix was in New York, and Paul and Dita had recently arrived in Australia.

Soon after war broke out, my status as an enemy alien in France deteriorated. Rather than every two weeks, I now had to go to the police every week to get my *permis de séjour* (residence permit) stamped. I was authorized to remain in Paris, but Mother, who had entered France with her Austrian passport after a certain cut-off date for Austrian refugees, could no longer get permission to live there. Obliged to leave Paris, she found a room in a private home in Versailles an hour away. There she established her legal residence. Trying to approximate a regular life, she came to Paris every morning on the train and returned to Versailles at night. So that we could spend some time together, I came home for lunch from school every day.

Clearly worrying about our future, Mother acted especially tense. She felt particularly discriminated against because none of our Austrian friends had been banned from Paris; they had, however, arrived in France earlier than Mother. Tempers were raw and flared easily. I recall a shouting argument between Mother and me when she wanted to go out somewhere; I was keeping her waiting because I could not put down the book that I was reading, the French translation of *Gone with the Wind*. I had rarely seen her that angry with me.

Meanwhile, I continued with my pattern-making studies, eagerly awaiting the June completion of the course. My friendship with Jean Pierre continued happily unchanged. We went out together on Friday nights, holding hands as we walked through the narrow streets of Paris admiring the old, ornate buildings hidden in quiet neighborhoods on the Left Bank. He was in the army reserves and wondered worriedly when he would be called up. The few hours we spent together each week were particularly lyrical; our walks became a peaceful oasis in the dangerous turmoil in which we were living.

Most of our friends who were Czech citizens had left for England, for Morocco—wherever they could go. The French did not treat the Czechs as enemies. Perhaps they felt guilty that they had not fulfilled their treaty obligations and had not come to the rescue of Czechoslovakia when the Germans invaded it. The French felt no such sympathy for the Austrians. They simply treated them as unwanted refugees and enemies.

On May 9, 1940, the German army invaded Belgium, Holland and Luxembourg. The newscasts on the Paris radio became more and more ominous, increasingly talking about German soldiers penetrating French lines. However, we still believed the French propaganda that these were only temporary setbacks. On May 12, the Germans broke through the French lines, bypassing the supposedly "impenetrable" Maginot Line at the French–German border. Was it possible that the allegedly unbeatable French army could give way so quickly?

Jean Pierre was now called up to join his regiment. I accompanied him in a taxi to the railroad station. In the cab he held me and sang a lilting love song that I have never forgotten. The melody stayed in my ears long after the sound of bombs or sirens vanished. We said a heartrending goodbye, certain we would never see each other again.

A few days later when Mother got back to her room in Versailles, she found a notice from the police commanding her to report to a certain assembly point in three days. She could bring whatever belongings she could carry, a blanket and enough food for three days. The notice said that she was going to be evacuated to the South. The next day she came into Paris and gave me 10,000 francs—from where, I did not know, but enough to last for several months—and the address of a Monsieur Weil, who would help us both leave France. With that she left, with a small suitcase and a bundle on her back.

These events all happened so quickly that I hardly comprehended what was happening. Too stunned to be frightened, I had no idea where she would be taken or where to contact her. Now it was clearly up to me to go into high gear and try to get both of us out of France.

5

ESCAPE

I HAD NEVER heard the name of Monsieur Weil before. Mother told me only that our acquaintances the Junks had given her his name before they left Paris a couple of months earlier. Gerhard Junk and his wife were German bridge-playing friends of Uncle Robert's. Christian anti-Nazis, they had left Germany in the early '30s and moved to Barcelona. At the outbreak of the Spanish Civil War in 1935, they fled from Barcelona to Paris. Uncle Robert saw them frequently; Mother and I knew the Junks only casually. During the days of the *drôle de guerre,* when Robert had left for New York and Mother and I were debating our future moves, the Junks promised they would try to help us get into Spain. But before their help materialized, the shooting war started on May 10 and they quickly went back to Spain. As they were leaving, they reiterated that they would try to help us from there.

As Mother prepared for internment, and intent on leaving me with as many resources as possible, she remembered Monsieur Weil. I was thankful for the contact but waited before using it. My own situation rapidly grew more harassing. I was now supposed to go to the police daily to prove that I had not escaped. Frustrated with their inability to stem the advance of the German army, the French authorities increased their monitoring of aliens. They were bent on cleansing France of people like me whom they considered to be spies. My request for permission to leave Paris was categorically denied. The French authorities could not have been more hostile.

In the first days of June the noises of detonation and guns were growing louder. The smoldering fires of burned documents in the courtyards of the French government offices started to cloud the Paris sky. The war had finally arrived. I was now in it and for the first time felt personally threatened. By now, all our Czech acquaintances had left Paris. With Mother gone I was all alone.

The only friends who were left were Sophie Freud, Sigmund Freud's granddaughter, and her mother, Esti, Freud's daughter-in-law. As Austrian citizens, they were in the same position as I. Sophie was the cousin of one of my good friends in Prague. When she had come to France, she stayed with me at Chatou. We had enjoyed cutting out paper dolls together and designing clothes for them. We now agreed to make common cause and try to get to Brest in Brittany. The Freuds hoped that from there they could get a boat to England to rejoin the rest of the Freud family, who had fled from Vienna to England earlier. I did not know what I would do in Brittany; I just wanted to leave and be with someone I knew.

I went to see Monsieur Weil, who immediately promised to help me get a travel permit if I came back the next day. I had to keep checking in with the police. They had threatened that if I ever left Paris without a travel permit, they would put me in jail as soon as they found me. Not waiting for Monsieur Weil, I went to the railway station to obtain a ticket to Brest just in case the police relented. The train station was closed. No trains were running. The blackout of Paris was complete, and the streets were deserted. The eerie absence of sound and activity was alarming. I was scared and felt trapped.

On June 14 Italy joined Germany and declared war on France. I went back to see Monsieur Weil that evening in a state of great agitation. He said he was sorry about not having been able to get anything for me. The room was crowded with others who apparently had also come for his advice or help. Among them was a handsome lieutenant who turned out to be Monsieur Weil's son, Albertito, whose mother was from Argentina. In uniform, he was on his way to the train station to rejoin his regimen. Despite my anxiety, I noticed he was tall, dark-haired, dark-complected and dashing in his neatly pressed officer's uniform. As I was leaving, feeling very dejected, he offered to accompany me home. Gratefully I accepted.

We waited for the Metro. I was impatient because it was getting late and I had to be home before the Paris midnight curfew. When the Metro finally came, the train was almost empty. Albertito sat next to me on the bench and started embracing me. His arms felt good. He asked me in a sort of muffled voice, *"Tu veux faire l'amour?"* (Do you want to make love?) I did not understand what he meant, but my response must not have seemed negative.

When we got out at the station of the huge and normally bustling Place de la Concorde, we were the only passengers exiting. We had to traverse the entire huge, cobblestoned square to reach my street. Past curfew by now, the square was deserted. I was petrified. Sure enough, a gendarme approached us and asked for our identity papers. I thought I was finished. I would now be arrested! But my escort showed the gendarme his officer orders and then he winked, saying, "And this lady is my friend." The gendarme understood and went away. The relief and gratitude I felt were indescribable.

Arriving at my house, he said he wanted to come up. Because in Paris no one ever had a house key, I had to ring the bell for the concierge to peek out of her window and buzz the door open. Though I thought that it was totally improper for me to come home at that hour of the night with a strange man, I knew I could explain if she or anybody else asked.

Upstairs in my apartment we were alone. Maria, the housekeeper, slept on the floor above in the maid's room. Keenly aware of how unseemly it was to be with this young man by myself at this late hour, I offered to make him tea. But before I could put the water on the stove, he embraced me and took me to the bedroom. I was startled but did not resist. I was not sure what we were doing, but I realized later that I had just lost my virginity. Afterwards he kept saying, "Why didn't you tell me that you were a virgin?" I became deathly ashamed. What had I done? How could I have let myself be carried away? I had enjoyed being in his arms, feeling protected and safe. But the elation that I had thought I was supposed to feel escaped me.

After I regained my composure, I told him to leave. Now, right away! He was stunned. It was about 2 a.m. and I knew that his troop train would not depart until 6 a.m. The Metro and the buses were no longer running, which meant that he would be out on the street during curfew. Without pity I made him leave at once and never saw or heard from him again. I have often wondered what he must have thought about my behavior and how he spent those three hours.

Despite my mixed emotions, this brief encounter made a crucial difference in my life. Now I was no longer a girl; I had become a woman, and as a woman I could permit myself actions that were unseemly for a girl. Strange that proper behavior was more important to me than saving my skin! During the next few sleepless hours I got up my courage and decided to leave Paris on my own, with or without permission. At daybreak I went to the police, determined this time to get a travel permit. I found the police station open but empty. The gendarmes were gone, having fled before the advancing Germans.

The streets were filled with moving humanity. People were pushing baby carriages loaded with belongings, some with a canary cage on top. Others had overloaded wheelbarrows. The mass of cars was all going in the same direction—south—and the roads were completely clogged. People who did not know how to drive tried anyway, with disastrous results. Others ran out of gas in the middle of the road and contributed to the already monumental traffic jams. When I looked at some of the people in the streets, they all seemed to have dirty faces, as if they had not washed for a while. I saw that I, too, had a black face. The French army had blown a smoke screen over Paris to try to cover the troop evacuation across the Seine before the Germans got there.

The Bicycle

Hurrying home, I found Maria in the kitchen and told her that I was leaving Paris by myself. I explained that I wanted to buy a bicycle so that I would not have to go on foot. She went with me in search of a bicycle, but we could not find one anywhere. Finally, quite far from our house at the Porte Maillot, we spotted a bicycle store. The store had only one men's racing bicycle left. I did not mind the high bar; I was desperate enough to want any bike. Luckily, Maria knew one of the salesmen and convinced him to sell it to me, although he had promised it to someone else. With part of the 10,000 francs that Mother had given me before she left, I quickly bought that shiny chrome bike with its racer handles. I also bought an inexpensive watch and a road map of France.

Intending not to return to the apartment, I had with me a little case that fit on the rear parcel carrier of the bike. The case held a change of underwear, two *pains au chocolat* (chocolate rolls) and the notes from my pattern-making course. Who knows why, but I also took along my box of oil paints. I can still see myself wearing a blue/green/white Scottish-plaid pleated skirt with matching top and a navy blue loden cape lined in the same plaid. I had just proudly finished making this outfit.

Waving goodbye to Maria on the square outside the bike store, I started pedaling. Since I did not know where I was going, I just followed the crowd. It did not occur to me to worry about the physical strain of cycling a long distance. I was just pleased that I had a vehicle and that I was moving. The southern two-lane road leading out of Paris was an unbelievable sight: a dense, unending line of cars, full of people and belongings, many carrying mattresses, motorcycles and bicycles; others were on foot, including families with children, some pushing whatever few belongings fit on carts and in baby carriages.

In that mob scene I felt very sorry for myself. Although frightened and alone and wondering whether I would ever see my mother again, I was mostly obsessed with leaving Paris. Equally troubling was the knowledge that I was doing something illegal. More than anything else, I was doing something that did not behoove a young lady of my station. Alone on the road? What would I do if a strange man started talking to me? And on a bicycle, which was such a slow and strenuous mode of locomotion! I had to remind myself I no longer was the young girl I was yesterday.

Before long I realized how lucky I was to be on a bicycle. On the congested roads where no cars could get by, I could always push my bicycle onto the curb and continue moving. Outside of Paris, the crowds lessened and passage became easier, even with army trucks going the other way. All the restaurants along the road had big signs saying, "Closed until the end of hostilities." They had run out of food and drink almost immediately after the exodus began. I did not mind. I was neither hungry nor thirsty. Not tired, I just kept pedaling. I did not even stop to look at the letter that the concierge had handed me just before Maria and I left the house to buy the bicycle. Given that I had not recognized the handwriting, I thought the letter could not be very important.

Finally near dark I entered the town of Étampes, thirty kilometers south of Paris. Policemen there directed the refugees to a shelter in a school. I wondered whether I should accept the offer. Would they arrest me if they found out I was a foreigner traveling without permission? The fear of being caught was as pervasive as the desire to escape the advancing Germans. But nobody asked for identification, and some civilian assigned me a space on the hard floor of a classroom.

As I lay down, I remembered the letter with the unfamiliar handwriting in my pocket and opened it. It was news from my mother. She had asked a stranger to send me a message that she was being held in a government reception center called Camp de Gurs, near Oloron in the French Pyrenees close to the Spanish border. Comforted by the knowledge that she was safe, I went to sleep.

The next morning I woke at the first light of dawn around 4 a.m. I jumped up, got my bike and started to pedal again. No more huge crowds, but still a steady stream of people going south. I did not need to figure out where to go, I just followed the crowd. Not realizing then how extremely lucky I was, only a day later I found out that at 6 a.m. the Germans had bombed the town and obliterated the school where I had slept.

Pedaling on, I still was not hungry or tired, just focused on continuing. In mid-morning I was going down a hill when a woman who did not know how to ride a bicycle ran into me. We both fell off our bikes. I injured my knee but paid no attention to the bleeding. Continuing on, I was more concerned that the police might stop me and, finding out I had no papers, arrest me than I was about my bleeding knee. Sometime later a young man started riding next to me. His attempt to get my attention was terrifying. What did he want? When he came alongside me, he pointed to my bleeding knee. Saying that I had to get my leg bandaged, he admonished me that I could not continue riding with that open wound. He motioned to some houses in the distance and told me where the pharmacy was. Hesitantly, I followed his advice.

The kindly pharmacist took one look at my wound and said that it needed stitches. Since he was not permitted to do that, he just bandaged it. The wound hurt, but I paid no attention to the pain. When he inquired where I was going, I told him I was going to Brittany; without trains I had to go by bike. He replied, "But in Orléans there are trains. That's just a few kilometers from here." Then he directed me to the train station.

When I got there, I found what looked like a mile-long line of people waiting to buy train tickets. In typical French bureaucratic fashion, only one ticket window was open. Many people wanted tickets to small places that the agent did not know. He painstakingly looked up the connections as though these were vacationers. It took an eternity to ticket each person. Meanwhile, hundreds of people waited in line—impatient, hungry, hot, and sleepless, with crying children and fainting women. Total bedlam! I was standing next to my bicycle, intent only on going ahead in the slow-moving line. I do not think I had eaten anything since I had left Paris the morning before, but I was not hungry. My badly bruised leg did not hurt. I was pumping adrenaline.

After several hours of inching closer to the ticket window, I heard the air-raid siren sound. Officials came and herded everybody waiting in line into a shelter underground. Although I was standing under a glass-sided overpass, I did not move. The thought of losing my place in line was more abhorrent than being hit by bomb-shattered glass. Perhaps five other people remained there along with me. We watched, fascinated and terrified, as German bombs fell all around us.

My patience and dumb audacity paid off. I got my ticket and was directed to the train to Brest. Astonishingly, despite the confusion, I was able to register my bicycle before boarding the train. Also to my great surprise the train, which I expected to be overcrowded, turned out to be totally empty. I guess nobody else knew that the trains were actually running.

Alone in the car in the now totally dark and blacked-out night, I shivered with fear. The train stopped and started several times and then stood on a siding for a long time. A troop train came by in the opposite direction and stopped. I went to the window to look out into the darkness. A young French soldier opposite me started asking questions across the open windows: Where was I going? Where did I come from? Why was I all alone? At first I hesitated to answer lest I give away my origin. Fortunately, my French accent was so Parisian that I could not be identified as a foreigner. We talked for a while and he told me his tale of woe. His outfit had been overrun by the Germans, but he and some of the other French soldiers got away and now he was going back to fight some more. Just before his train started to move, he handed me through the window a round loaf of bread, saying that I might need it. He did not know that I had not eaten in two days. I was grateful for the bread and touched by his gesture.

In the ominous dark the train started to move again, stopping every few minutes on the track. After one of these stops a man entered the compartment. Again I was terrified. Who could it be? Did he want anything from me? Was he the police? Eventually we started talking. He was a Frenchman who had been in the army in the north of France, and when the situation had become hopeless, he deserted. After hours of walking and ducking around sentry posts, he had found a train. He was in civilian clothes on his way south. He said that he had not eaten since he left his outfit and asked me whether I had any food. I handed him the loaf of bread that the soldier had given me, thinking he would take a bite. Before I knew it, I realized even in the dark that he had eaten the whole loaf. I did not mind. I was just grateful that he did not suspect me of any illegality.

When daylight came, the train began to fill up. With light I felt much less anxious. Yet every time a newcomer entered my compartment, I was sure a gendarme was coming to get me. After a while I realized from the station signs and passenger chatter that the train was not going to Brittany after all but was heading south toward Bordeaux. Many of the passengers were locals who were not fleeing, because the war had not come close to them yet. Meeting up with the Freuds now seemed unlikely. But since I knew that French friends of mine had gone to Salies-de-Béarn in the Pyrenees and that Mother was somewhere near the Pyrenees, I thought that the change of direction was serendipitous.

On the train, passengers discussed the war constantly. The consensus among the passengers was that France had gotten into this mess because of giving asylum to all those "dirty refugees" from Germany, Austria and Eastern Europe. One beefy Frenchman was particularly vocal about the *sals métèques,* the dirty foreigners who brought on the French debacle. People were telling each other their stories. I kept my mouth shut until the big, fat Frenchman asked me point-blank, "And where are you coming from, mademoiselle?" I could think of no answer other than telling him how I had left Paris on my bicycle and that I was hoping to join my mother, who was already in the south. He was very complimentary and said, "You see, mademoiselle, you are the epitome of a brave young Parisian woman, and I salute you." I said nothing. I did not have the guts to tell him that I was one of those *sals métèques* that he was spouting about.

Though he had called me brave, I felt that I was a coward for disguising my true origin. I have never quite forgotten that moment. Whenever I remember that incident on the train, my thoughts veer to how I might have acted if I had been in a concentration camp. Would I have been honorable? Would I have sold myself for a piece of bread? Would I have borne humiliation or physical pain courageously? Wondering whether I might have been able to overcome the pain may be idle speculation, but it is an undeniable aftereffect of my experiences.

Finding Refuge

I must have changed trains in Bordeaux without my bicycle; it never reappeared. Somehow I got to Salies-de-Béarn and the house of my friends. Although they were more like acquaintances than friends, they received me most cordially.

As their house was full, they helped me find a room in the home of a peasant woman nearby. The short, heavy-set woman with a black shawl around her shoulders was brusque and unfriendly. From the beginning she gave me distrustful, questioning glances but said nothing as she led me upstairs to the garret where I was to stay.

It was mid-afternoon, and finally I was able to go to sleep. I had not slept more than an hour when a knock on the door woke me. Two gendarmes, looking like country boys stuffed into uniforms, stood at my door asking for my identification papers. The surly, suspicious old peasant woman had denounced me to the police. I could hardly fathom that. They insisted that I go to the police station with them. Though they did not handcuff me, they sternly took me by the arms and led me across the cobblestoned village square to the police. The reality of my situation suddenly sank in. Here I was fleeing from the Germans only to be caught by the French police. For the first time in my escape I started to cry. Would I now be sent to jail? Was this what my life had come to? Actually, the police chief turned out to be very nice. He accepted the guarantee of my friends that I was not a spy and he let me go.

After a good night's sleep back in the garret, I returned to my friends' house and showed them the letter about Mother. Miraculously, it turned out that the Camp de Gurs, the center where Mother had gone, was less than ten kilometers away. Although gasoline was rationed and circulation of private cars was forbidden, my friends were kind enough to take a chance and drive to Gurs to find Mother. Unable to find her, they left a message telling her where I was. Given the chaotic conditions they found at the camp, I was fatalistically sure that Mother would never get the message.

Like everybody else, I was glued to the radio at my friends' house, incredulous that France was losing the war. One day, to get away from the radio news, I decided to go past the small town into the foothills and sketch the beautiful landscape. After all, I had my paint box from Paris and I continued to be interested in studying design.

I sat engrossed in my drawing when somebody tapped me on the shoulder. A gendarme from the border patrol wondered what I was doing. The scene was very close to the Spanish border, and the border patrol was watching for spies. He scolded me for not having permission to be in this area and took away my drawing in case I had sketched something classified. I was shaken. My confused mind began to consider whether I could really be an enemy, even a spy. If so many people believed it possible, maybe it was true.

A few days later, and before my fears could run even further afield, the unbelievable happened: On June 22 France capitulated and the war was over. France was going to be divided into two parts: the Zone Occupé, the Western section where I was, to be administered by the Germans; and the rest of the country, which the Germans handed to the puppet government of Hitler collaborator Maréchal Henri Petain in Vichy, the south-central capital of "independent" France. These changes happened so fast I could hardly believe them.

Gurs

A few afternoons later as I was sitting in the garden, I saw two women approaching, one of whom seemed to wave to me. I thought I did not know them, so I did not pay much attention. As they came closer, one of them called out, "Margit!" The voice was my mother's! Because I did not expect her and her appearance had changed so, I had not recognized her. She had lost a lot of weight and was very sunburned. My reaction was a mixture of amazement that she had gotten my message and found me, shock at her appearance, and relief at our reunion. Later, Mother said that my not recognizing her was one of the most traumatic moments of the whole camp experience.

She reported the following about the camp: Gurs was a *centre d'acceuil*, a "collection center" created by the French government in 1938. The center originally housed the thousands of Spanish Republicans who had fled across the French border to save themselves from the Franco fascists. When the French had realized the magnitude of the exodus from Spain, they built ramshackle facilities surrounded by barbed-wire fences across a muddy plain near Oloron in the foothills of the Pyrenees. At the end of the Spanish Civil War, the French government had sent most of the Spaniards back, many of them straight into Franco's jails. Eventually the French built sturdier wooden barracks with minimal sanitation facilities. Narrow, muddy paths ran between the barracks with no shelter anywhere. The French then used the facility to house a series of undesirables, first mainly Communists, then refugees escaping from Hitler.

Mother recalled that arriving in Gurs was a relief after a horrible three-day train trip with practically no room to move and totally inadequate toilet facilities. A feeling of utter gloom pervaded the packed cars. The primitive women's barracks to which Mother was assigned was an improvement! Like the other women, she had slept on a straw mat on the muddy ground with barely enough space between the mats for her meager belongings. Several of her Austrian acquaintances from Paris were also there, so at least she knew she was not the only one from her background in the same awful position. Housed in separate barracks, Communists and Nazi prisoners were removed from the refugees.

The food was almost inedible. The daily ration was 15 or 16 chickpeas in a brown, watery base, sometimes with a moldy carrot or cabbage leaf in the liquid as well as a round loaf of bread. The women learned to hide their bread during the day so that no one would steal it. Constant hunger was their companion.

The latrines consisted of a long wooden plank attached to heavy wooden poles at a point about two yards high. Raw, unfinished wooden steps without any railing to hold on to led to a platform that contained a plank with several round holes and no privacy. Under the holes were enormous iron buckets that the remaining male Spaniards emptied every morning. Climbing the steps to the platform, one could notice the pained expression of the women squatting over the holes without support. The climb was particularly hard for the older women, who could barely manage the stairs, let alone squat. A large pipe ran along the platform. At one end was a spigot from which water was available for only two hours in the morning. Most of the time, the flow was no more than a trickle. Those were the washing facilities for both the personal hygiene and the laundry of more than a thousand women.

Since newspapers and mail were forbidden, the women heard only gossip about what was happening in the outside world. Then one day the regime in the camp changed. The guards stopped their hourly vigils, and the whole tone of the camp became looser and less threatening. The war was over and France was to be divided. Nobody knew whether Gurs would be in the occupied or the unoccupied zone.

No longer sure of his authority, the French camp commandant decided to open the camp gates. He summoned Mother and asked her, of all things, why she was there. Was she a Communist or a common criminal? Did she have a police record? The commandant apparently thought he could at least foil the Gestapo's efforts to round up innocent people. Actually, the German army group that came to occupy the camp was not interested in holding unarmed civilians. For no discernible reason, the commandant now told Mother that she was free to leave.

Mother was lucky. Since, incredibly, she had gotten my message and knew where I was, she had a destination. Many others in similar circumstances could not leave, because they had either no money or nowhere to go. Mother enterprisingly found a farmer with a wagon who was willing to take her and her acquaintance from the camp to Salies.

Mother did not speak about Gurs very often thereafter. She did, however, emphasize that her time there reinforced her conviction that one needed self-control to survive tough situations. She was glad she had not coddled her children and had taught them to be resilient as well.

After Mother's amazing arrival in Salies, my suspicious landlady had become a bit more pleasant and consented to let Mother have the *mansarde* adjacent to mine. Without any time to enjoy our reunion, we now had to plot our next move.

Leaving Occupied France

We heard that Salies was going to be in the German-occupied zone. We were only a few kilometers east of the border between the two zones, but how could we get to the French-administered zone? Although the war in France was now officially over, confusion surrounded the division of the country. Without being restrained by official orders, local bureaucrats enjoyed demonstrating their power over the helpless and intimidated refugees. The local police refused to give us permission to leave Salies. Boldly we decided to leave anyway. We found out about an abandoned farmhouse just across the nearby border on the Vichy side where we could stay.

Before leaving, we decided to obliterate our identities, in case they could be used against us. In a nook under the roof in the farm woman's house we hid our Austrian passports and our French *cartes d'identité*. Reluctantly, we also decided to leave behind our expensive Costa Rican passports, acquired illegally in Paris a few months earlier through a murky transaction. We naively had thought then that we could transform ourselves into South Americans and thus avoid further harassment by the French authorities. I also stored a few letters under the roof that I had been carrying with me; they were from a young German refugee whom I had met in Paris. I did not know him well, but we had started corresponding when he joined the French Foreign Legion in Africa to escape Hitler. These letters could have been incriminating for both of us. I do not remember the young man, but I still recall the feeling of loss when I parted with the letters. To this day, I feel pain when I attempt to throw away old mail. I hoard it instead in various filing cabinets.

We left Salies on a brilliant summer day. Gendarmes guarded all roads out of town. Carrying only jackets, Mother and I walked by the gendarmes, greeting them casually but with our hearts pounding as we left the peaceful village pretending we were going on a little walk. Of course we never went back. We had recruited another farmer with a hay wagon who was willing to take and hide our belongings under the hay and then meet us outside of town beyond the view of the police. Mother gave him her rucksack and I the little suitcase I had attached to my bicycle when I left Paris. As I write this, our escape plan does not seem to be a big deal. Yet, as I try to recall the moment, I can still feel the tightening of my throat; we were gripped by fear that we would be caught. The French government was frightening because in its disintegration, it was completely unpredictable.

The empty farmhouse that we found was little more than a shell. The roof was only partially intact; what remained leaked and the windows were all broken. The scant furniture was barely usable. We found a bucket with which to bring up water from a well. Close by was a smelly outhouse. We were grateful to have even the semblance of a roof over our heads and decided to make the best of our newfound safety. The lovely Pyrenees countryside lent itself to long walks and the picking of wildflowers, for which we had no vase. I cannot remember what we did for food; I remember only the constant fear and the uncertainty. What next? We could not stay there for very long.

A few days after we arrived, a group of men appeared. On edge as we were, we could not have been more surprised that they turned out to be, of all people, a group of Czech Protestant clergymen who also were running away from the Germans. They had managed to get there legally! They said they were going to Marseilles on the Mediterranean coast, where they would get a French exit visa and a boat "to somewhere." They encouraged us to do the same. We did not have many choices.

Again we did not have the necessary papers. The only document we had not hidden in the roof in Salies was the bread ration card, which looked just like that of any Frenchman and could not identify us as foreigners. With just that card, the remnants of the 10,000 francs that Mother had given me before she was interned and the encouragement of the Czech clergymen, we embarked on the train trip to Marseilles.

Fortunately, no one examined papers on the train. But at the exit of the station in Marseilles the police were checking travel documents. We hid in the station until the last passengers were gone and the station police had finished their job and left. Getting past one more potential crisis, we crept out of the station and into the chaos that was Marseilles.

Marseilles

On leaving the station, we met some of our refugee friends who had been with us in Paris. We immediately felt less alone. With their help, we found a room in a flophouse near the Canebière, the busy, noisy waterfront. The room had running water and a shared toilet in the hallway. The best feature of our room was a little balcony that Mother turned into an outdoor kitchen with a sterno cooker on a stool. Since we had what passed for cooking facilities and the markets were full of wonderful fresh produce,

Mother cooked. A bunch of young refugees often came and paid us to eat at our place.

We were all in the same situation, trying to obtain visas to go to some safe place and permits to exit France, which were becoming harder and harder to get. The atmosphere in Marseilles was unreal. The town was full of life, with sailors happily picking up girls and enjoying their shore leave, contrasted with refugees desperately trying to leave France.

Soon I met and fell in love with Willi, a charming, dashing Austrian whom I had casually known in Alt Aussee as a member of the Austrian national tennis team. Now that I was no longer a virgin I was a different person, but not that different yet. I remember that Willi and I went out to a modest seafood bar to eat. In the middle of dinner I was too embarrassed to tell him that I had to go to the bathroom; one did not speak of that. So I excused myself and ran all the way back to my hotel in a cold sweat, afraid I would not make it. The kind of restrictions and manners that I grew up with—or that I put on myself—seem incredible to me now, but the memory of the anxiety is still very real more than 60 years later.

Most of my time in Marseilles was taken up with trying to get a visa. The United States was out, having closed its Austrian quota. Australia would take two years. People were considering going to strange places, countries on different continents that no one knew anything about. Listening to the other refugees, who would meet in certain cafes and trade experiences, Mother became totally paralyzed. When she heard that one had to cajole or bribe or bend the truth to get a visa, she said that she could not play that game; she just could not. So she stayed home and prepared meals, and I assigned myself the task of visa hunting.

I met all sorts of interesting people in the process. The discussions about the present and the future were stimulating, and I felt that I now belonged among the grown-ups. Infatuated with Willi, I had a great time. We decided to get engaged. I believe he thought I was a good catch because of the contents of Mother's small leather jewelry case, which had survived her internment. Mother asked Willi to pawn some of the jewels for her. We used the money for daily living expenses. Whatever arrangements Mother made to retrieve the pawned jewelry, I know only that she lost it and held Willi responsible for the loss.

While we were in Marseilles, my cousin Peter Tritsch, who had been living with Uncle Robert in Nice until Robert left for America, joined us. He and Willi became friends and planned to join the French Foreign Legion in Africa if they were not able to leave France.

By September, none of the visa leads had produced results. In desperation, I remembered Paul once saying that Father had owned shares in the Union Minière du Haute Katanga, a copper mine in the Belgian Congo (now Zaire). I cannot recall how the idea originated, but I went to the consulate of the Belgian Congo and explained that I was a shareholder in their largest mine and that therefore I wanted to go to the Belgian Congo. I must have been convincing; I got the visas for Mother and me, though not for Peter and Willi, who by now essentially belonged to our family.

Helping Hands

Having hidden our Austrian passports under the roof in Salies, we did not have a passport in which to stamp the visas. It occurred to me that I could ask the local Czech government-in-exile to issue us Czech passports. When the Germans occupied Czechoslovakia, the government of Czech President Beneš had fled to London. There they set up a government-in-exile as well as a consulate in Marseilles. At the Czech consulate I explained in flawless Czech who we were and asked them to issue us passports. They did. This was a heartening step forward. But we still needed to obtain the French exit permits required for all aliens, regardless of nationality, who wanted to leave the country.

With the visas to the Belgian Congo in hand, we were able to get Spanish and Portuguese transit visas valid for a month. Next we needed the impossible-to-get French exit permits. Daily attempts to obtain them at the French police station were fruitless. The Spanish and Portuguese transit visas were about to expire. So was our money. With only a little additional cash obtained from pawning some jewels, we had managed all this time on the 10,000 francs that Mother had given me in May.

At this critical juncture, we were again fortunate to find help from an unexpected source. We met an American Quaker, Varian Fry, who had come on his own to Marseilles to help famous German artists and writers to escape. He had heard in the United States that the Vichy government in league with the Nazis was preventing these notables, many of them Jewish, from leaving France and saving themselves. Also battling the American authorities that were opposed to letting Jews enter, Fry created the American Rescue Committee with support from Eleanor Roosevelt. That essentially one-man organization helped dozens of prominent German anti-Nazis and Jewish intellectuals—such as authors Franz Werfel and Lionel

Feutchtwanger, philosophers Hannah Arendt and Walter Benjamin—cross the Pyrenees with fake papers. Fry had the money without which the whole operation would have been impossible. Although we were not among the notables, Fry lent us the money, later repaid by Uncle Robert, that enabled us to reach Portugal. Another obstacle hurdled!

(In 1993 the United States Holocaust Museum in Washington, D.C., organized a magnificent exhibit on Varian Fry and his American Rescue Committee. From this exhibit I gathered many of the details of our escape. A large wall photograph of the crowds leaving Paris before it fell confirmed the scene that I had retained in my mind. I thought I could have been one of the women on this wall, shown bicycling among the dense crowds of frightened people. Here, too, were the first pictures of Gurs that I had ever seen. Viewing the exhibit was an emotional experience. I was sad that Mother was no longer here to see these scenes 55 years later in the safety of Washington.)

Our situation was becoming even more desperate. All attempts at getting French exit permits had failed. Our Spanish and Portuguese transit visas were valid for only two more days when we met an acquaintance on the street in Marseilles. He had heard that the day before, the French authorities in Cerbère, the French–Spanish border station on the Mediterranean coast, had allowed women with Czech passports to leave France without the necessary exit permits. Armed with this encouraging information and with the money from Varian Fry, Mother and I decided to try our luck. We set out for the border without exit permits and again without police permission to travel.

We would have marveled at the beauty of the landscape along the coast had we had not been so scared. Close to the border, the police checks became more frequent. At one point a severe-looking gendarme in his navy blue uniform with its visored cap was almost at our seats; just then, the train entered a station and stopped. We darted out of the train and quickly hopped back on at the rear, where the gendarme had already been. Another time we hid in the toilet when we saw the gendarme entering our railroad car and waited until we knew that he had finished examining each passenger's travel authorization and had left.

Every time I entered a toilet I remembered for a second that my period was long overdue. That I could have gotten pregnant the last night in Paris had occurred to me, but I was too preoccupied with the danger of our present situation to worry about that possibility.

We arrived in Cerbère together with other passengers who had valid exit permits. All of us had to get off the train. When we approached the border

114

control with the rest of the group, the gendarme asked for our exit permits. We told him that yesterday the border police had let Czech women cross the border without exit permits. He said that was yesterday; today is today.

All the other passengers were allowed to board the train to Spain, leaving us at the station alone and despondent. Mother was totally passive and uninvolved, but I was determined to figure out how to get across the border. Instinctively, without thinking, I went up to one of the young porters. I explained that our Spanish visas would expire tomorrow and we had to get out of France. He looked me over quizzically, then finally took me aside and said, "Yes, maybe I can help you. Go into the village. Go to the third street on the left and to the second house on the right, and find Monsieur Girard. He might be able to help you."

We took our possessions and hurried into the village of Cerbère to locate Monsieur Girard. We found a swarthy, fierce-looking, elderly man who looked to us like a smuggler. He listened to our predicament and remained ominously silent for a while. While we awaited his response, I wondered whether this was a trap and if he would now call the police. Fortunately, he turned out to be helpful and told us about a contact who might be able to assist us in Portbou, the Spanish border station. Instructing us how to leave town unseen, he described how to cross the mountain without using the road. Next he alerted us about spotting border patrols and the best way to get into the tiny village of Portbou without being noticed. Then he said, "When you get to Portbou, go to the restaurant to the right of the little hotel on the beach, enter via the back room and tell the owner that you want to speak to Señor Jesus. Señor Jesus has very good contacts with the Spanish police."

Glad to have some directions, whether trustworthy or not, we set out up the mountain. A beautiful fall day, the meadows were still green, the sky blue. The mountains were shimmering in the background. Our ascent could have been a lovely vacation outing had we not been so strained. We climbed and I do not remember either one of us being tired. Mother, who was 47 at the time, was luckily in good shape. Our anxiety was palpable, but the beautiful surroundings helped to relieve some of the stress.

We must have taken a wrong turn, because we could not find a road into the village. We had no choice but to take off our shoes, hike up our skirts and wade into Portbou, Spain, via the shallow bay. We located the cafe next to the hotel and found Señor Jesus. When we told him who had sent us and what we wanted, he started to curse. Had not Monsieur Girard gotten his message that his Spanish contact was in deep trouble and the border was being carefully watched? "How could he have sent you? I cannot do anything for you; otherwise, I will go to jail." Sensing our desperation, Jesus became less hostile. He confirmed that we would need a Spanish entry stamp in our passports before we could leave Spain for Portugal. His only advice was that we should try to go to the railroad and there, unnoticed, catch a train to Barcelona, where we had said we had friends. All along we had hoped that we could link up with the Junks, our German-born friends from Paris who were living in Barcelona and had promised to help us. However, he sounded pessimistic about our chances of success.

Caught in Spain

Discouraged and bedraggled from the effort of the border crossing, we struggled up the hill to the railroad station. At the station a border guard immediately stopped us. He said we had to go back to France. He could not let us enter because we had crossed the border at an illegal entry point, even though we had valid entry visas. When he saw our expressions of utter dejection, he told us to wait while he talked to his boss. We slumped on a bench in the deserted station, all alone there. I remember very distinctly the feeling of complete desolation that overtook me. My spirits plummeted as the full impact of our hopeless situation struck me, and I despaired. It was the end. We could not possibly go back to France; we would be apprehended immediately. I sat there, sinking into myself as though I could make myself invisible. The absent, expressionless look on Mother's face made me realize that I was now truly responsible for both of us. She who had always been a pillar of strength now relied on me entirely.

After a while, two disheveled and lost young men appeared who had also crossed the border illegally. They turned out to be Americans caught in the fighting between the French and the Germans farther north. Always on the run and avoiding contact with people, they did not know there was an unoccupied zone of France where they could have gone. They had been walking for days believing they had to get to Spain in order to save themselves. Such was the confusion at the time.

Soon two border guards came, took away our passports and told us they would escort the Americans and us to Gerona, the district capital. At least it was still in Spain, not France. They did not handcuff us but held us by the elbows and firmly put us on a train. We arrived in Gerona after about an hour, and the guards led us to the district police headquarters. The people in the waiting room, mostly Spaniards, looked at us with interest. None of the four of us spoke any Spanish.

It was dark by now as we sat in the stuffy and overcrowded room. The prospect of spending the night in that grubby police station waiting for the day shift to arrive was not enticing. I started talking to one of the guards who spoke some French. Asking him whether we could go to a hotel to spend the night, since nothing was going to happen until the next morning, I reminded him that they had our passports anyway. He went away and came back after a while, motioning us to follow him. I thought he was going to lead us to a hotel.

In the darkness, we crossed the cobblestoned main square, passed the beautiful old cathedral and headed away from the town center and from any buildings. We walked for quite a while in total silence. Suddenly I heard a signal call and somebody answering the call. We continued walking toward an imposing, squat building standing in a large courtyard and surrounded by a high wire fence. A man approached the gate from the other side of the fence and with a huge metal key unlocked the gate. The guard motioned us inside and the man with the big key locked the gate behind us. Soon we were standing in a noisy, brightly lit hallway, the entrance to a jail. So that was our hotel!

When I realized we were in jail, my first reaction was disbelief. How could someone like me—an upright, honorable person who would never commit a crime—end up in jail? Going to jail was not part of my life's script. I did not know then that many of the most honorable people in Europe went to jail during the war and that having been in prison did not blot your record indelibly. I felt more humiliated than afraid, more violated than ashamed.

No officials were on duty at night. The jail guard took away our belongings and motioned us into a large, high-ceilinged hall where dozens of women were sleeping, two to a bed. The matron, angry that we had awakened her, assigned us hurriedly to a bedstead with a straw pad that served as a mattress. The latrines, mere holes in the ground, were in a large room with an open archway close to our bed. Despite the overwhelming stench and the bright lights, which were on night and day, we fell asleep.

Awakened at 5 a.m. by the matron bellowing commands that we could not understand, we had to file into the yard and stand at attention while everybody sang Franco's national anthem. Without understanding the words, I learned them phonetically and still remember them today: *"Cara al sol con la camisa nueva que tu bordaste en rojo ayer."* (Your face toward the sun with your new shirt that you embroidered in red yesterday.) After the singing we went to the day hall, where all the women lined up with their cups or bowls to receive what passed for coffee. We had no bowls.

Following breakfast, the jail director called us to his office to find out who we were and how we got there. When he heard our story, he said, "So you're Czechs. Czechoslovakia is now part of Germany, so we will inform the German consul in Barcelona that you are here." Just what we wanted to hear after the perilous escape from the Germans! He gave us back our belongings minus the little mauve leather box containing Mother's jewelry. He wanted us to open it, but Mother had lost the key. So he just kept the box.

Most important for us was to get in touch with the Junks in Barcelona so that they could help us get released. We had arrived on a Thursday, but Wednesday was the only day when the prisoners were allowed to send out mail. That was a real blow. Looking for some help, I approached a slight, red-haired, blue-eyed prison guard who spoke a little French. After I explained our situation he was very kind, giving us a sheet of paper, an envelope and a stamp and promising to mail our letter on the outside. Of course we did not know whether the letter would ever reach our friends, but at least it had a chance of getting there. The tension was mounting as we speculated whether the Germans would get to us before our friends could.

At noon as we waited, we saw the same procedure of holding out one's cup for a ladle of soup. Two simply dressed country women who noticed our situation came over to us and handed us a life-saving cup and a spoon. The soup was a vile, watery liquid with noodles that tasted like felt. We were not yet starved enough to swallow more than a few spoonfuls, but we were thankful that someone had come to our aid.

That evening I got my period. As I had not told anybody about my last night in Paris, I kept my relief to myself. But I had nothing to protect my clothes and absorb the blood. Panicked and embarrassed, I went up to two prostitutes. The prostitutes, whom the Catholic Franco regime could not tolerate, were in one of the two groups of women among the prisoners. The other group was former schoolteachers who had belonged to the Republican opposition to Franco. The prostitutes gave me some washable sanitary napkins. What a precious gift! They had saved me from a terrible predicament. But how ironic that I, who never expected to meet or talk to a prostitute anywhere, found myself eternally grateful to these two women and in awe of their generosity.

118

We all suffered from a lack of decent hygiene. After breakfast the inmates were obliged to roll up their straw mattresses. On most of the bedsteads one woman balancing on top of the rolled up mattress would look for lice in the hair of the other woman sitting on the iron bedstead. Such was the morning's entertainment. For local women, prison life was slightly less onerous. Their families could visit and bring them food and bedding. Families seemed to go in and out of the jail without much supervision.

After a couple of days, both Mother and I got eczema and started having scabs on our skin. Of course we had nothing with which to treat them. But none of the physical difficulties was as stressful as the uncertainty, the waiting to know whether our pleas for help had been heard.

Rescue

We were doubly lucky. Our friends received our message and called the jail to let us know that they would be coming as soon as they could get the papers necessary to free us. And once the jail director realized that we had Spanish connections, he did not notify the German consulate.

After five or six days the Junks came to visit just to reassure us. I do not think they ever knew how much that visit meant to Mother and me. A couple of days later they returned by car with the necessary permission, and we were allowed to leave with them. It was high time because our physical systems had really not been able to adapt to the jail conditions. As we were leaving, the jail director returned Mother's jewel case unopened, probably not realizing that jewelry was inside. Driving away from the jail was an indescribable relief. From prison the Junks took us directly to a restaurant in Gerona, where I had what must have been the tastiest ice cream cone of my life.

We stayed in Barcelona for a few days until the Junks were able to legalize our entry into Spain and to extend our Portuguese entry visas, which had meanwhile expired. Our friends had good connections. At that time in Spain, a bribe and the right words could overcome all sorts of legal obstacles.

We thanked our friends profusely when they took us to the train for Lisbon. Though they told us that we still needed Spanish travel permits, we managed to get by without them and arrived in Lisbon without further problems. I felt that a boulder had been lifted from my shoulders

Less than four months from the start of the "shooting war" in France, when Mother was interned and I left Paris, we arrived in Lisbon. Scary months with enough excitement to last a lifetime, but an uncanny number of fortuitous coincidences and the help of many kind strangers.

Much later, when I could reflect upon what incarceration had meant to me, I realized that the jail experience was truly transforming. I became aware that I had many preconceived but useless ideas about what was appropriate behavior. Although I had so disapproved of the bourgeois values of my Prague world, I now recognized how strongly I had been formed and trapped by them. The prison experience stimulated me to rethink who I was. I began a slow and ongoing process of challenging these concepts and developing my own values.

Portugal

Arriving in Lisbon was like stepping into a new world. We left behind the blackouts, the furtive glances at the policemen in the street and the worry that the Germans could catch us. Situated on the river Tagus, Lisbon is a lively and lovely city built on many hills, with 16th-century squares and patrician houses. Tourists could spend days exploring its riches. But we were not tourists. Almost out of money, we first had to find a way to survive and then a safe destination overseas.

We located a Portuguese family who was interested in taking us in as paying guests. Our apartment was on the top floor of an old building on Avenida Almirante Reis, a main street leading away from the center of town. Our landlady was a stout, dark-haired widow whose name I do not recall. She had lived most of her life in Luanda, the capital of the then-Portuguese colony Angola. Her husband, who was in the Portuguese army, had been killed there. Afterwards she returned to Lisbon with her two children, Didi, a girl about my age, and João, a boy a few years younger. She could supplement her inadequate war widow's pension by renting us a room.

We knew that many of the Czech and Austrian refugees who had left Paris and then Marseilles would be in Lisbon. Indeed, we met a number of them on the street soon after our arrival. We learned that the refugees met at the *Chave d'Ouro* (Golden Key Cafe) on the Praça Rossio, a large square near the waterfront and an important nerve center of Lisbon for many centuries. The Chave d'Ouro had been a famous meeting place for Portuguese writers and intellectuals but had become run-down, the red plush on its benches worn thin and the floor mosaics chipped and hazardous to walk upon. The lights were dim and the atmosphere slightly gloomy. It was a convenient meeting place for the emigrants. We frequently congregated there, enjoying the inexpensive but delicious *bolos de Berlin*, a wonderful jam-filled doughnut. With the other refugees we commiserated about the difficulty of finding a haven somewhere and passage to get there.

Quickly I figured out how to earn what we needed. Many of the refugees had lost much of their luggage during the escape and needed new clothes. Through word-of-mouth I became the dressmaker to the refugee crowd. Our landlady had a treadle sewing machine that she put in our room and lent us an iron that was heated with hot coals. One had to swing the iron around in a circle to keep the coals burning and the iron hot. This strange way of ironing took a while to master.

Some of the women brought me pictures from fashion magazines to copy. One of my specialties was making pleated skirts from pre-cut and pre-pleated material prepared by another emigrant woman; she had learned to work a pleating machine to have a transportable skill when she arrived in America. I turned these skirts into dresses by attaching the blouse top from the matching material.

My reputation as a good dressmaker grew among the refugees, and pretty soon I was busy enough to support Mother and me. Mother helped me by sewing on buttons, hemming and overcasting seams.

In addition to earning money, I was eager to learn Portuguese. My friend Joseph Handler found a young Portuguese singer who was willing to give me lessons for free as a way of doing his bit in the war effort.

Joseph and his wife, Edith, whom Mother had known casually in Marseilles, became close to us in Lisbon. Joseph, originally from the Hungarian part of Slovakia, had moved to France in the 1930s and there became a well-respected journalist. Edith was a commercial artist originally from Prague, where Mother knew her parents. Edith had gone to France to get away from Hitler and then, although a Czech citizen, found it impossible to obtain an exit permit to leave to join Joseph in Portugal. She, too, walked across the Pyrenees but managed to avoid our prison experience. The Handlers made a distinctive pair. Edith with her beautiful, long, blond hair was tall and svelte. Joe, in contrast, was shorter than she, stocky, broad-shouldered and bald. She was pessimistic and he was always full of hope. We became lifelong friends. Joe not only found the Portuguese tutor for me at this time but also helped me find jobs much later.

Several times a week, swarthy, heavy-set João Brandao came to our house to tutor me. The jovial and witty singer found that I was adept at learning languages, and I quickly picked up enough Portuguese to get by.

Mainly I needed to know how to buy fabric and the notions for my dress-making business and how to converse with the family where we lived. We must have arranged for the landlady to cook for us, because I remember eating a lot of codfish, which was not exactly my favorite.

Once settled in Lisbon, we were able to communicate via telegraph with our overseas family—Felix and Uncle Robert in America, Bruno in Canada and Paul in Australia. We were thrilled to hear that Anita, my first niece and Mother's first grandchild, had arrived in Melbourne. The birth of the baby signified that life was continuing. All the family had been concerned about us since the fall of Paris. Each of my brothers had his own difficulties in adjusting to a new country, but each one eventually succeeded in making a good life for himself.

Uncle Robert sent us some money. Even more valuable than the dollars, he sent us an affidavit that allowed us to apply for American immigration visas. He put enough money into an American bank in Mother's name to ensure that we would not become a burden on the government after our arrival. The sum of $8,400 sufficed at the time! With this guarantee, we applied for what had seemed totally unobtainable: American immigration visas.

Soon we heard from Felix that the Austrian quota for immigration to the United States had opened because none of the previously registered people could leave Austria anymore. Thrilled at the prospect of being able to come to the United States, we easily discarded the idea of going to the Belgian Congo. We had only to wait until our application was processed in the U.S. The American consulate would not predict how long it would take.

Although I may have been impatient awaiting our visas, I enjoyed being in Lisbon. Different from what it had been in Prague or Paris, my life was full of new experiences. At the time, young, middle-class Portuguese women were not permitted to go out by themselves. By custom they had to be accompanied by siblings or other family members. I, on the other hand, felt perfectly free to come and go and was therefore frequently accosted on the street by Portuguese men. Most had a very long nail on the little finger of their left hand, an odd fashion they must have thought sexy. I had fun letting them follow me, listening to their come-ons only to pretend in the end that I did not understand Portuguese. I was delighted to be deemed desirable, particularly in view of the uncertain and surreal refugee environment in which we lived. My landlady's daughter, Didi, a plain, morose, depressive girl, used to lean out of her third-floor window, enviously watching me walking freely down the street. She spent most of her day at the windowsill.

Much of the shopping was done from the windowsill. The fruit or fish vendor would pass by advertising his wares in a lovely singsong voice. When the family members wanted to buy something, they shouted their orders down to the street and lowered a basket with money in it on a long rope. After the vendor filled the order, they raised the basket, the transaction completed. This was Didi's entertainment for the day. She could leave the house only when accompanied by her brother, João, who was not keen to be seen with her on the street. João was a chubby 13-year-old. Fresh, arrogant and trying to be the man of the house, he spent much of his time slicking his hair with a greasy, smelly hair lotion. His mother was constantly trying to humor him. I can still hear his mother's pleading voice, "O *Joãzinho*" (little Joao), asking him to run an errand for her and take his sister along.

Although I was busy sewing, I had time to worry about my fiancé, Willi, and my cousin Peter, whom we had promised to help leave France. None of my efforts bore fruit. When I was particularly downhearted, I went to the Chave d'Ouro to seek out the Handlers. Joe always said to me *"Tu auras ton Willi."* (You'll have your Willi.) At the time I believed it.

During one of the futile efforts seeking a visa for Willi and Peter, I met the charming, young and elegant Costa Rican consul in Lisbon. Thinking that it would help get visas for the boys, I told him that we had been able to purchase Costa Rican passports in Paris. Not impressed by our scheme, he was more interested in me. Suggesting that I accompany him on a business trip to Vichy, he assured me that I would be completely safe and that he would make every possible effort to show me a good time. The flattering offer sounded appealing. When I told Mother about it, she was horrified that I had even considered the idea of going off with a stranger and especially to Vichy France. So I stayed in Lisbon and continued sewing.

I did go on an outing with two young Portuguese men whom I had met somehow. But I do remember that the way I met them was more legitimate than if I they had been street acquaintances. They took me to the *Boca do Inferno* (Mouth of Hell), a promontory on the Atlantic coast where the sea rushes into clefts and caves in the rocks, making an ominous booming sound and sending up spectacular sprays of water. One of the highlights of my stay in Lisbon, the excursion took place on a sunny, cloudless day close to my 19th birthday in February 1941.

Preparing for our eventual departure, I ventured into the sinister shipping line underworld to get a booking. The few ships that still made transatlantic voyages were solidly booked and had long wait lists. But if one knew where to go, with whom to talk and whom to bribe, one could always find scalpers. I spent a lot of time learning how to operate in this shadowy environment. My being a young girl was a definite advantage. All the people with whom I negotiated were middle-aged men who apparently enjoyed flirting with me. No longer shy, I was not above toying with them to get our tickets. Even so, the negotiations were nerve-racking and consumed time that seemed short. We knew that the sea lanes were dangerous, with German U-boats patrolling the Atlantic Ocean, and we were not sure how much longer one would be able to reach America by boat. Obtaining passage was no longer the dangerous quest that getting a French exit permit had been, but the process still was treacherous. Eventually and triumphantly I got two tickets on some nondescript ship. I was not sure whether the visas would arrive in time for us to use the tickets; but if not, I knew I could always get rid of them.

On my way home from the shipping scalpers' office, I ran into Frederick Kraus. The son of my dentist in Prague, Frederick with his Viennese wife, Anny, and their three-year-old retarded son, Mikey, were desperately searching for ship tickets to the United States. I felt sorry for Anny going through the traumas of emigration with this unmanageable child, who would not sleep. The first retarded child I had ever seen, Mikey screamed at the slightest provocation and could not be pacified. I knew that the Krauses were not *débrouillard* (resourceful) about ways of navigating the shipping underworld. On the spur of the moment and without hesitation I offered them the tickets in my hand. I thought they needed them more than we did. At the time I was quite cavalier about my action, but the Krauses, who became lifelong friends, have never forgotten my gesture and have remained eternally grateful.

When the time for our leaving came several weeks later, I was sorry to leave Portugal although happy that we would be going to the United States. Long evaporated was the concept I had brought with me from Prague of a country of gangsters and skyscrapers and lacking culture.

We had arrived in Lisbon in September 1940 and were able to travel to America seven months later, in April 1941, on a Portuguese cork freighter, the only ship that had any space at all. When I first saw the size of the boat, it appeared improbably small for an ocean crossing. Once on board and having come to terms with the primitive accommodations, my elation at going to America took over.

During the more than two-week voyage, Mother and I shared one of the five tiny cabins on the ship. The only young girl on board, I became very popular with the Portuguese crew. Unfortunately, the incessant tossing and heaving made me almost constantly seasick, so I was not able to profit much from their attentions. When seasickness overcame me, I was sure I was going to die. I swore I would never go on another sea voyage. On the rare occasions when I was not lying in utter misery on my bunk, I played pingpong with the crew, improving both my game and my Portuguese. As the ship entered the Chesapeake Bay, the seasickness forgotten, I could feel the excitement in my bones at arriving in America.

With Portuguese admirers at Boca do Inferno

Madame Dubourguez

Château de la Pièce d'Eau

Bruno, cowhand in England

Cousin Peter Tritsch

Willi

126

PART 3
A NEW LIFE

6

AMERICA

CONTRARY TO THE experience of most immigrants at the time, we were not greeted by the Statue of Liberty; we arrived in April 1941 at a little port in Delaware. Even without the traditional welcome in the far more impressive New York Harbor, our landing was a moment of great exuberance. We had finally arrived! Also, good riddance to the incessant heaving up and down and no more noise from the ship's motor!

What an overwhelming feeling of relief to have made it to the United States. Although the odyssey from Paris to Portugal had lasted only four months and we had spent only seven months waiting in Lisbon, the intensity of those experiences was searing enough for a lifetime. Only now, in the safety of the United States, could we permit ourselves to feel the enormous strain of leaving Prague, leaving everybody and everything that was dear behind and becoming refugees. The fearful uncertainty about how we would survive, added to the many perilous escapes between Paris and Portugal, started taking its toll only now. But it was overshadowed by the excitement of arriving in America.

Felix met us at the dingy commercial port in Delaware. We were thrilled to see him. He had borrowed a car from a friend so he could pick us up in style. Fun-loving, he was eager to show us the lights of Broadway even before taking us to his apartment, where we were going to stay. What an unforgettable impression the bright lights made at night—especially in contrast to Lisbon, where all lighting had, of wartime necessity, been browned out.

New York

Debonair Felix was a great guide to the new world. After showing us Broadway and delighting in our thrilled responses, he took us to his apartment at 222 East 72nd Street. The one-bedroom apartment that he shared with his friend Otmar Gyorgy was on the ground floor of a brownstone house. To make room for us, Otmar moved out. The apartment had no air conditioning, and when the windows were open, all the soot from the street came in along with the noise from the 3rd Avenue El, the elevated train. New and different as everything seemed, we easily become acclimatized because we had a positive attitude. We were grateful to be in America and relieved to feel secure.

Since I had last seen him nearly six years earlier, much had happened to my attractive, now 26-year-old brother Felix. After his disastrous experience of investing and losing Mother's money in a get-rich-quick scheme, he had tried all sorts of other avenues of making money. None of them panned out, including the job at IBM. That is where he had gotten the idea of studying stenotype, which he was doing when we arrived. Felix was then living on $30 unemployment insurance a month. To ensure that he would make it to the end of the month on this small amount, he had a shoebox with thirty white envelopes—one for each day of the month—and one dollar in each envelope. Though he tried to limit his expenses to the allotted dollar a day, sometimes he had to borrow from the envelope of the thirtieth day if he had overspent.

Felix had completed a course in stenotype and was practicing to increase his speed. Having decided to enlist in the U.S. Army, he thought that good stenotyping skills in addition to his excellent language abilities would help him obtain an assignment in military intelligence. A combination of shorthand and typing, stenotyping produced a typed shorthand copy that could be read by anyone knowing the special shorthand code. This skill was worth more pay than shorthand, which generally was decipherable only by the person who wrote it. Before the advent of tape-recording machines, stenotyping was a highly valued skill; nowadays it is used primarily to yield verbatim rendering of court proceedings.

On my second day in New York, Felix suggested that I walk around in the city. The enormousness of the buildings was impressive. These were the skyscrapers that I had seen only in movies! I felt so small in this gigantic city, not sure what I was doing in the midst of the hustle and bustle on the sidewalk, alongside the large number of cars, buses, trucks and the El. People rushed by, as almost everybody seemed to be in a hurry. New for me also was seeing people sitting on fire escapes. The open garbage cans with half loaves of perfectly good bread or half-eaten chickens appalled me. Such waste was inconceivable to a European brought up in an economy of scarcity. I have never gotten used to such wastefulness and the abandon with which Americans throw away perfectly serviceable household or food items.

Walking the streets of New York, I noted that people dressed quite differently than in Europe. In Europe, one was able to recognize people's station in life by what they wore. Country folk were easily distinguishable from city folk. People who worked with their hands looked different from those who worked in offices. From their appearance, one could frequently guess the ages of passers-by. Here in New York, at first glance people from all walks of life seemed equally elegant; they seemed to be wearing their Sunday best to work. The salesgirl could not be distinguished from the store owner. Older women were as colorfully dressed as younger ones. All the women seemed to wear high heels. But my overriding impression of New York was of a palpable sense of freedom, a sense that everything was possible. No rules or restrictions based on family position seemed to hamper the individual attempting to reach his or her goal. I was eager to try that concept out myself.

My First Job

Knowing that we lived on borrowed funds, I felt pressured by the need to find a job and start making money. Daily I looked at the want ads in the *New York Times*. Soon I found a job opening for a dress finisher in a couture salon on Madison Avenue. Beginning to learn the layout of the city, I first had to find my way to Madison Avenue and then to the salon for an interview. Everything was an adventure. Never having been to a job interview, I imagined I would have to show my dressmaking credentials and respond to lots of questions about my work experience and myself. Instead, the only question the forelady asked was, "Do you have a Social Security number?" I had no idea what that was. The forelady said I should get one and return the next Monday at 9 a.m.

Obtaining the Social Security number was a quick introduction to the United States. I again had to find the right building, understand all the signs and directions to various offices, answer all the questions and fill out forms.

Temporary Social Security card in hand, I proudly returned to the salon the next Monday expecting to be properly interviewed. In good European fashion, I brought along the diploma from the Paris school of dress design and pattern making that I had received just before leaving Paris. I expected to recount my professional experience. Instead, the forelady told me to take my things and showed me to a sewing machine. I had no "things." She lent me a pair of scissors and a box of pins and told me to sew seam binding on the hem of a dress she handed to me. I looked at the dress. The design was a style out of *Vogue,* one that I had copied for one of my customers in Lisbon. Amazed at the coincidence, I was excited that I knew this design. How fabulous that I had gotten a job on the first try!

The elation did not last long. I sat down at the machine and realized that I did not know how to thread it. I had never seen an electric sewing machine; in Europe we had only treadle machines. When I asked one of the other seamstresses to show me how to thread it, she was not overjoyed. All the seamstresses there were elderly women who looked suspiciously at this young thing, obviously a newcomer who might take work away from them. After sewing a few inches, the thread broke. Again I had to ask for help to thread the machine. After another 15 inches the thread broke again and I was beside myself. At that moment the forelady appeared and said, "We really cannot use you. Please leave." I tried to explain that I knew how to sew but had never seen this type of machine, that I had made the same style dress myself. She was not impressed. It was only 10 a.m. and already I was fired.

I took the elevator down, in itself an experience because I had never been on this kind of automatic elevator. On the ground floor, where I had noticed a pay phone, I called my mother. Sobbing, I told her that I had been hired and fired all in one hour. I was completely dejected over my dismissal for incompetence, having considered myself pretty capable after the dressmaking successes in Portugal. Hurt and demeaned, I was also incensed at the unfairness of it all.

Thirty years later, when I had my own dress factory, I was just as unfair to someone whom I was trying out on the sewing machine. I could tell just by the way the applicant held her hand and held the fabric under the needle whether I could use her or not. I needed experienced help, and I was not about to train anybody. So I, too, dismissed someone who might have become

132

useful eventually. Memories of my own firing made me feel guilty about letting her go, but I did it anyway.

A day or so later, I found a job in another couture salon on Madison Avenue. This time I knew I would not be interviewed and that I had to bring my own basic sewing kit, including scissors, needles, tape measure, ruler, pins and chalk. Though I had learned to thread the sewing machine, I did not last more than a couple of days there either. I was not nearly as devastated this time, because I had learned an important American lesson: Easy come, easy go. The next day, I found another job that lasted a few more days, but there I quit before they asked me to leave. I was just too inexperienced for the level of work required. After that, I was able to keep the next job. I had learned enough in those first five days to keep my head above water. My wages of $12 a week were enough to survive on in 1941.

Mother, meanwhile, got a job as a salad cook at Horn and Hardart's, the famous cafeteria on West 57th Street. This was quite a life change for her, since she had never held a job nor spent much time in the kitchen while I was growing up. We felt we were doing well, amazed by the vast number of opportunities that existed. Nobody asked about your credentials; employers just wanted to make sure you could do the job. And despite having to adapt to a new life, what a relief not to have any more identification cards and residence permits to worry about.

Otmar Gyorgy

I met Otmar Gyorgy, Felix's roommate, soon after I arrived. Of course I had been thinking about Willi, whom I wanted to bring to the United States; but my ardor for him was gone and with it the urgency to do something about helping him to come to America. Soon Otmar and I started dating. I was smitten with him.

Otmar had come to the U.S. from Budapest in 1937 or 1938, helped by his Uncle Arpad, a wealthy Hungarian financier who lived in Switzerland. As a result of Arpad's intervention, the large New York stock brokerage house that managed Arpad's stock portfolio offered Otmar a position. When I met Otmar, he was just about to quit his job and volunteer for the U.S. Army. Although he was not a U.S. citizen, he felt he owed it to himself to fight against Hitler. At about the same time, Felix also decided to volunteer. They joined the Army in the fall of 1941, a couple of months before Pearl Harbor.

Physically attractive, Otmar was bright, sophisticated and worldly. Of medium height with brown hair, his brown eyes had a melancholy expression. He was always stylishly dressed. Very musical, but with almost no music training, he played the piano beautifully by ear. Otmar had finished the gymnasium in Budapest; as a Jew suspecting that the anti-Semitic policies of Hitler could reach Hungary, he jumped at his uncle's suggestion that he go to the United States. Otmar's widowed mother, with whom he was living in Budapest, was not overjoyed that he would leave her alone.

He welcomed the opportunity to improve his future. Though his father had never been a good provider, his two uncles on his mother's side, both very wealthy, adored their sister and supported the family in style. Otmar felt that his father had been sidelined and overshadowed by his prominent brothers-in-law. While Otmar enjoyed the physical comforts and the educational advantages derived from the uncles' contributions, he vowed that nobody would ever treat him as the family had treated his father.

From the beginning, Felix discouraged my relationship with Otmar, saying that he had a bad character. Even I could see that he was selfish, stingy and often critical; he could be very curt and cutting. Otmar frequently made derogatory remarks and acted superior to people of lesser education and lower socioeconomic conditions. Although these behaviors bothered me, I was willing to overlook them. My awareness of these negative traits should have warned me. But I was naïve at the time, had not read anything about psychology and knew next to nothing about long-term relationships. I was convinced that I alone understood Otmar and that I could change him by giving him the love he had never had.

Mother and Bruno in Canada

While I was preoccupied with my feelings, Mother had left the cafeteria job and found work as a finisher in a sweater knitting shop. She stayed there for only a short while. I believe she contacted the Viennese trustee of my father's estate, who was now also living in New York, and found him quite unhelpful. Although he invited us to lunch a couple of times at the luxurious hotel where he lived, he treated us like paupers. Whether he would have been able to save some of Mother's money is questionable. We assumed at the time that, as with all our property and belongings, the Germans had confiscated our money. So when, soon after our arrival, Bruno asked Mother to keep house for him on his primitive fruit farm in Canada,

134

she agreed to go. With no particular reason to remain in New York, she was eager to help him. Since Felix was about to go into the Army, and not wanting to leave me in New York by myself, Mother arranged to have friends invite me to Black Mountain College near Asheville, North Carolina, to participate in a summer construction work camp.

Black Mountain College

Mother's friends Johanna Jalowetz, a graphic artist and weaver, and Heinrich Jalowetz, a musician and conductor of the Cologne Symphony Orchestra in Germany, had found refuge in this experimental college in the North Carolina mountains. The community attracted many émigré intellectuals who had come to the United States without financial support. A number of them came to teach at this unique institution. The combination of committed faculty, first-rate intellectuals and vibrant sense of community created an outstanding atmosphere for learning. Interested in all things American and not thrilled at working as a dress finisher, I saw the invitation as a unique opportunity to get out of humid New York and see and learn something new, without having to pay for my livelihood.

Black Mountain College sounded interesting. In the 1930s, a group of professors and students from Rollins College in Florida had wanted to create a more humane, less competitive learning environment than existed at Rollins. With little money, the Rollins utopians were able to lease a building in the lovely Smokey Mountains overlooking the town of Black Mountain. The founders believed that living and learning should be intertwined and that education should take place everywhere, not only in classrooms. Faculty and students ate together. Their working together in community activities blurred the traditional distinction between curricular and extracurricular activities. With all aspects of community life thought to have a bearing on an individual's education, the faculty emphasized responsibilities inherent in being a member of a community but without suppressing the individual needs of each community member.

The college had no fixed regulations, no required courses, no system of frequent examinations, no formal grading. The students themselves were responsible for deciding what shape their education would take. Without the customary academic requirements, each student had to determine when he or she was ready to graduate. Those who felt ready then underwent rigorous examinations by outside experts. Not many students graduated; many left after a year or two, and others never felt ready to graduate. The approach to studies was certainly unconventional.

Having lost the lease on the building in which the college had started, the founders decide to renovate an adjacent property and construct a new building using free faculty and student labor. I was one of the summer students who could take courses free of charge in return for working in the construction camp.

When I arrived at the college, I was assigned a bed in a double room, handed a set of sheets and towels and told to come to meals at given times. No further instructions. Once in the room in this unfamiliar environment, I felt lost. Soon a tall, slender and beautiful young woman arrived and said hello. She told me she was a piano student of Dr. Jalowetz's and said nothing more. Surprised by her silence, I thought that as the newcomer, my initiating a conversation would not be polite. We did not say a single word to each other for two days. Already feeling isolated and uncertain about how to interpret her behavior, I was totally perplexed about how to react to my roommate.

Eventually when we broke the impasse and started talking, Maude told me that she knew I was a refugee from Europe and thought I would prefer not to be questioned. Later I understood that it was this tremendous respect for personal privacy at Black Mountain that made living in such a small, tightly knit community possible. She had kept her initial silence out of consideration for my feelings, not realizing how distraught that silence made me feel. After clearing up this misunderstanding, Maude and I became lifelong friends.

Soon after Maude left Black Mountain, she married Robert Haas, a much older, well-known Viennese photographer who had come to Black Mountain to take pictures of the famous European intellectuals there. Incredibly, his mother and my grandmother had been good friends in Vienna!

Maude was not part of the summer work camp. She was a regular student who continued her piano studies. But I, with the other work camp students went to the construction site every day at 6 a.m. and worked until 11 a.m. My first job was to pull rusty nails out of boards to make the boards reusable. I had never before had a hammer in my hand and found the assignment difficult and exhausting. Eventually I learned, but not before my hands became full of blisters. The few paid, skilled construction workers wore work gloves while overseeing the work of the volunteers, but none of the students did, in a show of pride I supposed. Eventually I bought work gloves for ten cents. Some mornings my assignment was another totally unfamiliar task, such as hoeing corn, mixing cement, building a stone wall or other masonry work. I even survived the back pain from the constant bending.

After work we went for a quick dip in the lake and had lunch. Classes started at 1 p.m. I took nature studies and American literature. The professors did not lecture; they held seminars. As the professors did not take attendance, students were on the honor system and felt free to skip classes. Completing assignments was optional. Everybody was on a first-name basis, with faculty and students on the same social level. I was in awe of the concept of the professor being one of us—an example of life in a democratic country, I thought. For someone like me, used to the strict European caste system, this camaraderie was exhilarating.

Students knew that no one was going to coerce them. Some students thrived under this regime; others just wasted their time. Nobody knew whether a student came from a rich family or was on scholarship because discussing one's personal financial situation was discouraged. The concept of ignoring social class was noble, but it did not prepare people for living in the real world. Some of the students who had spent four years there found adjusting to a normal competitive environment extremely difficult after they left. I learned much later that what I took to be a normal American college environment was highly atypical.

Among my many lasting impressions of the American South during that hot summer, food was primary. I was startled to see meat served with sweet condiments, ham with mint sauce, or candied yams with beef. At first I found such combinations totally unacceptable, but eventually I got used to them. Even today, Europeans who come to the United States have similar reactions to the mixture of sweet and savory main dishes served here.

Toward the end of my summer stay I experienced one of the most triumphant moments of my life. Another female student and I had been assigned to construct a scaffold so that we could wire a building that was to become the chemistry lab. We did as told and lo and behold, I stood on the scaffolding and it did not collapse. What an accomplishment! Putting in all the switch boxes and wires later was much less rewarding.

Living in the South, away from the refugee environment and melting pot of New York, I became aware for the first time of the powerful issues of segregation and the history of slavery. I did not know that the college leaders were careful not to get involved in local segregation issues. Already, college critics called Black Mountain "the college of communism and free love." The college leaders did not care to aggravate their precarious standing in the broader community.

In 1956 Black Mountain College closed its doors. During the 23 years of its strife-ridden existence, the tiny college with never more than ninety students at a time had attracted an amazing number of influential Americans—architect Buckminster Fuller, composer Jon Cage, dance choreographer Merce Cunningham, and artists Willem and Elaine de Kooning, Paul Goodman and Josef and Anni Albers, to name a few—who would help shape the U.S. cultural climate of the 1960s.

When I think of that summer at Black Mountain, I am disturbed at how the war in Europe left me basically untouched in my rural cocoon. I was not aware that during the same summer of 1941 the Nazis murdered hundred of thousands of Baltic Jews in a few nights. With the help of Baltic and Ukrainian sympathizers, the Germans dug mass pits just outside of Riga and Vilnius within earshot of the city population. The Nazis herded the Jews into long lines at the edges of the pits and then simply shot them so that the victims tumbled into the pits. When the pits were full, the executioners bulldozed them and started all over. Most of the Jewish population of the Baltic countries perished in those few nights. I think it was then that the Nazis became aware that shooting so many people was an unsavory and expensive method of mass murder, and they started to look for more efficient ways, such as using Cyklon gas. Though the *New York Times* reported the shocking news when it happened, few outside New York seemed to notice. Certainly not I in the remote Smokey Mountains of North Carolina.

Meanwhile, Otmar had joined the Army. As luck would have it, his assignment took him to Fort Bragg near Fayetteville, North Carolina. When he once had a weekend pass, we each took a four- to five-hour bus ride to spend the weekend together in Charlotte, halfway between Black Mountain and Fort Bragg. He had the low basic salary of a private and I was not earning anything, but we scrounged around for inexpensive food, took the Greyhound bus and stayed at the cheapest possible hotel, probably a flophouse. I remember the 100-degree weekend with no air conditioning, sweating but happy to be together. Because telling anyone would have been embarrassing, no one at the college or my mother knew about my meeting Otmar.

Married Life, 1941–46

At the end of the summer I returned to New York and Otmar remained at Fort Bragg. Felix was still at home waiting to be called up, so I continued living with him and working as a seamstress.

Mother was in Canada keeping house for Bruno on his Niagara Peninsula fruit farm and helping him with harvesting as well as canning fruits and vegetables. She was willing to put up with the hardships of living without plumbing and with having to draw water from a well. She did not complain. She was proud of herself for standing by her son and for doing work she certainly never expected to have to do. She derived great satisfaction from being able to help Bruno establish himself, and he was glad to have her help. The farm did not bring in much cash, and he had to work the nightshift in a nearby basket factory to earn enough for daily expenses. Money was scarce.

Shortly after my return to New York, Otmar and I decided to get married. I do not think we discussed the idea with anybody. Felix continued to discourage my relationship with Otmar, but we were very much in love. Even so, Otmar and I fought a lot over what seemed to me to be silly things. He was upset if I did not wear the dress that he had expected to see me in or if the fried chicken he was looking forward to turned out to be roast chicken. Unable to handle the slightest disappointment, everything became a big deal for him. Much later I understood that he was a very insecure person and that he compensated for his feelings of insecurity by being bossy and nasty. But at the time I constantly felt guilty that I had disappointed him and so took on the burdens of the relationship. I would not have married Otmar had I known that I could not change him.

To be fair, the political circumstances in 1941 played an important role in our decision to marry. Otmar was in the Army when the war was going badly for the Allies, and the future was uncertain. As with many wartime couples, emotion had replaced reason. Getting married and enjoying whatever time we could have together seemed logical. I was not yet twenty, but the thought that I was too young to marry never entered my mind. Two of my good friends from Portugal days, Edith Handler and Anny Kraus, both now living in New York, had met and disliked Otmar; they warned me against marrying him, but I did not listen. If I had doubts, I quickly extinguished them.

Pearl Harbor

We got married on December 10, 1941, three days after Pearl Harbor. The bombing of Pearl Harbor was a watershed event. The December 7 Japanese air attack demolished parts of the U.S. Navy anchored in the Hawaiian harbor. Earlier, President Roosevelt had unsuccessfully urged Congress to consider a more active role in the war for the United States. The shock of the attack changed the political climate. Everybody now rallied around President Roosevelt, and without further debate, the country prepared to go to war.

Otmar had obtained a ten-day leave from his unit for our wedding. We were married by a justice of the peace in New York City with Mother, Felix and Uncle Robert as well as Edith and Joseph Handler present. Otmar's mother was in Hungary. I wore an aqua-blue winter coat, bought for the occasion, with a matching wool turban made by a hat designer friend. The wedding luncheon took place at an Upper East Side restaurant that was upscale for our circumstances. From there Otmar and I went to a borrowed house in Manhasset, Long Island, for our honeymoon.

Two days later, Otmar received orders to return to Fort Bragg. The plan was for me to follow as soon as possible. Stoically I accepted the inevitable interruption of our honeymoon and returned to Felix's apartment, which we once again were sharing with Mother. She had returned to New York from Bruno's farm in Canada and was working at odd jobs, sewing and helping in the shops of acquaintances. Whether or not Mother was pleased that I had married, she did not say. In any case, my marriage did not affect our relationship. Felix maintained his misgivings but had resigned himself to the fact of our marriage.

Fayetteville, North Carolina

As soon as Otmar found out that he would stay there for a while, I followed him to Fayetteville. Although Fayetteville with its Army base had become a boomtown virtually over night and housing prices had soared, I found a nice furnished room in a private home. Locating a job as an alteration hand in The Capitol, Fayetteville's largest department store, I was greatly relieved to find work right away; we simply did not have any money. Otmar's pay as a private was not enough to support a dependent. With my salary of $12 a week and his pay of $30 a month, we had a combined monthly income of almost $80—just enough to cover our basic expenses.

Though being there was his choice, Otmar was unhappy in the Army and complained continuously. Most of the time he had nothing to do, slept a lot and was often dispirited. Fortunately, he was frequently allowed to leave the base and we were able to spend more time together than most Army couples. We played gin rummy, Otmar's passion, and quiz games, another one of his interests. I hated gin rummy and considered the game a monumental waste of time. But I went along, trying to please him. Although

Otmar was very demanding and I constantly felt pressured, in my letters to Mother I reported only happy episodes.

After my landlady and I became better acquainted, she started inquiring about my escape from France. In January 1942—a month after the Pearl Harbor attack, when the United States had entered the war—the war was not yet a reality for most people in Fayetteville. They saw me, a refugee, as a novelty, since there were no refugees in Fayetteville and nobody had ever heard a story like mine. One day the owner of the department store came into the alteration room and told me that my landlady, a schoolteacher, had called him asking him to give me time off that day to give a speech to the PTA. I did not know what a PTA was and I had never given a speech, but my boss urged me to accept the invitation. I thought it was a good omen that I had just picked up my one and only good dress from the cleaner's during my lunch hour. During the speech I was nervous, but the PTA ladies were encouraging and seemed interested in what I had to say. I enjoyed the experience.

My boss now became aware of me and promoted me to the position of office worker. I learned how to operate the switchboard and do accounts, and I tried to improve my typing. Eager to learn, I did not intend to be an alteration hand for the rest of my life. The most fun was being a cashier. The cashier's booth was on the mezzanine overlooking the sales floor. Money was sent up from the floor in pneumatic tubes. I had to make change and send the tube back down. Every time I heard the tube arrive downstairs, I felt a thrill. I was grateful that I was able to learn new skills while being paid for learning.

During that time I became a sought-after public speaker. The Lions, the Rotary and other groups, including churches, invited me to speak. I never got paid, but some groups gave me presents. I still have a flower vase from those days that I cherish. Remarkably, the press often seemed interested and covered some of my speeches. Otmar was pleased with my sudden prominence but did not want the social commitments that ensued. People invited us to hear more about my experiences, but such invitations bored him. The attention was a great boost to my ego, but the resulting conflicts with Otmar took away some of the pleasure.

Despite several attempts, Otmar did not succeed in getting a better assignment in the Army. We lived with a continuous sense of uncertainly about the future that pervaded our seemingly idyllic, self-absorbed home life. We tried to keep up with world news as best we could in a town like Fayetteville. If I was upset about the way the war was going, my letters to my mother do not show it.

Life assumed a sort of routine. I went to work; Otmar went to camp. He came home almost every night and we had dinner out somewhere, since we had no cooking privileges in our furnished room. I used the excellent public library in an attempt to compensate for my truncated formal education. I was keenly aware that stopping high school in the middle of tenth grade had left me with insufficient *Bildung,* the intellectual and classical education that was a must in the Prague of my youth. That I knew so little about America also rankled, although most of the people I met in Fayetteville seemed no better educated than I.

Frequently I sent letters to Mother, at first to New York but soon back at Bruno's in Canada. My comments show that I was amazed at how friendly and welcoming people were in Fayetteville. I also appreciated learning so many new skills, though I reported that my typing was not yet good enough to land a job at the Fort Bragg post, where the pay would have been much better.

One visit to Fort Bragg stands out in my mind. Once when I waited for Otmar in the enlisted men's mess, I sat down next to a black soldier who was sitting by himself at a table in a corner. I did not know that the Army was completely segregated. The dirty stares I got did not bother me, because I was interested in meeting this soldier. With no black students at Black Mountain College, I had not had an opportunity to know people of color in the South. That meeting in the mess hall was not particularly significant, and from our conversation I did not find out much. But the negative reactions to my crossing the color line stayed with me.

Lawton, Oklahoma

In June 1942 the Army assigned Otmar to Fort Sill, Oklahoma, near Lawton, a sleepy southwestern town whose population had tripled from 12,000 to 40,000 almost overnight due to the Army influx. I followed by bus with a stop in Chicago. Instead of sightseeing in Chicago I had to resign myself to staying on the bus because I could not afford a hotel room. Even just from the bus window seeing a new part of the country was still thrilling. To get to Lawton, the bus traveled through what seemed like endless miles of open, unpopulated stretches of dusty nothingness. In Lawton proper, nothing green grew anywhere unless some optimistic inhabitant watered it. At least the sunsets were quite spectacular.

We were able to find a little white clapboard house on the edge of the town, overlooking an expanse of dirt, with nothing between the horizon and us. We shared this house with young Lieutenant Hart and his charming wife, Mary. Although newly married and taking care of a house for the first time, Mary knew all about housekeeping and cooking. She was the oldest of many children and had been helping in her mother's household for years. I was lucky to find such a congenial housemate who was willing to take me, a housekeeping neophyte, under her wing.

Promoted to corporal, Otmar now worked in the office and was happier than in North Carolina. Finances were still tight. I soon found a job as a saleswoman in the town's finest ladies' dress shop, but I disliked my bosses. They did not like me either, because I was not willing to flatter customers just to make a sale.

After a couple of weeks I quit and, encouraged by Mary, started my own dressmaking business. I had made a dress for her that she liked. In the midsummer heat, customers were scarce so I spent a lot of time keeping house.

For the first time in my life, I was washing, cleaning and cooking. Unexpectedly, I enjoyed it. I had never before cooked and felt very unsure of myself in the kitchen. Mary Hart helped me patiently. Otmar was less understanding. All too often dinners turned into catastrophes. Either the meat was raw or burned or I was burned. The more critical Otmar was, the more uncertain of myself I became. Food was extremely important to him, and he looked forward to home-cooked meals. So when I presented him with a half-raw fried chicken, he became insulting. I would be crestfallen, always feeling that he did not love me enough or he would not have been that nasty.

That was the beginning of a pattern that lasted throughout the ten years of our stormy marriage. I was always feeling inadequate, because I was not blond or thin enough or pretty enough or a good enough cook. Trying to improve myself did not bring great results. He was always apologetic after each outburst, but the contrition lasted only a few days until the next crisis. I ascribed these outbursts to the general atmosphere of war and uncertainty. Otmar forgot his temper tantrums immediately, but they resonated within me for a long time. I tried to ignore them as much as I could. Most of the time we enjoyed being together having good conversations or listening to music.

Mother and I exchanged letters frequently. We wrote mainly about mundane occurrences, although I remember Mother's remarks about the anti-Semitism she encountered in Canada. I reflected that I had not felt any in either North Carolina or Oklahoma but had heard derisive remarks about the appearance of Orthodox Jews. These comments did not shock Otmar or me, because privately we would make similar derogatory statements. Otmar was less uptight about being Jewish than I was. I don't remember much discussion about anti-Semitism, although he knew how ambivalent I was about overt Jewishness. I was Jewish and therefore permitted to be critical of Jewish behavior or appearance, whereas I would classify the same remark by a non-Jew as overtly anti-Semitic. I did not understand then that anti-Semitism in Germany had started with such seemingly harmless derogatory statements that in short order enabled Hitler to convince the German nation that it was all right to treat Jews as if they were ants to be stepped on.

Toward the end of the summer my dressmaking business picked up, but the pace was erratic. Sometimes I had too much work, then not enough. In the fall I finally had enough work regularly to hire a helper. Much of my business consisted of retailoring men's suits for women. Such a wartime economic adaptation, atypical for the States, would have been commonplace in Europe, where people were more frugal. I became quite adept at these makeovers.

While we were in Oklahoma, we heard from Felix that he was now in North Africa assigned to U.S. Army intelligence. Mother wrote that Bruno had volunteered for the Canadian army. The war in Europe was going full blast, and many Canadians enlisted to contribute to the war effort. In 1943, two and a half years after he bought the farm, Bruno sold it. When he had started on the farm, he had $1,000 in the bank; after selling the farm, he had $2,000. He and Mother marveled at the unexpectedly favorable result.

Mother as Baby Nurse

With Bruno gone, Mother was at a loss as to what to do and how to make a living. Since she no longer had a place to stay, she returned to New York to move in with friends temporarily. She was toying with the idea of becoming a baby nurse, a skilled helper who stayed at a new mother's house for the first six weeks of a baby's life to take care of mother and baby full time. Baby nurses were not expected to do housekeeping, but they did get up at night with the baby.

I tried to persuade Mother to give up that idea because it sounded too strenuous. Suggesting that she try to become a translator instead, I wanted her to go to Washington and get a government job that would use her language skills. But she did not heed my advice and took a baby-nursing course at a hospital in New York instead. When I reread the letters I wrote her at the time, I am amazed at how I tried to persuade her, as if I were her mother and not her daughter. My relationship to Mother had normalized. During the emigration I was clearly the decision maker. Once in the United States we were on a more equal footing, each independent of the other. We kept in close touch as we went our separate ways. We had never been a demonstrative family, although we were a loving family, clearly loyal to one another.

After completing the training, Mother immediately found employment. The pay was excellent and the work rewarding. She had no expenses, since she lived in and could save her wages. Her employers were primarily European professional women who had delayed childbearing until their late thirties. These women were delighted to find an older European woman who came from a similar background and who was reliable and skilled. It seemed that Mother had made the right choice.

With Mother in New York and me in Lawton, I was forever asking her to send me things from the city such as stored clothes, household items or sewing supplies. These requests created endless money transactions. I always seemed to owe her $2 here or $5 there. At the time these sums seemed very important and called for a constant accounting between Mother and me.

Otmar was also concerned with our finances. He had borrowed small sums of money from the bank account that his uncle had left in his name. He used the money only as a loan to cover some of our expenses, which increased during the frequent moves. Now that I was making more money, both of us tried to settle our debts.

Unfortunately, Otmar and I were having frequent arguments and our lives were no longer idyllic. I became increasingly disenchanted with Omar's behavior and his imperious attitude about people. I was embarrassed that he felt so superior to most of his fellow recruits and to the typical townspeople. The critical attitude was exacerbated by his lack of challenging work. He was bored to tears because again he had nothing to do in his Army job. He became more and more disillusioned about his career's progress. And I with him, though I was too busy to give it much thought.

Battle Creek, Michigan

Otmar repeatedly tried but never managed to obtain better assignments. Finally in March 1943 he was assigned to the Military Police Officers Candidate School at Fort Custer near Battle Creek, Michigan. I stayed behind in Lawton for a few weeks to finish the work that I had started. Because visiting was not practical, I then went to New York for the duration of the OCS training. After he had completed the training and received his second lieutenant's bars, I moved to Battle Creek to be near him. He now had a lieutenant's pay, and we were not so poor anymore. We bought a car so that I could visit him approximately twice a week in camp because he was not able to come home every night as before.

I did not know how to drive. Otmar was my teacher. He was so impatient that on the second or third try in the middle of the city of Battle Creek, I stormed out of the car crying and causing a major traffic jam. I do not remember how I got home, but I will never forget the utter sense of frustration with him and my own inability to master the clutch. After that I took the car out by myself to practice on deserted streets and eventually took my driver's test at 8 a.m., when there was no traffic. Somehow I got my license, but it took me months to dare to make a left turn against advancing traffic. I think this experience helped me be more patient coaching my own children and others many years later when they were beginning drivers.

Otmar tried to get transferred out of the military police and into civilian affairs. I could understand that he did not like most of his fellow officers; they were basically cops who liked to drink and chase girls. Neither he nor I fit among people who drank heavily and who were interested only in sports. Our aspirations were more intellectual. Restlessly he whiled away the day and came home grumpy to the detriment of our relationship. So negative and so opinionated was he that I found it difficult to sympathize with him.

I considered leaving him but always rationalized that the situation was too fluid to make any major decisions. Who knew what would happen when he was sent overseas and how he might change? This type of swaying back and forth, of wanting to get out of the relationship but not doing it, lasted as long as the marriage did. Regularly I deluded myself into thinking that I could change him into a kind and warm person. I was plagued by a sense of failure at not making the marriage succeed, even to such a difficult person.

Otmar did not want me to work anymore, because he could now support me. But I could not stand the idleness. I started again as an alteration hand at Jacobson's, the finest store in Battle Creek, where I graduated soon to the office as I had in North Carolina. Again I gave many talks about my European experiences but became bored by repeating my own words.

Life was too full of uncertainties. One day Otmar was going to be sent overseas to Europe; the next day the orders were canceled. Two days later he was going to be sent to the Pacific and that fell through; and so it went— a nerve-racking time. My salvation was a new job in a large, inexpensive department store where the labor shortage was so desperate that I was promoted to credit manager after three days in the office. A supervisor from the firm's headquarters came to Battle Creek to teach me how to interview applicants, evaluate prospective creditors, and obtain credit references; I also learned to understand budgets. This job opened up a new and fascinating world and I loved it. Finally I was doing something that really taxed my brain. What I learned there in a very short time about people and about accounting has stood me in good stead all my life.

Greenville, Pennsylvania

Like all my other employment experiences during these years, my tenure as credit manager ended when we moved again. The next move took us to Camp Shenango near Greenville, Pennsylvania, a staging area for troops going to Europe. Instead of being sent overseas immediately as he expected, Omar's assignments again kept changing, from going to the Pacific to becoming a training officer in the United States to going to Europe. I joined him in the godforsaken hick town, where there was nothing but mud and cold and no decent place to eat. However, I found a college nearby that was willing to let me audit courses. I took my first course in American history there and several other courses in literature and political science. Always eager to learn, studying helped me overcome the discomfort of our uncertain situation. Otmar finally went to Europe in early 1944 for training to become part of the army of occupation. I do not remember the parting. If I was sad I must also have been relieved that the waiting was finally over.

Again I returned to New York and joined Mother, who did not have a permanent place to live, since she was able to stay with friends for the few days between jobs. Now that I was there to stay, we rented a nice apartment on East 73rd Street in Manhattan. Happily, our high-rise building with a doorman was in the same block where Uncle Robert lived. We had come quite far in the two years since our penniless arrival in the States.

Mother did not come home except on her days off. She was in great demand and could pick and choose among cases. At times she selected the wrong family and the people were unfriendly, demanding and arrogant. Not usually a quitter, when she did make the difficult decision to leave such a family, she usually found a harmonious and satisfying relationship with another family. To have found a well-paying profession where she was appreciated was a great boon to her morale. Who would have predicted in her circles in Prague that she would be living in other people's homes and doing some of the housework! To her great credit she never felt demeaned.

Office of War Information (OWI)

Soon after we settled in our apartment, Joseph Handler, my very good friend from Lisbon days, suggested I apply for a position in the Office of War Information, where my language skills would be useful. Joe was a Hungarian-French journalist who had joined the OWI at its inception in 1941. Although I was not yet an American citizen, the OWI was able to hire me because I had that rare combination of proficiency in a Slavic language, Czech, and a Latin language, Portuguese, both relatively unusual in the United States. People who knew French and German were a dime a dozen. I became responsible for listening to Czech or Portuguese radio broadcasts and simultaneously typing an English summary of what I was hearing, to be handed immediately to a supervisor. The job paid well, but my inadequate typing skills were a hindrance. I enrolled in an intensive typing course during the day because my work shift was either from 6 p.m. to midnight or from midnight to 6 a.m. After I broke my left clavicle in a car accident, I had to stop the course with only enough improvement to get by. To this day I regret not having completed that typing course.

The work was interesting, but I was apprehensive about walking to or from work at midnight on the streets of Manhattan by myself. Gladly I soon moved to a day job in the OWI's Long Range Planning Division. Although the term "propaganda" was not used in any of the OWI lingo, clearly the organization existed to further U.S. foreign policy aims by distributing promotional materials. "Long range" meant propaganda publications in print and pictures that were not dependent on day-to-day news and that had an indefinite life span. The Radio and Cable Wireless Divisions produced the "short range" news in 1943, shortly before the advent of television and decades before the Internet. The job of my division was monitoring all OWI print publications to ensure adherence to State Department foreign policy objectives. All 12 of us had to be conversant with State Department policy documents distributed and amended almost daily. We each had a different language specialty and a different region of the world for which our publications were destined. For example, it was U.S. policy to refrain from making hostile statements about the Soviet Union and to emphasize our friendship. OWI magazines and the articles talked about all aspects of American life and showed the level of effort the United States was making in the war. Sometimes, for example, we would take a statement about agriculture and recast it for the foreign readers as a story about "how American agriculture helps us win the war."

My job was to edit the drafts of our publications in Czech and Portuguese in view of daily policy changes and ensure that long-range publications continued to be responsive to U.S. propaganda aims. When they were not, I had to write memos suggesting changes. My English and my writing skills improved during this period. The work was fascinating and I loved it. I felt I was in the middle of important things. As the youngest in our group, my highly educated, experienced colleagues from all over the world initially intimidated me. But I soon overcame my anxiety when I realized that I could hold my own.

One particular experience stands out in my mind. Policy people from Washington were coming to New York to an important meeting in my boss's office to discuss the latest propaganda initiative. My boss had asked me to prepare a position paper for him for that meeting. The day of the meeting, he found that he could not attend and asked me to take his place. When my topic came up, the Washington people wanted to know the opinion of my boss. I spoke up and described the content of my position paper. The visitors asked no questions and nobody seemed to need to go further. They were glad that somebody knew something about the subject. Without opposition, the group adopted the position as I had written it, and the meeting proceeded to another topic. I had expected a thorough discussion or debate and was flabbergasted that government officials could dispose of an important issue in such a cavalier manner. I had not realized that my ideas, the thinking of a nobody in the hierarchy, would result in a major policy shift. In this my first encounter with policymaking, I remember thinking that if this was how government decisions were made, God help us. What really counted was that I had more information than the others. Knowledge coupled with the willingness to take responsibility gave one authority: what a valuable lesson! I put this insight to good use in later jobs, especially when I was trying to effect change within a large school bureaucracy.

Meanwhile, Otmar was in England preparing for assignments in the U.S. Army of Occupation. We wrote loving letters to each other every day, and all the doubts and disappointments that I had felt vanished. Distance was a great facilitator! In addition to working, I was busy sewing, making myself a trousseau for our real married life after the war. I also found time to attend courses at the New School for Social Research, where I studied literature, history and American government. My life was full with keeping up with old and new friends as well as the situation in the world at war. I never had enough time to do everything I would have liked to do. Just like today.

During this period I became a U.S. citizen. I did not have to wait the customary five years because I now was the wife of a U.S. citizen; Otmar had been naturalized in the Army. The brief but solemn ceremony moved me deeply. I no longer was a newcomer or an outsider. By now pretty self-assured, well-regarded by my superiors and my colleagues, I felt good that I had a meaningful occupation and that my life was so satisfying.

One day my office assigned me work in Spanish on the assumption that if I could read Portuguese I could understand Spanish. That was not quite true either for professional work or for living. On my own I took Spanish lessons from the director of the Museo de Bellas Artes of Santiago, Chile, who had come for post-graduate training at Columbia University. The lessons did not last very long but long enough to make me interested in Latin America, to which I had paid no attention until then. Reading editorials in the Chilean newspaper that my tutor brought helped me in my work. However, such study did not prepare me to deal with the food market when I lived in Argentina later.

As the war in Europe was winding down but the Pacific war continued, my office tried to interest me in learning Chinese by enrolling me in the China Institute in New York. After very few lessons it was disappointingly evident to me that I could not master the range of intonations indispensable in Chinese. However, the brief exposure to the language motivated me to read about China and to keep abreast of the developments in the war against Japan. I had not followed these events closely until then. I thought that in case the war against Japan continued after the end of the war in Europe, knowledge about the Far East might be useful.

During the last year, my responsibilities in this job included reviewing movies for the OWI. The office was stockpiling films for use by what was to become the United States Information Service after the war. I had to alert producers of commercial movies to scenes that could offend the sensibilities of the intended audiences around the world or would portray the U.S. in too unfavorable a light. Every day at 9 a.m. I went by my lonesome self to our large projection room, and by noon I had completed a rating on the film to forward to the producers. For example, I had to be sensitive to America's wastefulness. A movie showing Mickey Rooney throwing a plate of pasta or a pie into the face of his enemy seemed inappropriate to show to an Italian audience that did not have enough to eat. Although a fun assignment in the beginning, I grew tired of going to the movies every day. I could not have known that this experience would enable me to get a job in Hollywood when we moved there a year later. But with every new assignment I was gratefully aware of how much I was learning at the OWI and was eager to soak it all up.

Given my position in the OWI, I had to be well-informed about the progression of the war. I read the newspapers, the many government bulletins and recommended books. I had unusual opportunities to meet knowledgeable individuals and listen carefully to insightful discussions. Sometimes the news was overwhelming. I remember, for example, the jubilance I felt when we firebombed Dresden in the spring of 1945 and killed a huge number of German civilians. Having just seen the first newsreel photos (the closest we had then to TV news) of the liberated concentration camps and the broken bodies of their prisoners, I felt no remorse for our action. Two years later, when I went to Germany and saw the destruction we had wrought, I was more conflicted about our use of firepower.

Felix During the War

I followed Felix's whereabouts during the war closely. His first overseas post was in Algiers, where he was attached to the Free French government then under General Charles DeGaulle and stationed in North Africa. His assignment was to act as liaison between U.S. intelligence units and Jean Monnet, a key member of the Free French government. Monnet had been deputy secretary-general of the League of Nations. When Felix joined him, Monnet was coordinating an arms-buying program to enable the Free French to support the British war efforts. Felix got into some kind of scrape there and was wrongly accused of espionage or another sinister act. Although unsure of the details, I do remember him telling me that he was going to be jailed, that for the first time he was really frightened, and later that he had had a harrowing time. After enduring this terrible episode and eventually being totally exonerated, from North Africa he was sent to England and attached to SHAEF, the Supreme Headquarters for the American Expeditionary Forces. He became one of the aides to General Walter Bedell "Beedle" Smith, General Eisenhower's chief of staff. This assignment propelled him into regular contact with the highest echelons of power.

When SHAEF moved to France, Felix went along. Because he was charming and intelligent and had excellent manners, the generals assigned Felix to welcoming visiting VIPs. Well-connected in the Army, he rendered valuable personal service and was well-liked. He used his charm to ask some of these VIPs upon their return to the States to write a letter to his mother reassuring her of his whereabouts. As the mail was very slow and delivery irregular during the war, we often did not hear from Felix for weeks. So Mother was particularly pleased when she received a letter in October 1944 from James F. Byrnes, President Roosevelt's advisor and later secretary of state, saying: "He [Felix] is a most accomplished man and because of his knowledge of German and French was of great help to me. All of the officers have the highest regard for him, and I share their good opinion." Bernard Baruch, also an advisor to President Roosevelt and a special advisor to Byrnes, had written to Mother earlier, stating, "You can well be proud of your son. He was extremely efficient, likable, well-mannered, pleasant and intelligent; in short, all the fine qualities one likes to see in one's son. He was in good health and liked what he was doing." General George C. Marshall, U.S. Army chief of staff—who eventually created the Marshall Plan, which enabled Europe to get back on its feet after the war—also wrote a glowing letter about Felix to Mother.

When SHAEF later moved to Germany, Felix remained in his position. To avoid the embarrassment of having a sergeant hobnobbing with the generals, he received a "battlefield commission," becoming a lieutenant in the field, a very rare occurrence. While serving as the generals' social troubleshooter after the war, he bought German china on the black market, flew to Algiers on a private plane if the cook needed tomatoes for a special dinner and was an all-purpose fixer, much appreciated by those he served. Among the other dignitaries that he escorted were Prince Bernhard of the Netherlands, the queen's husband; Conrad Hilton, who was starting the Hilton Hotels; Louis Marx, who was launching a toy empire; and of course all the top brass who visited SHAEF. It was a heady time for Felix.

At the end of the war, when total chaos reigned in Germany, a short window of opportunity allowed servicemen to make a fortune on the black market. I think the way the scheme worked was that if one converted travelers' checks into cash or scrip, the Army currency, one could make a huge profit. Felix wired Mother to send him as much money as she could spare so that he could take advantage of the scheme. But Mother was not willing to send him money. She did not trust him and sent him nothing or very little, which upset him greatly. He always reproached her for her unwillingness to help him. He did, however, come out of the Army with much more money than he had had going in. When the time came for him to leave the Army, Felix asked to be demobilized in Paris. He had enough money to buy an apartment there. He took advantage of the chaotic post-war conditions in France, when with American dollars and American cigarettes you could buy almost anything.

Felix's extraordinary Army career, his closeness to the most powerful people in the Army and his unusual promotion, led him to adopt a totally cynical approach to the world. He said that he had met all the high and mighty. His impression was that they were no smarter than he was, that they behaved unethically and were only out for themselves. Thus, when Conrad Hilton and Louis Marx offered him excellent jobs upon leaving the Army, he did not accept either offer. He did not want to become an organization man. Felix particularly did not want to be associated with people who banked on connections rather than know-how and who were willing to use unscrupulous means to get ahead. He refused to be anyone's lackey. Not willing to take orders from anybody, he wanted to live life his own way. He did just that when he settled in Paris.

Paul During the War

Felix was not the only member of the family who had gotten into scrapes with the authorities during the war. While the war was being fought in Europe, Paul arrived in Australia in 1940 with an Austrian passport. He did not realize that he would be classified as an enemy alien because Austria had been annexed by Germany, with which the British Commonwealth was at war. The Australian government subjected enemy aliens to a number of petty rules and regulations that were a great nuisance to immigrants who were trying to establish themselves in a new country. Paul's battles with the authorities are well-described in his biography, *What a Life*. As part of his life's story, the book contains interesting details about Paul's early years in Australia.

Six months after the end of the war, Otmar was also demobilized. He returned home to New York in January 1946 just as my OWI job ended.

After the War

Otmar's return to New York was a happy occasion for both of us. On top of our reunion, on the first day back he found out that he had become quite a wealthy man. The shares in his name that had amounted to a couple of thousand dollars at the beginning of the war had now increased in value by some 500 percent. These shares had been put in Otmar's name by his rich uncle Arpad, who had never explained the purpose of this transfer. Otmar assumed that Arpad, his sponsor, had wanted Otmar to have a nest egg in case of an emergency. When we first were married and had no money, Otmar was hardly ever willing to touch that money, unsure about whether it was his. During the war we had no way of contacting his uncle to find out, so Otmar let the money sit. Perplexed by Otmar's sudden change of heart, I accepted his explanation about why he no longer doubted that the money was his. I could see that he felt important as a rich man.

Honeymoon

Ready now to spend, we decided to go to Mexico on our long-delayed honeymoon. We bought a huge, black Buick from a car dealer in New Jersey without waiting to have the car checked out. I packed all the clothes that I had made for myself as a trousseau as well as the jewelry that Otmar had "liberated," obtained on the black market in Germany, and we headed for Washington. Staying at a hotel near Union Station, we parked our car in front of the hotel, leaving the luggage on the back seat.

We went sightseeing and were impressed by Congress and the majesty of the Mall, feeling like two kids on their first trip away from home. Excited to visit the nation's capital, we saw the many buildings that played such an important role in the life of this country. Before the trip, we had viewed them only in movies or newsreels. We thought that this stopover was a fitting beginning for the long-postponed honeymoon.

The next morning when we were leaving, we found the left side window of the car shattered and our luggage gone. We raced to the nearest police station, where we received an incredulous reception: "You did not really leave your luggage on the back seat overnight!" I think we might have gotten more responsiveness from the police if we had announced that we had indeed left the luggage during the night in full view of passers-by and reported the items still there!

After our outrage subsided and reality set in, we felt even worse that we had been so stupid. I am not sure whether I was more upset at losing the clothes that I had spent so much time making or about our naiveté.

We continued our trip without luggage. Shortly after crossing into West Virginia, we heard a sudden loud noise coming from the motor, and the car broke down in the middle of nowhere. We could see no houses, no phone nearby, just wide stretches of meadow. So soon after the losses in Washington we were really not well-primed for another such blow. Eventually, we managed to get the car towed to a garage, only to be told that the motor was burned out and the car was ready for the junk heap. That beautiful, stately, elegant black Buick! We left the car there and licked our wounds, having learned a hard lesson in how not to buy. Another investment gone. Good thing we did not have any luggage. We continued our trip to Mexico by train. Our destination was Cuernavaca, a small, lovely, lush resort town near Mexico's famous volcano, the Popocatépetl.

We rented a charming villa with a view of the volcano. Hibiscus trees in bloom and fragrant jacaranda bushes surrounded our pool in the garden. The house came with two Mexican maids, delightful but illiterate and inexperienced young girls. I had to teach them everything, from setting the table to how to store food in the refrigerator. They were willing to learn and eager to please, but my OWI Spanish was not up to the task. I had to be patient.

After a couple of weeks in Cuernavaca we spent a few days in Mexico City, where we had friends. We loved it. I bought some clothes, just enough to get by. The need to be elegant had somehow vanished with the stolen trousseau. We found Mexico picturesque and seemingly unspoiled, where one could accomplish a lot by applying well-placed energy and creativity. Life seemed so much more relaxed than in New York, and Otmar thought that with his money we could live better there than in the United States. Although probably true, the prospect of living like the rich among the many poor did not appeal to me. The class differences in the States were not so obvious as in Mexico. In the short time we were in Mexico, I experienced enough broken promises that I knew I would find it difficult to live in a culture where time did not matter. *Mañana* meant maybe later, maybe never, but not tomorrow unless a bribe were involved. We debated whether we should stay or return to the U.S. In the end we decided to go back but opted for leaving New York to escape the summer heat. New York without air conditioning could be brutal; air conditioning then was rare except for movie theaters.

Moving to California

From Mexico City we flew to Los Angeles to stay with my cousin Mimi's mother, Marianne Roberts, and consider the possibility of living there. Just like my flight from Prague to Paris eight years earlier, the plane was not pressurized, and again the pain in my ears was excruciating. Similar to Mexico City, the Los Angeles area had beautiful residential districts, a pleasant climate and lush vegetation. Life also seemed less hectic than in New York. Southern California had all the advantages of Mexico without its drawbacks. We decided to move there and thought that Mother, who was still baby nursing, might join us once we were settled.

Feeling optimistic, we went back to New York to gather our belongings and buy another car. The leisurely cross-country drive—with no break-downs—was a unique opportunity to see new parts of this vast land.

A friend of my aunt's, a real estate agent, suggested that we live in Bev-erly Hills. We bought a house on South Elm Drive, between the major streets of Olympic and Pico, a good but not exclusive neighborhood. We both liked the green-shuttered, white wooden bungalow and its all-enclosed patio with a huge, old walnut tree in the middle. The oleander bushes in the garden reminded us of Mexico. What a change from sooty, hot New York.

Otmar suggested that he would furnish the house while I looked for work. I never questioned this arrangement. I took it for granted that I would work. My wages would cover our expenses. I would hand over my paycheck to Otmar, while he contemplated his investments and decided what to do with his life. He never considered being somebody else's employee. During the almost two years that I lived without Otmar in New York, I had become more self-assured and multi-skilled. Yet in spite of sur-prising myself by being successful at the OWI and not lacking admirers (whose favors I rejected, being a faithful wife), I was still very unsure of myself vis-à-vis Otmar.

Story Analyst at MGM

Believing that I could not build on my OWI experience in Los Angeles, I decided to return to my former trade and applied for work as an alteration hand at Saks Fifth Avenue in Beverly Hills. But before I was due to start working there, a more interesting employment possibility materialized. Once again the job opportunity arose through Joe Handler, albeit indirectly. Joe had suggested that I call his childhood friend from Slovakia, Emery Kanarik, who was a story analyst at Paramount Studios. On the phone I told Emery about Joe's continuing work with the State Department and about my work reviewing films at the Office of War Information. He was very welcoming and promised to invite us for dinner the next week. A couple of days later, and before we had met socially, he called again and said, "I noticed on the phone that you have a foreign accent. Do you by any chance speak Czech?" He told me that Metro-Goldwyn-Mayer was looking for somebody who could review Czech books and stories and write summaries in English. Louis B. Mayer, the head of MGM, had bought a number of Czech properties. According to MGM's policy, the studio had to have a summary of every property it had purchased to protect itself against charges of plagiarism.

Emery and his wife, Rose, became lifelong and beloved friends. An architect by training, Emery was working in films only because he could not find work in his field in Los Angeles. As soon as the economy improved, he went back to architecture. Charming, short and bald, Emery reminded me of Joe. Both men had a great sense of humor. Wherever they were, they excelled at telling jokes in Hungarian that only Hungarians understood. Through the Kanariks, Otmar met a number of amusing Hungarian writers and directors who were prominent in Hollywood films at the time.

Sweet, even-tempered, patient Rose also came from Slovakia. Modest, yet with a brilliant mind, she had been the first woman to obtain a Ph.D. in mathematics at the University of Pittsburgh in the early 1930s. One of the first professional women I had met, she was balancing her life between caring for their two small children and teaching at a community college. Accomplished as she was, Rose nevertheless had difficulty obtaining a university position because in the 1940s women did not teach mathematics. As I write this, Rose, now in her nineties, still tutors mathematics students.

I was grateful to Emery for the tip about the MGM job. Immediately hired and installed in a plush office with a thick, white carpet, a reclining chair for reading and a beautiful desk with a typewriter, I could not believe my luck. Before leaving New York, Joe had jokingly said to me, "Next time we hear from you, you'll be working in Hollywood." I had dismissed that comment out of hand, but here I was! Walking around the studio, looking at the sets and passing by famous people felt quite exhilarating.

After my story editor boss saw my first review, he said, unforgettably, "Margit, you do write well. But you do write with an accent." I was glad that he liked my summaries.

HUAC

Soon after I started at MGM, the Screen Actors Guild went out on strike led by Ronald Reagan, then the head of the guild. Story analysts, too few in number to create their own guild or union, had joined the Painter and Paper Hangers Union. In sympathy with the striking actors we, too, went on strike. Most of my friends in Hollywood were great leftists, so I was pleased to be able to demonstrate my commitment to labor causes. I walked the picket line proudly for one day. The next day MGM and the union settled the strike. We received a 25 percent pay hike, and Ronald Reagan became the great hero of the labor movement for a while.

On the picket line I met people who were deeply disturbed about the actions of the House Un-American Activities Committee. HUAC had been inactive during the war years but became more prominent during Harry S Truman's presidency. Truman, regarded by some of his Republican opponents as being soft on communism, had put into effect the first of many of the so-called anti-Communist loyalty oaths. In 1946 HUAC's greater power reflected the increasing Cold War suspicions by the government and the public about the Soviet Union. Anti-Communist feeling was growing rapidly in the United States. The committee launched multiple investigations into Communist infiltration of organized labor, the federal government and, most audaciously, Hollywood. In September 1947 HUAC subpoenaed 41 witnesses, 19 of whom declared their intention to be "unfriendly" witnesses. Of these, ten, almost all Hollywood screenwriters, claimed their rights under the Fifth Amendment. Suspended without pay by their Hollywood producers, they became the famous "Hollywood Ten" who were sentenced to a year in prison for contempt of Congress for refusing to testify about their political affiliations. They also received a fine of $1,000 for their refusal to admit or then disavow their affiliation with the Communist Party.

Once blacklisted by the film industry, the Ten were barred from working in Hollywood; to sell scripts, they resorted to using pseudonyms. The atmosphere in the film industry was fearful, full of suspicion. During this divisive and rancorous time, many Americans were jailed and suffered personal and professional exile because of their political viewpoints. Others who might have been outspoken about world politics became timid and self-censoring to keep their paychecks and avoid public condemnation. The witch-hunts continued into the early 1950s, when Senator Joseph McCarthy began his own Red-scare rampage.

By the time the influence of HUAC and McCarthy declined in the late '50s, the whole country had been tarnished by the vicious pursuit of those McCarthy identified as Communists and subversives. Careers in government, academe and business were ruined. This dark chapter in American history left deep scars on everyone who had lived through the madness.

Dress Shop in Beverly Hills

While I was involved with the film industry, Otmar had decided to invest in a real estate venture from which he expected to make a huge profit. But that project did not fill up his days. To find something to do, Otmar suggested that we buy a dress shop in Beverly Hills. His plan was for me to leave MGM. I would be the designer/dressmaker, and he would manage the business end of the shop. I acquiesced reluctantly; I liked my job at MGM and would have preferred to stay there.

Innocently, and without looking into the size of the clientele, we bought an existing shop off Rodeo Drive, even then a prestigious address. The shop sold clothes, accessories and costume jewelry to which I would add the "couture" component. Because we did not know that old inventories are generally heavily discounted, we paid full price for the store's inventory. We opened the store with great anticipation, but the euphoria did not last. Otmar sat in front waiting for customers who rarely came. I was in the back and quickly became very busy. An acquaintance with figure problems was pleased to find someone who could custom-make clothes for her and recommended me to her friends. Other women came and ordered dresses.

Otmar continued to sit morosely in front watching people go by, hoping that when a woman stopped in front of the window, she would come in even just to look. Though the purpose of owning the store was to give him something to do, he was again idle. Just as it had during his Army service, idleness brought out his worst characteristics. He became rude and abusive. When a day went by and nobody entered the store, he would say, "Let's get rid of it; it was a mistake." When he made a sale, he would say, "Let's give it another try." The seesawing went on for days.

To fill the increasing number of orders, I had to hire a helper and could not take the time to argue with Otmar. Although buoyed by my success in the shop, I realized that I was no longer interested in being a dressmaker. I had been genuinely energized by the work at the Office of War Information as well as the story-editing experience at MGM. Now I had come to view dressmaking as an insurance policy that was no longer needed. The worst part of staying in the shop, though, was the wearisome coping with Otmar's temper.

During this difficult time we followed Felix's activities from afar. Felix kept writing from Paris what a wonderful time he had living on PX rations in an impoverished city. He suggested that we come and share in the spoils of war. These reports tempted Otmar. But as we had just started a new venture, I thought we should give it a chance. However, Otmar was too impatient to sit around long waiting for the dressmaking business to become interesting for him. We had serious disagreements about the business. Personal conflict persisted as well.

One day a man came into the shop and asked Otmar whether he would consider selling it. This representative of Burlington Mills said his company needed a storefront in a good location. Burlington Mills had just produced a new miracle, nylon stockings, which created a fashion sensation. The company knew it would make a fortune, so it offered to buy the store for what we had paid. It was an incredible deal because the store had lost much of its value in just the few months we had owned it. Inexperienced, we did not know that store inventory loses a portion of its value every month it is not sold.

Otmar accepted the offer unhesitatingly, because then we could soon go to Paris. Not as pleased as Otmar, I finished the dresses I had on order. Once we had rented out our house, we were off first to Canada to visit Mother and Bruno and then to Paris, lured by Felix.

Bruno

Bruno had started to study at the University of Western Ontario in London. While in the Canadian army, he had first taught the use of weapons and then physical fitness. Toward the end of the war, because they thought he was an outstanding and helpful instructor, a group of university students urged him to make use of the Canadian GI Bill to study psychology at a university. The father of one of these students, a professor at Western Ontario, helped Bruno get admitted even though he had questionable academic credentials. Bruno started studying psychology with the intent of learning to help youth become well-adjusted to life. He found that he constantly asked himself to what kind of life people should aspire. That preoccupation drew him into the study of philosophy as his major. After three years he left with a B.A. in philosophy and applied to the University of Toronto to continue his studies.

While Bruno was studying, Mother had moved to London, Ontario, to keep house for him. Paul, who had started a paint factory in Melbourne, Felix with his Army "loot" and I with a well-to-do husband were now in reasonably stable financial positions. We three agreed to contribute to Mother's support so that she would not have to depend solely on her income from baby nursing. Wanting to invest some of his money, Felix loaned Mother $12,000 to buy a house in London. With none of us in New York, her moving to Canada and living with Bruno was a good solution for both of them. Their neighbor next door to the new house was Gwen Jones, a fellow university student who would eventually become Bruno's wife.

Although he was now a university graduate student, Bruno had not given up his dream of becoming the owner of a summer camp for boys. He loved the outdoors. Being good at carpentry and other trades, and enjoying working with his hands, he envisioned a camp in a beautiful natural setting. Boys would learn several outdoor sports, work with their hands and become good citizens. Above all, he wanted to help shape the characters and influence the lives of young boys. Paul's unhappy boyhood experiences had never been far from his mind. Bruno was sure that a character-building camp experience could influence youngsters sufficiently to lessen the normal traumas of adolescence. With hardly any money but with an enormous amount of enthusiasm, he bought a piece of land on pristine Lake Baptiste, four hours north of Toronto. On that site he started what became Camp Ponacka, his life's labor of love. In California, Otmar and I knew of these developments and were eager to know more.

Family Reunion in Canada

The timing of our December 1946 departure from California to visit Mother and Bruno could not have been more fortuitous. It coincided with

Paul's first post-war trip from Australia to see his family in North America. Felix had come from Paris and Otmar and I from California to await the arrival of Paul, Dita and their two children, seven-year-old Anita and two-year-old David. I can still see Paul in a gray overcoat alighting from a Trans Canadian train. He had David on his arm and was helping blond, freckled Anita, who was behind him on the train steps in her own gray coat, smiling shyly. Dita followed, wearing a blue suit, arms laden with the children's hand luggage. Although I knew that Paul and Dita had two children, I had never pictured Paul in the role of father. After eight years of separation, the reunion was a moving experience for all of us.

During that visit, Paul and I grew close. We spent many hours catching up with each other. He recounted how hard the time in Australia had been when he arrived there as a penniless refugee in 1940. To his credit, he never lost his optimism, bearing up under the weight of several jobs that had ended badly. Eventually, together with a chemical engineer from Prague, he had started to manufacture paints and varnishes. The business had grown and become sufficiently lucrative that he could afford to take his family on a visit to Canada.

Paul and I were amazed at how similar we were in many respects. We found that we considered ourselves lucky to be enriched, rather than defeated, by the difficulties of transplantation. Both of us were risk-takers, outgoing and impatient. We were interested in other people and eager to see new places as well as amass impressions. Taking advantage of opportunities that arose, we both lived full lives. I was thrilled that Paul's plans included a visit to us in Paris and then to Prague, where I would join him.

That visit in Ontario was truly memorable. It would take another twenty years before Mother and her four children would reunite.

7

EUROPE AND
BEVERLY HILLS
AFTER THE WAR

A FTER OUR EXCITING family reunion in Canada, Otmar and I left for Europe in mid-January 1947. We sailed on the most luxurious ship of its time, the elegant H.M.S. *Queen Elizabeth*. We stayed in London for a few days, visiting Otmar's mother, brother and one of his uncles. Otmar's mother had survived the war in a Budapest ghetto and had gone to England as soon as it was possible to leave Budapest. The money issue never came up again with Uncle Arpád, who was then somewhere in Switzerland.

London

We also visited my good friend from Alt Aussee days, Uli Pulay. Shortly after Germany had annexed Austria in 1938, to escape from anti-Semitism, Uli and her family had left Vienna. They immigrated to England, where Uli continued her education. Her schooling was interrupted when Uli was seriously injured during the Blitz, the German bombardment of London early in the war that caused such enormous damage to buildings and hurt so many people. After the attack, Uli was evacuated to a country hospital. There she met Charles Lloyd Pack, an actor then in uniform, whom she married after her rehabilitation.

Uli and I had corresponded all during the war, and I knew that she and Charles had had two sons. She had written of the difficulties of raising two children in war-torn London amid great shortages of all kinds. I had sent her diapers, canned milk, soap flakes and whatever else I could to ease her life. We were thrilled to see each other again. Uli had not changed much; she was still petite with dark hair and expressive dark brown eyes that did not betray her wartime suffering. In her unheated home, our friendship warmed us during one of the worst cold waves that winter in England. Although thereafter we saw each other only occasionally and our correspondence was erratic over the years, our friendship never faltered until she died in 2000.

Paris

From London, Otmar and I took the train to Paris, returning seven years after my eventful bicycle escape. My situation now was very different from when I had left, a scared Austrian refugee fleeing both the German bombs and the pitilessness of the French bureaucracy. Now a well-heeled American tourist, I returned to a city impoverished by the war and its aftermath. Pleased to be back, I still could not rid myself of a somber feeling.

Back from Canada, Felix greeted us when we arrived. We stayed with him for the first few days in an apartment he had rented in an elegant residential district near the Etoile. He chose to be demobilized in Europe so that he could stay in France and take advantage there of the GI Bill of Rights. This great innovative federal program after World War II enabled millions of American war veterans to begin or continue their college education. The Army paid the students' tuition and gave them a stipend. With the stipend, the inexpensive PX rations to which he was entitled and the money he had accumulated through his schemes while in the Army, Felix was able to live in Paris much better than in New York at the time.

When we arrived, Felix was spending his time playing the piano, reading about current affairs and playing quiz games. His real interest was wheeling and dealing on the black market. Whenever it served his purposes in going back and forth between Germany and France, he wore his Army officer's uniform. He knew where to buy cheap gasoline with his PX card and where to obtain rationed items that were unobtainable in the Paris markets. Felix kept track of expenses in his unique bookkeeping system, which only he could decipher. Enjoying the ability to help people, he had made many acquaintances who often asked him for favors.

His lifestyle was very much of his own making. For example, he never locked his car, saying that the lock would not stop a thief or vandal and he preferred not to contend with broken glass. Felix's optimism was only partially validated. Thieves entering the unlocked car stole some of my jewelry that Otmar had "liberated" in Germany and that I had given to Felix to take to his German jeweler for needed adjustments. Given the widespread devastation and the strained atmosphere of the post-war times, when the majority of the population was hungry and cold, neither Felix nor I took these losses seriously. We were living in a sort of never-never land, profiting from the misery of others but not quite prepared yet to look at the questionable morality of our lifestyle.

Luckily, Felix never lost his "shock absorber." He had bought gold bars that he had melted and fashioned into the shape of a car shock absorber, painted it black and stored it in the trunk of his car. He believed that nobody would steal a shock absorber. When he needed money, he snipped off a piece of the fake shock absorber with pliers, removed the black paint and converted the gold into money.

During that time in Paris I became close to Felix, the adult. He had left Prague when I was 13 and not old enough to have a serious conversation with him. We now had much to talk about and enjoyed getting to know each other. I was glad to have him taking my side during the frequent spats with Otmar about money and sometimes food; Felix tried to use humor to mediate between us. Although his negative opinion of Otmar had not changed, Felix spent a lot of time with Otmar because they both liked playing the piano, gin rummy and quiz games. Each of them enjoyed scheming to get a bargain when changing money on the black market.

For me, fun with Felix was going to the opera. We frequently went to the Paris Opera that first winter of electricity shortage, when the opera house was blacked out except for the auditorium. Without Otmar, who was not interested in opera, we went to every performance of *Faust* and *Rigoletto*, always with seats in the first few rows. At that time one could drive up to the Opera, park a car in front of the entrance and leave it there for the whole performance. Parking restrictions had not been instituted, because there was almost no traffic in Paris. Though French citizens could not afford it, the French wanted to revive their cultural life, which had been almost extinguished during the war. We were so blasé in this unreal setting and could afford to go so often that we felt free to leave the opera house after our favorite parts were performed. We would walk out on *Rigoletto* after Sparafucile's big aria and on *Faust* after the ballet in the third act.

Jean Pierre

Wanting to be back in contact, I called my former landlady, Madame Paul-Boncour, who was pleased to hear from me. The next day I received a call from her grandson Jean Pierre, to whom I had been so attracted before leaving Paris in 1940. Jean Pierre and I had an emotional meeting in the Cathedral of Notre Dame. He showed me a packet of letters that he had saved during the war. The packet contained the letters that he had sent me after we parted; they had never reached me and were returned to him. He had kept them, certain that we would meet again—sometime, somewhere. When I read some of these touching love letters, in the middle of the awesome cathedral, I started to cry. He explained that he had been as much in love with me as I with him; but because I had been a minor at the time, he had felt that he could not take advantage of me physically. I was so overcome by emotion, joy on one hand, and sadness on the other, that I did not know how to absorb all the feelings I was experiencing. Although we went our separate ways, we have seen each other several times over the years, still keeping in touch today with brief notes and phone calls. We both cherish the memory of our deep feelings for each other.

Immediately upon arriving in Paris, Otmar and I started hunting for a place of our own. Felix had warned us even before our arrival that finding an apartment in Paris was unlikely. Not easily discouraged, we answered an ad in the Paris edition of the *Herald Tribune* that offered an apartment in exchange for an affidavit of support. Ginette Cosnard, the owner of the little apartment near the lovely Bois de Boulogne, needed the affidavit to obtain an immigration visa to the United States.

The ground floor apartment looked onto a dreary, paved, second inner courtyard of a large, elegant apartment building, but our little abode was far from elegant. Sun never reached our rooms, and during the many hours when electricity was cut throughout Paris, we would have been sitting in the dark if we had stayed at home. Whatever its shortcomings, we were pleased to have the apartment.

During the months before Ginette got her immigration papers, she used her savvy about her environment to help us. Short, stocky and energetic, she knew where to get cooking oil and butter as well as gas for our stove when absolutely none was to be had. Wounded in northern France during bombing attacks, she was nursing large burns on her legs; it was amazing that she moved so fast. When we took over her apartment, Ginette went to live with her mother to wait for her American visa. She eventually reached the States and married Paul Cox from Tennessee. Widowed and living alone in California now, she and I have remained friends ever since we met.

Shortly after we settled in Ginette's apartment, Paul and his family arrived in Paris, passing through on their way to Czechoslovakia. I joyously agreed to join them in Prague without Otmar, who was not interested in coming along.

Prague Revisited

In long letters to Mother in Canada, I described how thrilled I was to be in Prague, seeing it for the first time with grown-up eyes. Much of the time we were in the city, Paul and I were busy with restitution matters. We hired a lawyer to negotiate the return of Bruno's farm, which had been confiscated by the Nazis. The Nazis gave it to poor ethnic Germans who had worked it for a time, then had fled Czechoslovakia at the end of the war. They were among the Sudeten Germans whom the Czech government had mercilessly expelled in 1945. The now-abandoned farm had become the property of the community and managed by its rural cooperative as part of the Czech government's Communist-inspired scheme to collectivize agriculture. Because the Nazis had taken the farm from us in 1939, we had a claim to it.

We also tried to get Mother's pension reinstated. Upon contacting Father's now-nationalized bank, we found that the bank was willing to pay Mother's pension and reimburse her for the lost war years. Quite accidentally, a friendly porter at the bank told us that two large crates in Mother's name had remained in the bank's basement throughout the war. No one there knew their contents. When we received permission days later to open the crates, we found all of Mother's silver: her tea sets, coffee set, platters and plates—an amazing array of valuable items. Paul and I argued over what to do with these finds. I said I wanted no part of them; I did not see myself using that silver. My U.S. lifestyle did not approximate our pre-war Prague living conditions, and I was not going to clean silver and have it using up valuable storage space in a modest house somewhere. Paul decided to file restitution papers to retrieve the silver rather than leave it.

Some of our acquaintances were filing restitution claims for art stolen by the Nazis. With no record anywhere describing our paintings, we were unfortunately not able to claim compensation or restitution for them from Germany after the war. The paintings may well have ended up in some

Nazi home where they could have been bombed to bits. Or they may hang somewhere in a museum. We will never know.

While we were there, post-war Czechoslovakia had a sizable Communist Party that did not yet dominate the country's Socialist democracy. However, all restitution matters that were going through the courts came to an abrupt end the following year, when a Communist government took over Czechoslovakia and appropriated all middle-class property. We never got anything back, including the pension. I did not expect that disturbing turn of events at the time of my first visit back to Prague.

I wrote to Mother that I found everything about Prague much smaller than I had imagined, marveling that distances were so small compared with the United States. Although life was onerous for the average citizen, a feeling of excitement was in the air. With the Germans defeated, the majority of the Czech population agreed with the Socialist orientation of the government. The intellectual elite in Prague were enjoying an expansive cultural life. The first Prague Musical Spring was under way in 1947 with famous musicians from all over the world coming to Prague for the first time since the war. Through Paul's friendship with the Menuhin family, I became acquainted with then-unknown performers such as David Oistrach, the Russian violinist; Leonard Bernstein, the American composer and conductor; and Dmitry Shostakovich, the Russian composer. All three became world-renowned musicians within the next decade. I had the privilege of hearing them play in formal attire in the concert hall as well as in their shirtsleeves after successful concerts in the private homes of the Prague musical elite. The atmosphere was exhilarating.

My cousin Fritz, the son of my father's sister Luise, was in Prague at the same time to meet with the agents of Czech agricultural industries that he was representing in Turkey. Fritz, Paul and I spent many a wonderful evening renewing ties and savoring our new relationships.

I could have easily stayed there. I could see myself living in either Prague or the U.S., but I was not eager to stay in Paris because the atmosphere there was unfriendly to foreigners. But once Paul's visit was over, I had to return to Paris, where both Felix and Otmar had ordered American cars to be shipped to them. They expected to live comfortably there for a year on the profit from selling a brand-new American car in Paris.

Felix continued enjoying his life, free to do nothing if he felt like it. But I was becoming increasingly bored and uncomfortable with this directionless life. Otmar and I argued about major as well as inconsequential things, and the indulgent lifestyle was not conducive to improving our fragile relationship.

Nuremberg

Our aimless situation came to an end when life in Paris started to normalize and our "free ride" evaporated. With living growing more expensive, Otmar now felt he had to make money. He applied for and got a job with the Nuremberg war crimes tribunal as an economist, even though he was untrained in economics. Knowing German, having worked in the stock market in New York before the war, and being willing to accept a short-term appointment seemed to qualify him. I remember many unsettled weeks before his contract was finalized and before the court authorized my joining him.

Harboring too many anti-German feelings, I was not looking forward to going to Germany. I certainly was not prepared for what I found. When I drove there, Otmar was in Essen, the once proud industrial center in West Germany, preparing evidence for the trial against Alfred Krupp, head of Germany's largest heavy-manufacturing conglomerate. The American authorities had taken over the palatial Villa Huegel in Essen, the Krupp villa where we stayed. The villa was one of the few pre-war buildings standing in an otherwise bombed-out city.

Surveying the damage, I remembered how elated I had been in New York when I read about the Allied pilots' bombing raids on Essen. Seeing the destruction in person evoked very different emotions. The drive from Paris was preparation for viewing the sickening war damage in Essen. All along the highways were bomb craters. With all the bridges out and huge sections of broken road requiring detours, travel was cumbersome. I saw burned-out buildings missing walls, some with a piece of roof hanging over a room where dozens of people tried to find shelter. The streets were full of rubble. People with nothing to eat scrounged in the garbage. Children peeked out from behind mountains of trash or sat staring vacantly. The scene depressed me greatly. Unexpected emotional conflicts overwhelmed me. On the one hand, I knew that Hitler had to be defeated and that the Germans had only themselves to blame. On the other hand, I realized how our side had ravaged civilians who had lost so many of their loved ones as well as everything they owned.

Moving to Nuremberg for the trial after Otmar had completed the economics research in Essen, we found that our assigned billets were actually in Fuerth, about 12 kilometers from Nuremberg. Living in Nuremberg was impossible, because practically no houses were left standing in the devastated city. In Fuerth we had a comfortable apartment where we lived like royalty on the "cigarette economy." On the open market one could buy practically nothing. Inflation was so rampant that the real currency was cigarettes, not deutsch marks, the currency of the occupation. The Germans craved cigarettes, and we could convert non-smoker Otmar's weekly cigarette ration into whatever food we wanted with plenty left over for other purchases. Two cartons of cigarettes, worth a dollar or so in the States, could buy 12 place settings of fine Rosenthal china.

Living like millionaires compared with the Germans made me feel uncomfortable most of the time, although once in a while I let Otmar's joy at our relatively superior standard of living in the despised Germany seduce me. I found it hard to get my bearings. Belonging to the victors was complex. A few years before, the people who were now our neighbors might have reported us to the Gestapo. As Jews we would have been at best humiliated and most likely exterminated. Now we lived well and the Germans paid for their aggression. The average German citizen, whose main crime had been passivity, had no house to live in and little to eat. Was that justice? Were we to gloat over our victory? I could not get these concerns out of my mind.

When I arrived in Nuremberg, I was offered a job at the war crimes tribunal as a simultaneous interpreter, translating proceedings from English into German. The trials were held under the auspices of the American, British, French and Soviet governments. All documents were translated and speeches interpreted into English, French, Russian and German. Never before attempted on such a large scale, the whole profession of simultaneous interpretation started at the Nuremberg trials. With lawyers speaking the different languages of their countries, conducting the trials without simultaneous interpretation would have been almost impossible. I would have been happy to accept the job offer, but Otmar objected: suppose he did not like his job and wanted to leave and I had committed myself to staying on? He would be inconvenienced. I was disappointed but did not want to make an issue of this job. As was my custom in trying to stay married, I offered no resistance.

By the time we arrived in Nuremberg, the "big" trials—of Goering and the other leaders—were over. Ours was the second echelon of important but less prominent war criminals. The first time I went to the courthouse to observe the proceedings, a young American lawyer was trying to prove that a German defendant who was known as the commander of a concentration camp had been present at that camp. Witnesses had no doubt about the defendant's identity, but his involvement was hard to prove by the court's rules, since there were no existing records. Furthermore, the German defendant was a wily fox, whereas the American prosecutor was an inexperienced lawyer. The session was most frustrating to watch because the German was running rings around the American. When I left a couple of hours later, the prosecutor still had not been able to prove that this man who was responsible for thousands of deaths had ever been at the site. I was furious.

As I got into my car to drive the dozen or so kilometers to my home, a mass of ordinary Germans was standing in front of the courthouse waiting for the streetcar. I felt like ramming the car into the crowd, I was so frustrated and angry. As I drove on, the anger dissipated. Closer to home I drove past the bombed-out houses, past a group of women and children clearing rubble to get to the garbage cans for food, past a pregnant woman who had fainted from hunger with a little baby next to her crying. I felt so sorry for them that I would have been willing to give them the shirt off my back. But I did not do anything of the kind; I just drove home. The conflict between my outrage at what the Germans had done and the effect of our response, justified or not, was eating me up. I had to do some kind of work; otherwise I could not stay mentally sane in Nuremberg.

German Youth Activities (GYA)

I applied for a job with the U.S. Army of Occupation, which hired me as a German Youth Activities specialist. Being bilingual, I was a good candidate for the GYA position. Additional qualifications were having experienced firsthand the authoritarian schools in Prague, similar to the German ones, and knowing enough about America to emphasize the difference. The significance of being entrusted with this assignment as a new American was not lost on me.

My job was to re-educate the Hitler Youth in democratic ways. What an assignment! In my view it was the most significant job of the occupation forces. I was not impressed that the main activity of most of the soldiers was guarding the huge stockpiles of materiel and issuing tickets to speeding GIs. Though the strict ban on fraternization with Germans was mostly disregarded, the GIs were still bored and wanted to go home. Their lack of

171

interest in reforming the Germans energized my efforts to attempt it. I was the only civilian in my unit. Before I arrived, the soldiers had been teaching the German kids baseball and buying them Cokes and ice cream. Believing that the U.S. Army could do better, I advocated the creation of a youth center where children could go after school. Living in half-destroyed houses without heat or much to eat, the children would find a warm place conducive to learning. After convincing my boss of this idea, we requisitioned a large, intact villa that stood in what must have once been a lovely garden and started an American-style youth center.

In addition to liaison and office duties, my job was to create and lead a teenage girls' group in the afternoons. I tried to run it like a discussion group with topics chosen by the girls, but I got no response at first. They were only willing to follow orders, and if none were forthcoming they just waited, staring into space. All their answers and comments were meant to please me and to agree with me. They were completely unwilling to show any initiative or take responsibility for anything. It took me a long time to get more than yes-and-no answers. When I finally got them to open up about war issues, they just reiterated that Hitler's only sin was losing the war. What had happened to the Jews was of no consequence to them. They had not known any Jews and knew hardly anything about their persecution. They did not know that I was Jewish and I did not volunteer it, because at that time I still felt uncomfortable about being Jewish. The young women in my group believed in Hitler, and if Hitler said that Germany had to become *judenrein* (free of Jews), they were not going to question the wisdom of the beloved Fuehrer. They heard the same message from the leaders of the Nazi youth groups to which they had belonged. Country girls, they knew little about what had gone on outside their local community. Since they were ignorant about almost everything, I was inclined to believe them when they claimed no knowledge of concentration camps. During the last phases of the war, they and their families had been mainly preoccupied with survival.

As director of the youth center, I had a free hand. My boss was busy with other things. I wanted to get books and start a library in the center because one saw no books anywhere. Non-Nazi books had not been published in Germany for years, and the occupation forces had destroyed or banned whatever books had survived the bombardment. I suggested organizing a book day for youngsters. Reading would be a useful activity where there was nothing to do but play in the rubble. For the book day, we invited children to bring an older, non-banned children's book to the youth center and get a Coke or an ice cream cone in return. We printed posters and stuck them on walls—a major effort. I was very apprehensive about whether anybody would come. Inauspiciously, the appointed day was a rainy, dreary, cold Saturday. But lo and behold, an hour before the starting time the yard was full of waiting families. We got enough usable books to start a children's library that we could build on.

To the great amazement of the German children, our library was a "free hand" library, meaning that the borrower could hold the book and look at it before checking it out. Until then, the books in German libraries had been off-limits in stacks, and the public had to select books from library cards.

Though my work was completely involving, I was constantly aware of my conflicted feelings about being in Germany. Every so often I needed to get away from the depressing sights in Germany and from Otmar, with whom I had increasing marital difficulties. According to several of the letters I wrote to Mother at the time, I was leaving Otmar one day only to return the next. Neither of us could let the other one go for good. The many such episodes led to a wearing accumulation of stress. The issues were never about a third party; the problem for me was Otmar's temper. His fits were over insignificant things—minor expenditures or whether someone had cheated him in one of his black market deals. That I never commiserated with him about such matters made him even angrier.

For respite, I sometimes went alone to Prague, which was close enough for a weekend trip. Another reason for going to Prague was to see about restitution of Bruno's confiscated farm. Progress on that front was very slow, but I was thrilled to be in Prague. I found old and new friends and tried to coordinate my stay there with my cousin Fritz Kandler and his Greek wife, who on occasion visited Prague from Istanbul on business. We had a wonderful time going to the theater and concerts and dancing together, and I was sorry to leave after each visit. As an adult I now saw the Prague that I had known only as a child or adolescent, and to my surprise, I felt very much at home there. Remembering how conflicted I had been as a teenager when I could not decide whether I was Czech or Austrian, I felt relieved that I no longer had to contend with that unresolved conflict. Earlier, that internal decision meant figuring out an identity while being Jewish without wanting to be Jewish, and being Czech some of the time and Austrian at other times. Now I was an American.

On one of those trips I met executives of the Bata Shoe Company, where Paul had worked before the war. I told them about my work with the children in Nuremberg, who had no boots for the coming winter. The Bata

Company generously agreed to donate hundreds of pairs of children's boots to our youth center. I then got the U.S. Army to transport them—a minor miracle! Thus we were able to start a shoe distribution event. To see the smile on the children's faces when they received a pair of boots made the effort worth it; but happy event that it was, it was heartrending. The distribution of boots and the acquisition of books were the highlights of my time with GYA.

Displaced Persons (DPs)

To commute to our respective jobs with only one car and no public transportation, we hired a driver, although after having been poor for so long, our having a driver seemed ludicrous. As soon as word leaked out that we were looking for someone, dozens of young men applied for the job. Getting to know our new driver, Paul Perich, turned out to be another significant experience for me. A displaced person (DP), Paul originally came from the Ukraine, then a part of the Soviet Union. When he was about 12 years old, the Communists arrested his parents and sent them to Siberia because the family was middle class and therefore considered politically unreliable. Paul never heard from them again. Without family or friends, Paul had to fend for himself. After the Germans overran the part of Poland to which he had fled, they captured him and forced him into slave labor. He had gone through the most awful times from then until age 22, when we met him. His story was harrowing.

Finally, he became a mascot of a U.S. Army outfit. That protective position ended when a new commander forbade displaced persons living in the camp and threw him out without any support. His American contacts promised Paul that he would be able to immigrate to the States, but as I found out only a few days before we left Nuremberg, his chances were slim. Because he was Ukrainian-born and could not document his past, in American official eyes he was suspect. The United States and the Soviet Union were now engaged in a cold war. I was outraged at the way our authorities treated him after all their promises, but I could do little for him before leaving. Although he went to work as a driver for friends when we left, I sadly lost contact with him soon afterwards.

Knowing Paul helped me become aware of the enormity of the problems of displaced persons. Thousands of DPs were living in Germany, including concentration camp survivors, war victims, orphans and released prisoners from both sides. Desperately looking for a new home somewhere where they were not unwanted, they all shared a frightening past, a present lack of money and a questionable future. The United Nations Relief and Rehabilitation Administration (UNRRA) was in charge of the many DP camps and through dedicated efforts for many years eventually resettled most of the people from the camps.

Developing a Worldview

We left Nuremberg in early 1948. Otmar's assignment had ended and he did not care to start another one in Germany. At that point I would have been happy to stay. Deeply involved in what I was doing, I thought I was having a positive impact through my youth work. I was upset about having to leave.

My stay in Nuremberg was pivotal for me. I had learned a lot about arranging events and being in charge of a significant activity that had not been tried before. I had also figured out how to create and run an organization. But especially important, I acquired a worldview. As had many others who had been in the war, I became convinced that war is an unacceptable way of resolving political differences. Although I did not doubt that we were justified in defeating Hitler, the idea of sending innocent young men to kill other innocent young men seemed the ultimate immorality.

The many scholars who claimed that the Second World War was avoidable persuaded me over time. If the West had seized the opportunities early, it could have stopped Hitler when Germany first occupied the Rhineland in 1932 or even later, in 1938, when Hitler annexed the Sudetenland. With England and France unwilling to oppose him and the United States staunchly isolationist then, Hitler felt emboldened to proceed with his aim of creating the thousand-year Reich.

I thought, too, that the typical German did not understand the extent of Hitler's reach. My contacts with dozens of German civilians eventually convinced me that most Germans did not know what went on in the concentration camps, although not many of my friends share my belief. Many Germans never saw columns of Jews walking through the town to the railroad station. And those who did were told that Jews were sent to the East to help the war effort. They chose to believe what they were told. I think the greatest crime of the German majority was apathy and passivity. The population had been bombarded by Nazi propaganda; moreover, the citizens who were more aware of what was happening felt that as individuals they had no power and that resistance was dangerous in a severely punitive state. Anyone caught helping the Jews could have ended up in jail. Like most other nations in Europe, it was easy for Germany to become a nation of bystanders.

It was an eye-opener for me to realize the way the world worked, that most people everywhere are passive when their governments act unjustly. This understanding influenced the rest of my life. I determined not to be a mere bystander but to become active in the community or in politics, to find solutions to conflicts before they escalated into war. Watching the Allied occupation also showed me that war effects do not stop when the shooting stops. The spiritual cost of total war was debilitating for both the victor and the vanquished. The corruption that the war spawned on both sides, although we were willing actors, debased us. The privileges of the occupiers were hard to resist and created an unwarranted sense of superiority in many of us.

During the time we were in Germany, the Marshall Plan, which was to reconstruct Germany, had not started. America had to come to terms with a devastated nation of fatherless children. Less than a generation after we helped get them back on their feet economically, this former enemy would become one of our staunchest allies. What folly to consider war a solution!

While we were living in Germany, France had continued to recover from the effects of the war and Felix could no longer profitably reside in Paris in style on the black market. Subletting his Paris apartment, he moved to Vienna, where he was able to obtain a bombed-out apartment in one of the few buildings that had been damaged during the war. With the condition that he would repair the damage, the apartment would be his for 99 years as long as he or a family member remained in it. He was not permitted to rent it out. Felix managed to make the ruin into a cute apartment. With its high ceiling he was able to add a spiral staircase leading to a new loft bedroom above one corner of the living room. The apartment continues to be used by visiting family members.

With Felix no longer in Paris when Otmar's assignment in Nuremberg ended, we had no reason to return to Paris and decided to go back to California.

Back in Beverly Hills

We left for the United States together, although according to letters I wrote to Mother, I had decided that our marriage was finished. In reality I was still vacillating. When our relations were at their lowest point, Otmar had a way of turning on his charm, and I always fell for it. In retrospect I cannot understand why I did not stay on in my job in Nuremberg; on my salary I could have afforded to stay on alone. But for some reason I ended up leaving with him.

After we landed in New York, we bought a new, red Buick and drove leisurely across the country, seeing new and interesting places. I was happy to be back in our lovely little house in Beverly Hills. During our absence, the tenants had taken good care of the house, so our re-entry into California was smooth.

Once again Otmar did not know what to do with himself. He decided to study architecture, but since he could not start until the next semester he enrolled in an art school to learn to draw and paint. The great pleasure he took in exploring a newfound talent was not enough to make up for the disappointments with his real estate venture. He had hoped to make a huge profit on the house he had built on spec before going to Europe and expected to sell it upon our return. But he still could not sell it at a price that satisfied him, and he was incredibly frustrated because he believed that he was entitled to make that profit. Apparently I had sympathized with him this time, according to the letters that I wrote to Mother, although I do not remember my reaction that way. I mainly recall his temper outbursts followed by the periods of reconciliation that continuously kept me off balance.

The seesaw of our marriage was extremely stressful. Whether I left him or not, I clearly had to do something to make money; I could not depend on Otmar's future support. I also needed to work as part of gaining some emotional stability, but I was not sure what I could do if I did not want to go back to dressmaking.

1948 Election

A different kind of opportunity arose with the 1948 presidential election, in which Henry Wallace, Roosevelt's secretary of agriculture, was challenging Harry Truman and, ultimately, Thomas Dewey, the Republican governor of New York. Through some fluke, during the same election I got a job as a campaign worker for Democrat Phyllis Ziffren, who was running for the California Assembly from Los Angeles. At first I was a volunteer, but after a few weeks the campaign paid me and I became her co–campaign manager with her friend Robert Deutsch. Not that I knew how to run a campaign, but I learned fast. The hustle and bustle of the campaign was thrilling, although it meant working 24 hours, seven days a week, because the candidate made speeches at night and on weekends. In between, we created and distributed updated literature.

This was also the year when Richard Nixon was running for Congress against incumbent Helen Gahagan Douglas, whom he defeated by unjustly branding her as a Communist. Outraged, I could not fathom how in this great country, people could run such a dirty campaign for public office. He used the slimiest smear tactics and such disinformation that he was despised by liberals during the years he served in Congress.

My friends in Los Angles were all committed Democrats and deeply involved in politics. Some were members of Wallace's third party, whose platform was more liberal than that of either Truman or Dewey. I also supported Wallace but in the voting booth voted for Truman, believing that against all predictions he had a chance to win. In my first-ever election I did not want to throw my vote away.

Incidentally, one unforgettable side effect of this election occurred when I registered to vote. I called the Election Office and said, "What are your hours?" The clerk answered, "From nine to five, and be sure to bring your naturalization certificate." So much for my hopes that I had no foreign accent!

On a more significant level, this intense and personal introduction to elections and the knowledge that every vote counts influenced my future voting behavior. In addition to voting in every election, I became and have remained involved in election politics by following the issues in the media and by participating as a volunteer in the campaigns of candidates I respected.

At Loose Ends

After the 1948 campaign was over, I accepted a seasonal job as a designer in the L.A. garment district. Although I was no longer interested in the dress business, the money was good and I needed it. While my previous experience had all been in retail sales and custom dressmaking, this was my introduction to a small American garment factory. I found the production end fascinating and learned a lot in a short time. I observed how a factory operated while I was designing blouses to go with Juli Lynne Charlot's circular felt skirts. I had met and liked Juli during one of the campaign events.

Again jobless at the end of the design season in early 1949, I wondered what to do next. I was not satisfied with the series of short-term jobs that seemed to create a pattern of employment for me, even if they suited our vagabond life. I did not want to be a dressmaker, but that was the only trade I had learned. Often feeling that I needed an education, as yet I had no particular interest or goal. While I had enjoyed each of the jobs that had come my way and had profited from every one of them, I was not centered. I felt buffeted by fitful winds. Though I was proud that I had always done a good job, I had attained no real career satisfaction.

At about that time, Otmar received an unexpected call from the FBI. The FBI wanted to interview him because the State Department was interested in offering him a position. By 1949 the United States, which had been isolationist before World War II, was well on its way to assuming its role as a major world power with strong sponsorship of establishing the United Nations. Since the end of the war in 1945, the Foreign Service had been expanding rapidly. Several months earlier, Otmar had casually filled out a federal job application form at the post office and sent it in without mentioning it. But the State Department staff members who had seen the application were sufficiently interested to request the routine FBI background check that preceded every hiring.

To our total surprise, the department offered Otmar a job as vice-consul at the American legation in Budapest, his former home. He loved the idea. Because both of us were floundering, this offer seemed like an interesting and prestigious solution. Otmar's job was not in the career foreign service. For that he would have had to pass the Foreign Service exam, but it was nonetheless a bona fide foreign service job. The idea of a foreign service job in a country I did not know sounded exciting. We were embarking on a new adventure.

The Foreign Service wanted Otmar to start immediately. Otmar left before me in June 1949. He drove across country alone because he was eager to take our shiny red Buick on the boat with him to Budapest. He had correctly surmised that there would not be another car like it in Hungary. I stayed behind to rent both our house and Otmar's dream house, which he still had not been able to sell. I finally had to rent it out for much less than the mortgage, and Otmar became upset that he was losing money every month. This loss did not improve his disposition, and I always felt guilty because I had not been able to perform the miracles he expected. I aspired to perfection of myself and was disappointed when I could not please him.

8

FOREIGN SERVICE

I WAS LOOKING forward both to going to Budapest and to living under a Communist regime. I remembered my high school teacher praising the Communist slogan "From each according to his abilities, to each according to his needs." In Prague I had been impressed by the policies of the Soviet Socialist government and influenced by friends who praised the Soviet Union. I wanted to see for myself how much of the anti-Soviet news so prominent in the States was based on reality.

The division of Europe between Communist and non-Communist countries, as though separated by an "Iron Curtain," in Winston Churchill's phrase, was becoming become more pronounced. Certain that East–West relations worldwide had deteriorated only because people did not understand each other, I thought I had a conciliatory role to play. I would bring the two sides together, interpret them to each other and decrease the threat of nuclear confrontation. After my Nuremberg experience I still had high, rather naïve ideals about the results attainable from nonviolent conflict resolution. My Office of War Information experience made me suspicious of any kind of propaganda, and I wanted the opportunity to fashion my own opinions about what was going on. Though the German-speaking Hungarian middle class would have interpreted for me, I was determined to learn Hungarian so that I would not have to depend on anyone else's interpretation.

Budapest

By the time I arrived in Budapest in July 1949, Otmar was well-established in a beautiful old *palais* that the American government had leased from an impoverished aristocrat. The mansion was located on the castle hill, the Buda side of the city that had been heavily damaged during the brief but violent siege at the end of the war. Hungary first became involved in battle in December 1944, when the Russians laid siege to Budapest. Until March 1945 the Germans occupied half of Budapest and the Russians the other half; bitter house-to-house fighting devastated much of the city. The population suffered terribly during that time: no water, no electricity, no gas, no food, no heat and many deaths. Undertakers had disappeared, and corpses lay unburied and rotting in the streets. If it had not been for the bitter cold, a ghastly epidemic might have followed. When we got there four years later, the several months' siege remained uppermost in the minds of the residents. All accounts of events were prefaced with "Before the siege" or "After the siege," and included tales about the barbarous behavior of some of the Russian occupiers. People you talked to began by recounting their siege experiences, hoping that the telling would make these experiences real for those who had not lived through them.

Our Jewish acquaintances also told of their harrowing war experiences. Until 1944, Hungarians had been left to the fascist rule of their own government. During the early years of the war, that rightist and very anti-Semitic government, while not deporting Jews, used Jews for slave labor. Conditions in slave labor camps were harsh and unforgiving. Many slave laborers were injured and their health ruined.

When the Germans finally took over Hungary, in a few short months they deported and murdered some 400,000 Hungarian Jews from the provinces. Deportations of the Jews from Budapest, the capital, started at the end of 1944, when the Soviet army was already near the city. Many of the Budapest Jews were able to save themselves, some with the help of the Swedish diplomat Raoul Wallenberg. Everybody we met had a tale of horror. I could not help being reminded of how lucky I had been to escape the war in Europe.

The street where our three-story palace stood was miraculously undamaged. The huge porte cochere opened onto a covered entrance for vehicles leading into a courtyard. In former times, the aristocratic house occupants descended from their coaches well-protected from the elements. A massive staircase led to grand reception rooms with walls featuring huge Gobelin tapestries and Rubens-like paintings to show off the heavy mahogany furniture. The American government leased the house for their personnel, thereby protecting it from confiscation. Considering the American government as a savior, the owners were happy to leave all their belongings, thus avoiding a takeover by the current Communist government. Beneath the building, an intriguing secret passage led to the Danube. I heard that the Turks were the last to use the passage, during their conquest of Budapest at the end of the 17th century.

Our elegant house was a metaphor for this time. As elegant as the living quarters were, so were the kitchen and the servant quarters shabby. The kitchen wing with two tiny rooms for the servants had no central heating. The kitchen did not contain any equipment such as a mixer; everything had to be done the hard way. The maids washed the laundry by hand in the unfinished basement, which was freezing cold during the winter. Without a washing machine, they had to heat the water on a wood stove and then carry the heavy, wet laundry up two flights to the attic to dry. The maids were used to the working conditions in this house and thought nothing of it. They did not know anything else. I was surprised by my own reaction. After all, this setup was similar to the one I knew growing up in Prague. But my years in the United States had influenced me sufficiently so that I was uncomfortable with the traditional class structure, which I now considered unfair.

Also uncomfortable was the location of the district police station in the former stables on the ground floor. We were dismayed by their proximity. But considering that the police were going to watch us anyway, at least the surveillance was in the open. The policemen on duty there were primitive, almost illiterate young peasants who had received this plush assignment as a reward for being good party members. To show their loyalty, they displayed a big photograph of Stalin in one corner of the room. Under the photo they had built a ledge that usually held a vase with flowers and two lighted candles, their altar to the new religion.

My immediate goal was to learn Hungarian quickly so that I could talk to the maids. Although they were deferential and seemed very efficient, I was ill at ease because I could not communicate with them. I was also motivated by my frustration at not understanding the writing on the ubiquitous red banners that adorned almost every major building. Without the language I felt shut out. I found a teacher who was willing to come to our house. Since contact with Westerners was frowned upon, if not forbidden, most Hungarians avoided being seen with us. But my teacher, Maria, was not afraid. Furthermore, she needed the money. At first she came twice a week, and I spent many hours by myself every day studying. Soon she came every day because I was passionate about learning Hungarian. In fact after about three months I spoke it fluently and almost without a trace of a foreign accent. With my typically Hungarian name—Margit is the Hungarian form for Margaret and as common as Mary is in English—people thought I had been born in Hungary. They ascribed my lack of vocabulary to having been abroad for a long time. But otherwise I sounded like a native.

Aside from feeling discomfited about not knowing enough Hungarian and being in a country where I was considered an enemy, my relationship with Otmar went from bad to worse. By the time I arrived, he had met a very pretty young actress with whom he was having an affair. She was one of the many theater people he had met through contacts from his boyhood days. He liked the amusing and well-educated theater crowd.

All of them had had a terrible time during the war, especially the Jewish ones, who were so fiercely persecuted during the last months of the war. The end of the war brought only a short respite before the Communist government took over. Considered untrustworthy, Jews were again discriminated against by the ruling party, which did not permit them to work in any intellectual profession. Members of the middle class who were not committed Communists were assigned to menial jobs. The theater people felt they had little left to lose by socializing with an American vice-consul.

When I found out about Otmar's lover, he said that this fling while he was alone was unimportant and would not affect our relationship. But I soon realized that he cared about her. He was very generous, giving her money and coffee or sugar or vital supplies from the legation's commissary almost impossible for people to obtain in war-ravaged Budapest. I was touched by his uncharacteristic generosity toward her, recalling the many fights we had at the end of the war when he objected to my sending care packages to my friends in Europe. Though hurt, I felt encouraged that maybe something had finally opened this stingy man's heart. In some masochistic way I encouraged him to help her.

Instead of focusing on our marriage, I concentrated on studying Hungarian and trying to understand what was going on around me. Few cars struggled through the torn-up streets; people were pushing carts and carrying heavy bundles. Two sights struck me: the tremendous amount of rebuilding and the equally large number of red flags. Every building displayed large pictures of Stalin and the Hungarian Communist leader, Rákosi. A new industry must have sprung up because most of these pictures had been hand-painted in the two years since Hungary had gone

Communist. Construction was visible everywhere. With practically no construction equipment, the government was rebuilding houses, bridges, factories and schools the hard way.

People frequently worked at night. I thought they were willing to keep such long hours because they were paid overtime. When I asked one of the workers nearby, he laughed at my idea of overtime. He told me that under the Communists' Stakhanovite system, named for an exceptionally productive Russian worker, each worker had a certain minimum to fulfill every day. If not skilled or fast enough, the employee would have to work nights to fulfill this quota. The system was designed to motivate workers to double their efforts. This particular worker was very bitter. A primitive peasant who had come to Budapest from the countryside to improve his lot, he said that even when he fulfilled his quota he made barely enough money to survive. He was fed up with the party-imposed deductions used to help pay for the red bunting everywhere. He resented having to contribute part of his salary for the Five-Year Plan, the Communist blueprint for economic development, and having to pay for the frequent special party celebrations. In the beginning he had been enthusiastic about the Communist takeover but had lost all his illusions after only a couple of years.

I was beginning to abandon my initial intentions of convincing Americans that anti-Communist news was just propaganda. I came to understand that the totalitarian system of government ruled every aspect of the individual's life. That the Communists had replaced the capitalist class system with its own class structure was particularly dismaying to me. The *nomenclatura*, the people in power, were loyal party members with little education and often crude behavior; this new elite had its own shops, its own fine villas and its own curtain-covered limousines, but these privileges were well-hidden and inconspicuous. At least the educated, decently mannered leaders of the old capitalist system had real class! Seeing the pitfalls of the Communist system, I became less critical of the Hungarian bourgeoisie who, although they had suffered terribly during the war, felt that a war would be preferable to communism. I still believed that war was the worst of all solutions to national or international disputes, but I could share their disillusionment.

Visiting Yugoslavia

Writing from across the ocean, Mother suggested I visit my cousin Lily, who had survived the war in Zagreb with the help of her non-Jewish Croatian husband, Pierre. Lily was the daughter of my father's brother Valentin, with whom Father had spent his student days in Vienna. Mother wrote that Lily and Pierre made barely enough money to avoid starvation in a country where everything was rationed. In Yugoslavia, unless you could buy food on the black market, you frequently went hungry. I was eager to follow through on Mother's suggestion and to take them food and other supplies available using my diplomatic PX privileges.

Our legation considered my trip a foolhardy undertaking. Otmar did not object; he looked forward to a few days alone with his sweetheart. Hungary had just broken diplomatic relations with Yugoslavia. Yugoslav dictator Tito had just left the Cominterm, the organization of Communist states, and was an outcast in the Soviet bloc. Legation staff told me that the American authorities might find it difficult to rescue me if I were detained for whatever reason. Even under these circumstances I was not averse to risk taking. Given the disparity in our situations, I felt that I owed Lily my help. After some arm-twisting I was able to get a visa and the other necessary documents.

I had our cook roast a goose, bake cookies and put together food parcels. Heavily loaded, I set out on the long and unheated train trip to Zagreb. At first the train was very crowded, but as it got close to the border, almost everybody got off. Hungarians were not permitted to go to Yugoslavia. By the time we stopped at the border station, I was alone in the compartment and the electricity was out.

In the dark I waited anxiously for the Hungarian customs control. Eventually two unshaven, shabby young men in military uniform came in with a torch and asked me for my documents. I had an American diplomatic passport, but my typically Hungarian name puzzled them and they kept questioning me. I had been in Budapest only three months, and I had a hard time understanding their coarse peasant accent. They kept saying that I was a Hungarian and only pretending that I did not speak Hungarian. Sitting in the dark with these two uncouth, threatening-looking fellows, I was reminded of the sinking feeling in my stomach during my escape from France in 1940.

I had visions of how I would be abducted and never heard from again. These men clearly had power over me. Living in a totalitarian society where the citizen had no recourse in the law could increase anxiety immeasurably. Finally, still suspicious, the Hungarian boys left and the train lurched forward a few meters to the Yugoslav border. I heaved a sigh of relief. The thought of the roast goose buoyed my spirits.

The electricity reappeared and the Yugoslav border guards, looking just like the Hungarians, entered my compartment. They greeted me very civilly. I was struck by the absurdity of the border. On both sides were the same kinds of people who could have been brothers but now were supposed to hate each other because somebody somewhere had drawn an artificial line on a map.

Again I was alone in the compartment for a while, but the train began to fill up. By the time we arrived in Zagreb, my car had become so crowded that I could not get through to the exit with my bundles. A couple of strong men came to my rescue and hoisted me and my goose out the window—quite a dramatic entrance into Yugoslavia! Lily and Pierre's delight with my coming amply compensated me for all my trouble.

I decided to return to Budapest by plane, although there was only one daily flight from Yugoslavia to Hungary, and that was from Belgrade. I had to fly all the way south from Zagreb to Belgrade to get to Budapest farther north, but I looked forward to seeing something new. Because I was married to a "diplomat," the official Yugoslav tourist bureau organized my travel. I flew to Belgrade in a rickety old plane, sitting on a bench without seat belts or flight attendants. The ride was so bumpy that I would have prayed had I known to whom.

To my great astonishment, an official of the Ministry of Foreign Affairs, dapper in his army uniform, met my plane and escorted me during the six-hour layover in Belgrade. I said that I had wanted to take a taxi and see the sights. Instead he drove me around Belgrade in a black limousine, the typical vehicle of the Communist government VIPs, with curtains drawn so that people could not see who was in the car. The driver usually was taking some big shot's child to piano lessons or a wife to a well-hidden beauty salon. I was duly impressed by my VIP treatment and by being chauffeured around in one of the Yugoslav government's few cars. In retrospect I had a fabulous trip and was able to report on what I perceived to be the difference between the two Communist countries.

Back in Budapest, I was again submerged in my marital misery. Additionally, I did not enjoy the diplomatic receptions to which we were invited almost every night. We always saw the same people at these events because the few Western diplomats in Budapest entertained each other quite lavishly and frequently to extinguish their boredom. They made little use of the vibrant musical offerings in Budapest. Among the Americans were few with whom one could converse meaningfully, and most of them drank too much to be coherent. When they were sober, they complained about life in

Budapest; they felt like colonials—superior to the natives. This attitude prevailed before the Foreign Service geared up for the important role the United States was to play in international affairs. Eventually everybody whom the State Department sent abroad had to go through language and country training.

I often felt more at home with the local Hungarians than with my fellow Americans. And I kept thinking that by mere accident I was now on the other side and how easily I could have been "one of the locals."

Otmar did not share these preoccupations. He was proud to be in a position of power and thrived on the admiration showered on him because of it. One day he reported triumphantly that his girlfriend had just had an abortion. This disclosure was a huge blow; I had tried to become pregnant all during our marriage and could not. My feelings were crushed, my ego destroyed. Did Otmar really have so little consideration for me that it had not occurred to him that his gleeful announcement would devastate me? He had always said that he would not see his lover anymore, but I had known that these were just words. He kept promising and I kept waiting for him to change.

Learning Russian

To keep myself sane, I decided to add another challenge. Planning to study Russian, I wanted to be able to read Dostoyevsky's *Crime and Punishment,* which had so impressed me years before, in the original. Now I had the opportunity. Thinking that I knew enough Hungarian to get by, I was ready to move on to the new project and searched for a Russian teacher. I found an impoverished, highly educated, highly sophisticated count of the old school, who had taken refuge in Hungary after the Communists took over in Russia in the 1920s. He had been educated in the czarist schools in Zarskoe Selo, the czar's estate outside of St. Petersburg, and was the most educated man I had ever met. His stories about life in Russia—and the then Soviet Union—were fascinating. Our lessons greatly increased my knowledge of and interest in things Russian. Unfortunately, I never mastered Russian enough to be able to read Dostoyevsky, but my interest persisted. When I visited Russia for the first time, in 1980, the count's descriptions as well as the tales of Soviet oppression told by my Russian-born French teacher in Prague, Madame Miagkov, still resonated.

Against the warnings by our legation, we continued seeing Otmar's Hungarian theater crowd. The American authorities kept impressing on us that they would not protect us if we got in trouble with the Communist regime. They did not want us to make waves by hanging out with groups the regime considered "unreliable." Around town we were particularly conspicuous driving the red Buick. Our acquaintances enjoyed our hospitality and were willing to risk the displeasure of the authorities. Contacts with the local population were not actually banned, only discouraged, and one could never tell what might lead to an arrest. The strain resulting from such uncertainty was constant. Otmar and I frequently fought, his temper continuing to worsen. Mostly I was very unhappy in a luxurious cage.

Pista

And then Pista (pronounced Pish-tah) changed my life. He was part of the theater crowd we had been seeing. Twenty years older than I, he was married to Muci, a pretty, much younger, but uninteresting woman. He spoke fluent German, like most of the Hungarian intellectuals, and had been a successful theater director before the war.

In 1942 the Hungarian Nyilas, the fascist party that collaborated with the Nazis, conscripted Pista. They sent him to a forced labor camp where the treatment was abominable. As punishment for some insignificant infraction, they hung him up by his arms tied behind him so that his shoulders were permanently damaged. But he survived. During the war, he had lost his position and most of his belongings because he was Jewish. The same thing happened again when the Communists came to power; they did not permit him—an intellectual and, as such, an "unreliable bourgeois element"—to work in the theater. They assigned him in 1946 to a job in a horticulture enterprise in the country, an hour's train ride from his home in Budapest. He and Muci could barely survive on his meager income.

One evening at a dinner party in our house, he and I sat in a corner of our large salon. He asked me how I could stand living with Otmar, whom he knew was continuing his liaison with the young actress. Thinking of myself as a sort of non-person in that crowd, I was surprised that anybody cared. I was touched by his concern and grateful for his interest. He had always struck me as very attractive. His beautiful blue eyes had such a sad look that I had wondered what they hid. Very soon we fell madly in love.

Arranging our meetings was most challenging. We had three strikes against us: Otmar, Muci and the police who followed the red Buick. Far from the city center and with no public transportation near our house, I had such a hard time getting around that I rarely left without the car. Furthermore, Pista had very little time. He left for work in the country early every morning and returned on the train around three or four o'clock in the afternoon. Otmar finished work at 5:30 p.m. and I had to pick him up most days.

In a workers' neighborhood not far from the railroad station, we found an inn where we would meet for an hour or so if Pista managed to come back a bit earlier. We spent many hours sitting there; I drank raspberry juice and he apple cider and we talked about our feelings. A friend of Pista's gave him the key to his apartment, and whenever we could arrange it we met there for a few hours. My heart was always pounding, not only because of the anticipation but also because even the circuitous routes we took to get there were risky and we had to avoid being followed. Of course I had a bad conscience, even though I felt I did not owe Otmar any loyalty.

These hours were magical, full of wonder for me to have somebody caring who understood who I was and appreciated me. For him, I think, I embodied youth, a zest for living and a ray of sunshine in a drab, hopeless situation. For a long time Pista and Muci had not been happy together, but neither of them saw a way out. Pista knew that Muci would not mind getting divorced if it meant that she could leave Hungary. Muci had urged him to leave illegally as so many Hungarians had during these years, but Pista would not hear of it. He had no contacts abroad and no money, and he was convinced he could never work in the theater other than in his native language.

When I appeared on the scene and we fell so unexpectedly and deeply in love, emigration became conceivable to him. I embodied the hope for a better future. For me, this liaison seemed like an equally unanticipated miracle. Our excitement was probably enhanced by the danger that enveloped us. We started talking about the future and struck a bargain. I would arrange to smuggle Pista and Muci out of Hungary, and they would then get divorced. I knew there were smugglers in Vienna who would for a considerable sum of money lead individuals across the border. Such an undertaking was very risky, and many who got caught went to jail. But many times the escape was successful. Naively, I agreed to look after them in a new country. Not sure how either one of us would make enough money, I trusted that I would manage. In moments of panic, the enormousness of my responsibility dawned on me; but when Pista and I were together, the fear disappeared.

As plans became more definite, Muci insisted that I smuggle some of her valuables out of Hungary so that she would have something with which to start a new life. A non-Jew, she had managed to keep away from the Germans and then conceal from the Communists exquisite jewels, beautiful linens and silverware and other things that she valued. I agreed to smuggle them out, since Otmar and I often drove to Vienna for the weekend. I knew that he frequently took along valuables that his friends had entrusted to him. Each time we arrived at the border carrying something that did not belong to us, we had an instant of alarm. The Hungarian border police were always suspicious of cars with diplomatic license plates and looked underneath the car, watching to see whether we were hiding people. Fortunately, we did not get caught. My aunt Grete, the widow of my mother's brother Gustl, helped us store everything at her apartment in the center of Vienna.

Now it was my turn to smuggle. These efforts were always associated with the utmost stress: picking up the bulky things unnoticed, stowing them in our house where they would not be discovered, then getting them into the car unobtrusively so that Otmar would not be suspicious. I had to invent reasons for going to Vienna by myself. My only confidante was my Hungarian teacher, who suffered through this ordeal with me. She disliked Otmar and was glad to help. Frazzled inside, I had to appear calm.

Meanwhile, the political situation in Hungary continued to deteriorate. The 1948 show trials of Communist leaders had created even more apprehension among the citizens than before. The regime now wanted to prove that nobody—not even the most trusted party members—was immune from persecution if it suited the party. Such actions did not augur well for relations with America. Unsure what would happen next, I had to act fast.

Expelled: Vienna and Smugglers

I made several trips to Vienna and smuggled everything across the border without incident. None too soon—shortly after I finished, an American businessman accused of being a spy was found guilty in a show trial. As a result, in the spring of 1950 the Hungarian government expelled the staff of the American legation and we had to leave practically immediately. Having to find a place for all the suddenly jobless officials, the State Department assigned Otmar to Patras, Greece. The U.S. government sent our belongings to Greece, and we took only hand luggage when we left.

Instead of accompanying Otmar, I declared that I was going to Vienna to see Felix and then to Alt Aussee to join Mother, who was traveling to our house in Alt Aussee for the first time since the war. With Pista's backing I had become more assertive with Otmar and no longer let him intimidate me as much.

Otmar knew nothing about Pista and did not suspect anything. I think he was mainly concerned about leaving his lover. By this time he and I had such an unpleasant relationship that he accepted my decision without arguing.

We left Budapest in such a hurry that I had no time to reflect. In the haste of our departure, Pista and I reaffirmed our commitment to each other, including my getting both him and Muci out of Hungary. I was so much in love with him that any other action would have been unthinkable.

Otmar was able to sell the red Buick quickly on the black market for a fortune before leaving. Luckily, when I arrived in Vienna to stay at my Tante Grete's, Felix kindly put his little Opel with U.S. Army license plates at my disposal. At the time, Vienna was still governed by the four-partite occupation forces, and I needed a car with American plates so that I could navigate in all four zones in my search for smugglers. Tante Grete's apartment was in the American zone, but the airport and the Eastern outskirts were in the Russian zone. Driving through the Russian zone was always risky, even if you had a diplomatic passport; venturing there with a U.S. Army–licensed car—especially as a single young woman—was not advisable. Rumors abounded about Russian soldiers raping young women. But I had become pretty adept at getting around border posts and talking my way through potentially unpleasant situations. Remembering the successes helped me became less tense about this new challenge.

I did not know how to go about finding smugglers who helped Hungarians cross into Austria illegally. Luckily, some Hungarian friends had come out that way only a few weeks earlier and had good contacts. They taught me how to read coded newspaper ads that advertised smugglers. I started meeting potential smugglers, going to their unsavory homes to check them out and arranging to have the money to pay them. Felix may have lent me some money, or perhaps Otmar had given me some before he went to Greece.

Needing to unwind with someone who could keep my secret, I was glad to have Tante Grete to come home to at night. Only Felix and Tante Grete knew about Pista and our plans. Though Mother was nearby in Alt Ausee, I did not want to involve her for fear she would be both critical and worried.

I had promised Pista I would keep a diary that I had no intention of mailing. Every night I wrote long descriptions of the day's events that I was planning to present to him when he came to Vienna. Normal mail was working, but it was very slow and censored. I missed him dreadfully and felt closest to him when I was writing. Meanwhile, he and Muci were getting ready to leave at a moment's notice.

At that time in Vienna, there was a huge smuggler culture with its own specific protocols. One could not alert the person who wanted to leave that the smugglers were coming. Instead, one had to pay the smugglers 50 percent of the price in advance and give them a prearranged password that would reassure the person trying to escape that it was safe to go with the smuggler. In several cases, "smugglers" turned out to be police spies who immediately arrested the persons in their care.

After several gut-wrenching weeks I found two men who seemed reliable, though I constantly feared that I might have already been caught in a trap. If the American authorities had found out that I was trying to arrange to smuggle anybody out of Hungary, I would have been in serious trouble. In addition, border crossings that were safe one day became dangerous the next. You never knew whether someone who led people across the border safely one day would get caught the next—like when Mother and I had tried to cross into Spain! I heard as many rumors about unsuccessful crossings as about successful ones.

Finally I contracted with the two men and received coded word from Pista that he and Muci were ready to leave. I arranged with the smugglers to bring Pista and Muci at a specified time and day to a cafe near the Vienna Volksoper, the theater that performed mainly operettas. The wait was interminable. I worried about the many things that could go wrong, and I could hardly stand the delay. The day of the scheduled meeting, I arrived at the cafe early and waited. And waited. And then waited some more. Nobody came. I replayed the past weeks in my mind and reconsidered all that had happened. Through my emotional kaleidoscope I viewed these recent turbulent months and weeks: my love, my fears, the risks, the future, Muci's life, Otmar, and the financial burden that I had placed on myself. Finally one of the smugglers showed up. Alone.

The man reported that when he and the other smuggler went to Pista's, Muci did not have the guts to chance the escape. She had stayed behind, and a friend of Pista's had taken her place. They got close to the border without incident, but when they were almost there Pista lost his footing and injured his ankle. Because Pista could not run fast enough, a border guard noticed him. The guards caught the whole party. Only the smuggler who came to meet me had escaped. Pista and his friend were to receive a sentence of several years in jail.

Hearing this account, I thought my life had come to an end. I was absolutely crushed; not only were my hopes for a life with Pista dashed, but he would now be in jail because of his desire to live with me. How could I handle the responsibility for his incarceration? We both knew how awful the conditions in the Hungarian jails were for escapees, and he had been willing to take the chance. But why could he not run fast enough? Perhaps he had been afraid of leaving. That thought plagued me, and the smuggler could neither deny nor confirm the hunch. Feeling the life drain out of me, I was only glad that Muci had stayed home.

Guilt-ridden, I castigated myself for failing to get them out, for having made a mess. With no energy left, I was too dead inside to even cry. It was similar to the moment in Spain when Mother and I had crossed the border illegally and been caught, but this defeat felt different. I had tempted fate and took as personal failure the tragic consequences befalling both Pista and me.

Numb, I stayed on in Vienna for a few more days. With no more reason to be there, I went to Alt Aussee to lean on Mother and Felix. They were both very supportive when I relayed my story. The first few days of September 1950 there are a blur.

A few days later, Otmar appeared. The Foreign Service had transferred him from Patras to the American Consulate in Alexandria, Egypt. He did not know where I was, because I had not written him since we parted. He knew only that he could track me down through Mother in Aussee.

Trying to be casual about his arrival, I was glad that Mother had put him up in the large third-floor room with the desk. His room would be next to my small *mansarde* under a slanted roof with just enough room for a bed. She knew that I would not want to sleep with him.

The next morning, beside himself, he approached me with a sheaf of papers in his hand. I had forgotten that I had written to Pista at this desk every night and had put all the unsent letters in the drawer. Otmar had found the letters and was completely stunned that I had been so much in love with this man and that he had not known about it. How could I have been unfaithful and humiliated him so! We had a very emotional session with both of us crying—for perhaps the first and only time during all these years.

We expressed no recriminations, only sorrow. He said sadly that since both of us had lost our loves—his in Budapest, mine in prison—I might as well go to Egypt with him. I thought, "What's the difference?" I did not care about anything anymore. Nothing seemed important. So I numbly agreed to accompany him to Egypt.

Egypt and Israel

When Otmar and I traveled to Egypt in October 1950, I had agreed to go with him on an interim basis, making it quite clear that I did not intend to stay married to him. He accepted this condition. We avoided speaking about anything personal and at first enjoyed a pleasant, casual relationship. I felt detached from myself, as though I were not quite there, as though the feeling part of me had been excised.

From Alexandria I wrote to Pista's family in Budapest. They were beside themselves that he was in jail. Held incommunicado for the first weeks, he was later allowed to write or receive only postcards with no more than twenty words on them. He became very ill and had inadequate medical care. Pista's family was upset that I had gone back to Otmar. On top of everything else, I had to tell them that many of the valuables I had held for Muci and Pista were lost, stolen by my cousin Peter, who never returned them.

Cousin Peter

I learned Peter's troubled story in pieces. My only cousin on my mother's side, Peter Tritsch was the son of Mother's brother Gustav (Gustl). Gustl was an officer in the Austrian army in World War I who was taken prisoner on the Russian Front. He returned to Vienna infected by a virulent syphilis virus that plagued him for the rest of his life. He and his Christian wife, Grete, had one son, Peter, born in 1922.

I had seen the family perhaps twice when I visited Vienna with my mother as a child, but they were not really part of my life then. Peter became important to me when Mother's other brother, my Uncle Robert, invited him to come to France in 1938 to protect him from Hitler's anti-Semitic laws. Robert and Peter lived in Nice on the Riviera and I in Paris. After Mother first came to Paris from Prague in 1938, she went to live with them in Nice for a while, and I heard all about Peter from her.

In the summer of 1940, when Mother and I were trying to get out of France, I had spent time with Peter in Marseilles. Uncle Robert was in England on his way to the United States and had asked Mother to look after Peter. So Peter lived with us during those tumultuous weeks when we were trying to get papers to leave France and a visa to some overseas country that would accept us. We had every intention of helping Peter get out as well. But before we could get papers for him, Mother and I obtained a visa to the Belgian Congo in a newly issued Czech passport, thereby changing our enemy status in France. Because our Spanish transit visa was about to expire, Mother and I had hurriedly left Marseilles to cross the French–Spanish border illegally. We left Peter behind with my Austrian fiancé, Willi, tearfully promising to send them both the necessary visas to get them out as soon as we could.

While Willi and Peter were waiting in Marseilles, the French authorities decreed that all Austrian men must report to a special assembly place to be interned. To avoid internment, both men enlisted in the Foreign Legion; this French colonial army in Africa, a known refuge for French tough guys in trouble, became a haven for refugees in trouble from everywhere. That was the last I heard of Peter until after the war. Willi, who eventually caught up with me in America, did not know what happened to Peter either.

I met Peter again on my first visit back to Vienna in 1948. He told me that he had felt abandoned by the family. In a hopeless position when he could not get out of France, and without contacting his mother in Vienna, he decided to return to Austria. There he joined the SS, the Nazi storm troops, as the best way to hide his half-Jewish identity. Like concentration camp victims, the SS men had numbers tattooed into their arms. Peter spent much of the war in Russia fighting with the Nazis. At the end of the war, when the Russians were about to enter Vienna, he deserted and went to the apartment of his mother, Tante Grete, in Vienna. He rang her doorbell at midnight and when she realized who it was, she nearly fainted. She had thought that he was in America during the war and had no idea of what had really happened to him. Peter insisted that she burn out his tattooed SS number so that the incoming Russians could not identify him as a Nazi and shoot him in retribution.

Then he found out that the Gestapo early in the war had taken his father away. Gustl had been sitting on a park bench in Vienna; in one of his syphilitic moments, without knowing what he was doing, he started cursing the Nazis in a loud voice. The person next to him denounced him to the police, who came and took him away. No one heard from Gustl thereafter. At first Tante Grete could not find out what happened until a witness gave her the sickening information. Apparently he died in Auschwitz.

Peter told me his story in great secrecy once and never mentioned it again. I only know that the trauma of Peter's war experiences left him psychologically incapable of resuming a normal life. Though he had no skills, he had tried various jobs but had not succeeded at any. He needed money. His mother did not have enough to feed herself, let alone him, so he next became involved in all sorts of illegal activities.

During that period, I was in Budapest and often traveled to Vienna with the valuables that I smuggled out for Pista and Muci. I always stayed at my Tante Grete's, where I stored the treasures. One day when I arrived she greeted me crying in utter despair. Peter apparently had taken the silver and the jewelry and pawned them, promising to retrieve them as soon as possible. Needless to say, he never returned them. I never saw Peter again after that.

He got into more trouble with the law, and before he was supposed to go to jail, he absconded with valuables to the Seychelles, the islands in the Indian Ocean. His mother did not hear from him for years. Peter stayed there until it was safe to return to Austria. Upon his return he became the driver of the Indian ambassador to Austria, a job he held until he died at age sixty. He had found a very nice woman with whom he shared his last years.

His mother had never gotten over the shock of his coming back from the SS. She went though terrible troubles with him and died a disillusioned woman. We had kept in touch with her and helped her financially. I was grateful to Tante Grete for providing a safe haven for me during those stormy months in Hungary and then in Vienna when I was trying to get Pista out of Hungary. I felt very sad for her but resented Peter's dishonesty and its consequences for his mother and me as well as for Pista's family. Yet at the same time I felt a certain sense of guilt about letting Peter down in Marseilles. Unable to cope with what he saw as abandonment, he never managed to regain enough equilibrium to lead a life free of crime.

Pista's family suspected me of having taken the valuables and profited from them. Their accusations were deeply painful for me. After numerous exchanges of letters, Pista's family eventually came to accept that I had been honest, but the atmosphere between us stayed poisoned forever. From Alexandria I kept sending parcels to his family and then to him— Hungarians could receive only one parcel a month from abroad. I wrote letters as well, but the glow of my relationship with Pista was gone.

I never saw Pista again. He and Muci were divorced while he was in jail. After he was released from jail, he wrote me a loving letter saying that he was marrying the widow of a friend. By marrying her, he was able to help her keep her apartment. He wanted me to know that it was not the kind of marriage that we had envisaged together.

I have kept the diary that I wrote for Pista before he was jailed and reread it for the first time fifty years later. Never looking at it all these years, I may have been afraid of what I would find. Even with the hindsight of fifty years, I still cannot fully understand my behavior in letting go of our relationship. Why did I think that I would never see Pista again when I knew that his sentence might be for only a couple of years? Why did I give up so completely? Had what I considered deep love been only infatuation? In retrospect I believe that I had been foolish and irresponsible to make such a binding commitment given that we hardly knew each other. We had never spent more than a couple of hours together at a time. At the critical juncture was I so afraid of the responsibility I had willingly taken that I was able to drop it—and him—in a moment? Was the only way to come to terms with my behavior to block him out of my future? In fact, that is what I had done. I am not proud of my actions.

Alexandria

Outwardly I acted normal. While we looked for a house to rent, I wrote to Mother frequently, describing Alexandria as a modern city, a long sausage of a town beautifully located along the sea with modern apartment houses and California-style villas. Ordinarily I would have felt energized by being in a new culture and would have been eager to immerse myself in learning about it. But now I was too preoccupied with Pista's fate and with the uncertainty of my own future to make the effort. I waited for mail from Hungary, but none came. I heard nothing from Pista's family. Concern about his fate made Alexandria seem irrelevant and remote from what was important.

I had never been to a Third World country like Egypt. The poverty shocked me deeply. Men sat on the sidewalk in the broiling sun waiting for Allah to give them some food or call them to him. Drowsing, they were unaware of the flies that flew into their open mouths. All too commonplace, the average Egyptian just walked by such sights without noticing. I had been disturbed in Hungary and in Yugoslavia by the shabbiness of life under the Communists, but the misery here was of a far greater magnitude.

I had heard of the high rate of illiteracy in Alexandria, but its effect did not sink in until one day on my way to look at a house for rent. Going up to a policeman directing traffic at an intersection, I showed him the piece of paper containing the address I was looking for. He looked at the paper and shook his head. Clearly, he could not read. No wonder there were no street signs anywhere! To find an address in Alexandria, one had to know both the general neighborhood and the craft of the neighbor; for example, the direction would be to a house near the mosque and two houses down from the shoemaker.

We rented a palatial villa in Smouha City, the beach resort of Alexandria. Our neighbor on one side was the queen mother of Italy; on the other, the sister of King Farouk, who was still ruling Egypt. The house had marble floors and was beautifully furnished. It had a very nice room with a private bath for the Greek maid of the former tenant. At that time, most of the maids in Alexandria were Greek. When we inspected the house, we found a space on the ground floor that I took for a storage room or a place for a dog. The ceiling was so low that one could not stand up straight in it. A naked light bulb hung from the ceiling, and a faucet drained into a hole in the ground. A barren iron bedstead was in one corner. I was shocked to hear that this was the room for my houseboy. To most locals, that seemed perfectly normal. The houseboys in the queen mother's house slept on the roof without anything over their heads. Refusing to accept such conditions for my houseboy, I decided not to have him live in. Even if his own home was no better than the one I could offer him, at least the poor abode would not be of my making.

Customs concerning the houseboy were contemptible. The boy could not enter the house until you called him, and he could not have a key. So at the home of a neighbor, one of the inside maids had to get up at 6 a.m. and clap her hands several times for the boys to descend from the roof so she could let them in. Besides giving our boy a key, I also left him alone at home when I went out—another taboo. I had to remember to give him specific instructions when I left him there alone. If I forgot to tell him something, I could not leave him a message; he was illiterate and he also did not answer the phone. Since he did the house cleaning and we were out at parties almost every night, I decided to dismiss the Greek maid. An outside launderer cleaned our clothes, and we did not have much to iron. After I let go of the maid, the boy thought I was eccentric because I insisted on going to the market with him. Upper-class ladies were never seen in the market, and he felt uncomfortable chaperoning me. At least I was able to view a real slice of Egyptian life, quite different from my normal routine as a foreigner and the wife of a diplomat.

Otmar refused to give me enough money to run the household. He and I were constantly arguing about money. Sometimes I had to sink to stealing money from his wallet. Although we had agreed to let bygones be bygones, our relationship kept deteriorating. Whenever I said I was leaving, he always said that I would never find a better life. He would quote the German saying *Selten kommt was Besseres nach* (Rarely something better follows). He meant that I would never find a more interesting life, a compelling argument I had believed several times before. Now I was no longer quite so easily dominated.

With my compulsive interest in learning languages I tried to learn Arabic, but it proved too difficult. Instead I took tennis lessons and spent time aimlessly at the country club. Depressed and dispirited, I was angry at Otmar for having lured me to Egypt and angry at myself for having come. The social life struck me as a chore. The diplomatic set held lavish cocktails and dinners. The Egyptian women were most elegantly dressed, showing off diamonds the size of walnuts. The food was sumptuous and abundant, and every one of these evenings reminded me uncomfortably of the contrast between the abject poverty of the masses and the amazing luxury of the rich.

At one of these parties, I met the commandant of the port of Alexandria. We conversed in French, as only a few Egyptians spoke English at that time. I remember him asking me how I liked the Egyptian hospitality. I answered that the hospitality was great, but how could he stand to go to such lavish parties and walk past a starving child on his way to the car? He put his hand on my shoulder and answered, *"Mais ma chère*, but my dear, it's been like this for two thousand years—and what do you think we Egyptians can do for our poor if we have to fight a war against our neighbors to the north?" As I knew that he had no idea I was Jewish and just saw me as an American, I was not prepared for his response. It seemed absurd that Egypt, a nation of 25 million, felt so threatened by the new and tiny state of Israel that it could not attend to its own development.

That statement piqued my interest and brought to mind a conversation I had had in Budapest with the Israeli envoy to Hungary. From him I had learned about the Israeli War of Independence and about the creation of the state of Israel. Although I had read about the problems of the new state, I had never been affected by its struggle. When I mentioned my ambivalent feelings about being Jewish, he said to me, "Margit, you really should go to Israel and see for yourself." I had heard the same suggestion in Prague from my good friends the Dagans, the family of Paul's wife, Dita, before they left Czechoslovakia to settle in Israel. With these suggestions in my ears, when I finally had the courage to leave Alexandria after only two months and against Otmar's wishes, I decided to visit Israel on the way home. Before I left Alexandria, I learned that Pista had received a two-year jail term. The part of me that had not shut down felt a keen sense of loss.

Israel

Two other thoughts went into my decision to visit Israel: my distress at seeing the dismal, impoverished living conditions in Egypt drove me to find out what it was about Israel that threatened Egypt so; and I was beginning to develop the secular Jewish identity that I have now. I was eager to see the Holy Land with my own eyes.

My American diplomatic passport was accredited to Egypt, so I could not fly directly to Israel. First I had to go to Cyprus to obtain a travel document from the American legation there. I received an official-looking document with a red tape on it that enabled me to travel to Israel without the Egyptians knowing. My travel companion on the plane was the British ambassador to Egypt, who had to go through the same rigmarole. Then I found out what "red tape" really meant.

Arriving in Israel in December 1950, I was prepared for an emotional experience. Landing at Lud airport, a tiny, dusty airstrip, I was thrilled that I was going to step onto Israeli soil. But the Israel I arrived in was not the Jewish state that I had envisioned. Instead I found a country that looked more like Egypt, with Sephardic Jews who resembled Egyptians, and Israeli Arabs dressed in robes and lounging around on the streets. I had expected Israelis to look like me, like Central Europeans. Tel Aviv was hot and dusty, and I remember sitting on a bench on the main street watching the crowds go by and feeling totally out of place. Was this the supposed "homecoming"?

Israel was still on a war footing. I stayed with the Dagans in their Arab-style house in the Arab section of Jerusalem. The fighting that continued on the road between Tel Aviv and Jerusalem had interrupted the water supply, and the population of Jerusalem lived with the scantest amount of water. The Dagan family of four was permitted to use one bathtub full of water per week. They had unscrewed the washbasin drain and placed a bucket underneath to capture the water used for washing or tooth brushing. That water was then used for flushing the toilet. On Fridays the whole family took a bath in the same water and then used it for washing the laundry. They cooked on a one-flame picnic stove. Keeping a family going was tough, but nobody complained. The spirit was wonderful.

Wanting to see more, I managed to get around the country with the help of Dita's brother, Hardy, whom I had met at Paul's wedding to Dita in 1938. He was now a student in Jerusalem and owned a precious commodity, a motorcycle. He took me around on it and showed me Jerusalem and its environs. I then rented a car—a minor miracle at the time—and Hardy and I drove up north to a Czech kibbutz, Naot Mordechai. I could never have found my way alone. During the war, many road signs had been deliberately eliminated to keep the Arabs from finding their way. The signs that remained, written in Hebrew letters, I could not read.

I found kibbutz life, developed by a group of highly educated Czech and Austrian Zionist idealists, fascinating. These kibbutz leaders had arrived in Palestine in the '30s to help create the Jewish state. Willing to do back-breaking manual labor to clear the malaria-ridden swamp and grow crops, they also built fortifications to defend themselves against the Arabs. Enthusiastic and dedicated, their egalitarian community embodied the best practices of ideal communism, not the kind that the Soviets forced on people in their bloc. The Jewish settlers had come voluntarily to build the future.

Their selflessness impressed me tremendously. The settlers lived in primitive shacks; only the children's house was a decent building with electricity and running water. Children lived there from birth to adolescence so that both their parents could work all day. Parents saw their children for only an hour or so in the evening. Kibbutzniks believed that his type of family arrangement would lead to the ideal Socialist society that they envisioned. After my disappointment with communism in Hungary and the excesses of capitalist feudalism in Egypt, I was truly elated. Except that my body did not cooperate. The dining hall with open windows where the bats flew in and out was not conducive to eating. The bathroom facilities, such as they were, were filthy and so objectionable that my bowels refused to function.

I spent every evening in fascinating discussions with some of the kibbutz founders. Despite their primitive living conditions and the exhausting physical labor, the kibbutzniks maintained a high educational level and a lively interest in culture and the arts. The new Israeli state, built on truly democratic principles, also emphasized advancing culture. Perhaps maintaining a cultural focus under difficult circumstances was one of the attributes of Israel that threatened the Egyptians.

When I got back to Jerusalem, Col Israel, the Israeli state radio that was just being created, offered me a job. I was tempted but not tempted enough to stay. I thought that if I had high enough principles and were a more generous person, I would chose to stay. But the memories of my comfortable and lovely little house in Beverly Hills, with its clean bathroom and screens on the windows, won out over my principles. What impressed me most about Israel was the Socialist idealism rather than the idea of a Jewish homeland. I think I reacted to Israel more as a leftist than as a Jew.

Turkey

After a couple of weeks in Israel, I flew to Istanbul to visit my Czech cousin Fritz Kandler and his wife, Celestine. They were living well at the time, although the situation in Turkey was unstable. They showed me around and took me to the grand bazaar in Istanbul, then still authentic and worth a visit to Turkey all by itself. They bought me a fabulous Turkish bracelet that was too big for my wrist and jingled when I moved my arm so that I had to have it made smaller. At an art exhibition many years later, I was amused to see the identical bracelet exhibited as a harem anklet. That explained its size.

I found out that illiteracy was still substantial in Turkey 25 years after Attatürk became its president. Kemal Attatürk was the charismatic nationalist leader and statesman who came to power in 1923, ending six centuries of rule by the antiquated Ottoman dynasty. He created the secular Republic of Turkey and introduced a broad range of sweeping reforms in the political, social, legal, economic and cultural spheres. Attatürk insisted that Turks henceforth use the Latin alphabet. He forbade men to wear the traditional red Turkish fez and forbade women to cover their heads. He knew that living conditions would improve only with increased levels of education. Turkey had made great strides under his rule, but the country still had a long way to go. I was interested in talking to Fritz about these reforms and comparing Turkey with Egypt. Both were basically Moslem countries that had taken very different approaches to economic development during those past 25 years. I was amused that many Turks were illiterate in four languages: Turkish, Armenian, Greek or French. In the few months since leaving Budapest, I had learned a lot about the Middle East from three different cultures, each with great political difficulties.

Going Home Alone

From Turkey I went to Paris before sailing to New York on my way home to California. Felix had rented out his apartment in Paris but had kept a maid's room that he put at my disposal. The maid's room was on the seventh floor without an elevator; one had to walk up along a winding staircase. The light buttons for the staircase were on the ground floor and on the top floor, but not in between. If you did not climb the stairs fast enough, the light turned off before you got to the top.

A couple of nights before I was to sail, I returned home late from dinner at the celebrated Tour d'Argent, invited by my rich cousin Walter Jahn, now of Los Angeles. When I got to the middle of the winding stairs, the light went off and I continued climbing in total darkness. At the top I saw a man sitting there. I was so frightened that I nearly fell back down the stairs. To add to the shock, it was Otmar.

I do not know how he found out where I was, maybe through Mother. He had traveled all the way from Alexandria to try one more time to get me to return. Though he used all his wiles to tempt me, I remained firm for once. By now I had made it clear to myself that I could live with him only if I were willing to humor him, be his nurse and put up with his temper, the way one puts up with someone else's illness without getting upset. Although my ties to Otmar were still strong, I had decided that the drawbacks outweighed the advantages of living with him. Unwilling to go with him to Kenya, his next post, I left for the United States the next day.

I arrived in New York on the French liner *Champlain* after days that alternated between the lows of seasickness and the highs of winning at pingpong. Uncle Robert, contrary to his usual fiscal conservatism, lent me $2,000 so I could buy a car and settle in upon my return to California.

My friends in Los Angeles welcomed me heartily, and I was very happy to be back. They were pleased that I came back without Otmar. They thought that I should have left him a long time ago. But Otmar and I were still not entirely through with each other. It was not until I married Frank that our relationship really ended.

9

A NEW BEGINNING

WITH GOOD TIMING, the tenants to whom we had rented our house had just left, so I could move immediately into my own home and resume my Southern California life. Uncle Robert's loan enabled me to buy a two-door Chevy coupe; living in Los Angeles without a car would have been totally undoable. As soon as I had overcome the jetlag, I had to consider how to support myself. Though Otmar now had enough money, he was willing to let me have only the house, nothing for my support. Moreover, he wanted me to delay starting divorce proceedings until he could return on home leave and we could settle things amicably. I did not believe that we could reach a fair arrangement, but I agreed not to hire a lawyer right away. First I had to make money to pay my basic expenses.

When I started recounting my experiences of the past year, friends and acquaintances became very interested in my descriptions. They were eager to hear about Israel from someone who had no Zionist leanings and who was coming from Egypt, or about communism in Hungary contrasted with communism in Yugoslavia. All sorts of Jewish groups invited me to speak. A friend of mine who worked in public relations suggested that I become a professional lecturer. He prepared a glitzy brochure and we strategized about promoting me. However, we ran into a roadblock: organizations usually booked lectures a year ahead, and I could not wait that long to earn money. I also started to write about my experiences, thinking that I might be able to sell some articles. I put myself on a strict writing schedule, knowing that unless I adhered to it I would never get anything done.

Juli Lynne Charlot

Just then, Juli Lynne Charlot, the woman for whom I had been designing blouses before I left for Europe, called me. She "desperately" needed help with designing and could I "please, please" come and help her. At first I said I could not, but she was so insistent that I agreed to help her out on a part-time basis. I was serious about trying to become a lecturer or writer. She accepted my terms, and I worked for her a couple of days a week, then came home to write. Little by little I spent more time at the factory and less time at my desk until I finally gave up the idea of becoming a writer or lecturer. Realizing that my knowledge was superficial and that what I was able to contribute was not sufficiently substantial for publishing, I reconciled myself to becoming a full-time designer. At least the money was good.

Juli was no stranger to the dress business. Her mother had a factory that created dresses for children. Gifted but temperamental, Juli was an attractive, statuesque brunette who had originally hoped to become an opera singer. She had lots of beaus among the movie crowd, but her affairs never lasted and she was constantly angry at some man and discouraged with herself. A couple of years before, while helping her mother in the factory, Juli had had the idea of designing circular felt skirts with hand-sewn appliqués. The skirts were an instant success.

A creative designer, Juli had no production experience. When I designed blouses to go with her skirts before going to Europe, her mother's factory had produced the skirts. But with an increasing number of orders, Juli now needed her own production. She tried to organize her own manufacturing, but she could not get along with any of the people she hired. Often irrational, she would flare up over a minor mishap, turning it into a major upset. She fired one production manager after another until she finally turned to me, her designer, one day and said, "I want you to become my production manager."

Juli and I got along well, since I knew how to humor her. More than her employee, I was also her shrink and her friend. I told her that I did not know anything about running a factory or managing a business, but I could not dissuade her. She offered to hire a consultant to tutor me if I agreed to become the manager. Reluctantly I consented. From the consultant, from observation and by necessity, I quickly learned about production and about running a business. Intrigued by the challenge of making a go of the business, which had potential but was suffering from Juli's volatility, I began managing it.

We produced interesting thematic circular felt skirts with felt appliqués, such as Theseus and the Minotaur in the Labyrinth, Romeo and Juliet, and April in Paris. The buyers raved about the skirts, but the business made barely any money. One day our luck changed. A picture of Princess Elizabeth, then in her twenties and heir to the British crown, appeared on the front page of the major newspapers. It showed the princess dancing a hoedown in a Juli Lynne Charlot skirt that someone had given her for the occasion. The publicity was a fantastic boost to our sales, as every major store in the country started buying our skirts. This once-in-a-lifetime chance presented a huge new production challenge. I worked 24 hours a day, but the success was energizing.

During that time, Otmar came to Beverly Hills twice, trying to lure me back with fascinating tales of Kenya and then Israel, his next post. He appealed to my sense of adventure and detailed the advantages of the life he could offer me. However, I was proud of the life I had made on my own. My self-esteem had grown sufficiently so that I had the strength to resist him. Although we still had a neurotic attachment to each other and he knew that I occasionally wavered, I filed for divorce and stuck with my resolve. The lawyer I hired said to me, "You know that in California you cannot remarry for a year after your divorce is filed." I replied, "No fear. If I ever get remarried, I will live with the guy for at least three years. No hasty decisions for me." He laughed.

I was dating men with a broad range of occupations, including a physicist, a scriptwriter and a commercial artist, but nobody that I would consider for a husband. Much too independent by then, I was hanging out with a crowd of Hollywood fringers. Some had had one big success with a screenplay or song and were now hungry because they could not get another job. Many were depressed, bitter and negative about the world. Most of the men I met wanted a nice woman who would look after them, who was pliable and whom they could dominate. No longer could I go along with that scenario. I was quite prepared to live by myself if I could not find the right man.

One day a Hungarian acquaintance brought Dita Nemes to me for advice. Dita lived in San Francisco, where she wanted to start a children's dress business but did not know how to go about it. She thought I could help. Dita and her husband, Count Vincent Nemes, had been wealthy landowners in Hungary. Though World War II had not particularly affected them, when the Communists came they fled to Egypt, where their cousin—the wife of the deposed Albanian king—had taken refuge. In Egypt they no longer had money. Vincent did not know how to do anything except shoot clay pigeons and play bridge. Dita had to support the family. Their little girl, Shoya, wore beautiful dresses made in Hungary, and friends suggested that Dita make such dresses in Egypt for the daughters of the refugee nobility. Her fledgling business came to the attention of King Farouk, who had three little girls for whom he had been buying dresses in Palestine. The king's Palestinian clothing connection vanished in 1948, when Israel became independent and the Arabs were fighting against the establishment of the state. The king was pleased to find a new resource in Countess Nemes. She became the children's dressmaker to the court in Cairo.

When Farouk was deposed, the Nemeses left Egypt for the United States. Again Dita had to figure out how to support the family. She showed her Egyptian samples to I. Magnin buyers in San Francisco, who were interested in ordering selected styles in larger quantities. In Egypt, dressmakers, whose pay was practically nothing, had made all Countess Nemes dresses by hand and each dress was an original, custom-made for the wearer. Dita had no idea of American sizes, how to grade patterns or how to produce dresses on a commercial scale. That is why she sought me out.

I enjoyed meeting this member of the Catholic Hungarian nobility. Dita was about my age with a round face and short blond hair. With her inquisitive gray eyes and eagerness to get on with life in America, she was determined to make a go of her new venture. I gave her as much general production information as I could, but I knew nothing about children's dresses. She kept saying how much she would like me to live in San Francisco, and I politely waved her interest off. The children's dress business did not interest me. Soon after, however, my interest was awakened.

Frank Meissner

It was August 1952. I was having lunch with Suzie Kanarik—the 12-year-old daughter of my dear friends Emery and Rose—whom I had invited for the weekend as a special treat. This was one of those times when I had just completed designing a seasonal collection and took time out to emerge from my hectic design schedule to reacquaint myself with my friends. We were sitting on the patio of my house when the phone rang. A man said he was Frank Meissner, a friend of my sister-in-law Dita's brother, Hardy, in Israel. Hardy had suggested that he look me up if he ever came to L.A. from Berkeley, where he was studying. Frank was in L.A. only for the weekend and wanted to meet me. My first thought was that I was too busy and that the last thing I needed was to meet this man; but then I remembered how helpful Hardy had been to me in Israel. How could I be mean and ignore his friend? As a good girl I invited Frank Meissner for lunch on Sunday.

No sooner had I hung up than I regretted the invitation. If I had known where to reach him I would have uninvited him on the spot. Suzie was not very pleased either about the disturbance of our time together. I soothed her, saying, "OK, we'll have him for lunch, but we will make no special preparations whatsoever for this guy."

Frank's Sunday lunch consisted of canned sardines and beer. That was what I had at home. The simplicity of the meal did not bother him in the least. He turned out to be delightful. We noted that he was balding but had the hairiest arms either Suzie or I had ever seen. Six feet tall, he was muscular and sturdy-looking, built along straight lines. His glasses did not hide inquisitive blue eyes. Somewhat to my surprise, his obvious and conscious Jewishness did not put me off. A graduate student in agriculture economics at the University of California at Berkeley, he lived with a family as a babysitter and dishwasher and also worked as a janitor at a synagogue. He also made money writing book reviews for the *San Francisco Chronicle* in his spare time. Both Suzie and I enjoyed his upbeat stories and marveled at the range of his activities. Talking a lot about his life, he seemed very comfortable with himself. His endearing sense of humor and positive outlook were a relief after all those frustrated Hollywood types.

Later that afternoon I was invited to a Hollywood open house to celebrate the host's receiving an Oscar for music. I asked Frank to come along. I did not know how he would fit into this volatile crowd, but he seemed comfortable there and I enjoyed being with him. Driving him back to the airport, I promised to visit him in San Francisco for a weekend soon; I frequently took long weekends to unwind at the end of each designing cycle and had already planned to spend the next one in a few weeks with friends in San Francisco. I told him I would let him know when and thought no more of it.

The day I was supposed to leave for San Francisco, my friends called to say that they both had the flu and that I should not stay with them. I decided not to change my travel plans except to stay instead at a small hotel near Union Square. My decision had nothing to do with Frank, although I called him later that afternoon when I arrived. Since I had not given him much warning, I fully expected him to say that he was too busy to see me. Instead he said, "If you're not doing anything this evening, I'll come to pick you up."

We had an informal dinner and a very pleasant evening. He asked me to join him for a drive along the beautiful coast the next day, Saturday. Knowing how many jobs he had, I was amazed that he had time. He was a wonderful tour guide, showing me all sorts of out-of-the-way places and telling me more about his life.

By that evening I knew a lot about him, but he knew very little about me. Not eager to talk, I was happy just to listen to him. He suggested dinner at a place where one could dance. Though I was not much of a dancer, I agreed. Frank turned out to be an excellent dancer, and I tried to follow his lead. I was not unusually attracted to him, but we had an instant rapport and I felt very comfortable with him. Unassuming and very funny, he made interesting comments on a range of subjects from agriculture to Czech history, from paper manufacturing in the Middle Ages to land reform in Sicily. A high school dropout long before the term was coined, he seemed unusually knowledgeable. Before the end of the evening I realized that he was seriously interested in me. I was beginning to be intrigued.

The next day, Sunday, friends had invited me for lunch at their home in the suburbs and I asked whether I could bring a friend. My friends said, "Sure, bring him." Frank came to my hotel as arranged at 11 a.m. Since I had not finished packing, I asked him to come up to my room. He sat in the armchair while I was in the large walk-in closet putting my clothes in my suitcase. Suddenly I heard him say, "Would you marry me?" I could not believe my ears. Stunned, I came out of the closet and he repeated the question. I did not know what to say. When the question sank in, I answered, "But you really don't know me." He said, "I am 29 years old; I was not born yesterday. I have seen lots of things in my life, and I know a good thing when I see it." I was speechless.

After a moment I countered, "Yesterday you told me that you wanted to have a lot of children. I have tried to become pregnant and could not. I may not be able to have children." Without hesitation he responded, "That's not a problem, we'll adopt them." I was flabbergasted. To me, the inability to conceive was a huge problem. Although Otmar had not been eager to have children, my failure to become pregnant rankled and was never far from my thoughts. If we had had a child, I would not have left Otmar and would have kept trying to make the marriage work. I had never even considered the idea of adoption. And here was this man I had just met who wanted to marry me and was willing to adopt a child if we could not have one of our own. His finding such an easy solution to such a major issue in my life was mind-boggling.

We did not talk about his astonishing proposal anymore that day, although I found my interest in him growing by the hour. I kept observing him as we went to lunch and when he took me to the airport. I kissed him goodbye at the gate and said that I would think seriously about his proposal. The whole thing seemed like a dream; I could not quite believe what was happening. However, I did realize that this man was different from my earlier romances and from Otmar. I could hardly believe that I had just encountered someone who was so nonjudgmental and unquestioningly accepting of me. Slowly awakening to the enormousness of this series of happenings, I began to consider that this relationship could be for real.

Frank's Story

During the 72 hours we spent together before he asked me to marry him, Frank told me his story. (Some of the information that follows is based on his later writings about himself.) Frank was born in September 1923 in Třešť (Triesch in German), an industrial town of about 5,000 inhabitants halfway between Vienna and Prague. Although 90 percent of the population was traditionally Czech, landed estates belonging to hereditary German-Austrian aristocrats dominated the agricultural sector.

By the turn of the century, Třešť had become a relatively prosperous industrial island located 12 kilometers from the old silver-mining town of Jihlava (Iglau) in the forest-covered Bohemian–Moravian Highlands. The harsh climate and poor sandy soil of this region, often referred to as the Moravian Siberia, made for low agricultural productivity and much rural poverty.

Several members of Frank's family were among the entrepreneurs who built bridges between subsistence agriculture and relatively prosperous industry. They set up a wood-processing shop in Třešť to make clogs, furniture and matches. Later the factory diversified into producing machinery for butchers and bakers. Those relatives who could not find employment in Třešť sought opportunities elsewhere in Vienna, Prague and Brno, and even North America.

Until the depression of the 1930s, the Meissners had a house with several bedrooms and a peasant girl as a nanny for Frank. After his father's furniture factory went bankrupt, they rented out all but two rooms and the living room. They shared these cramped quarters with Frank's maternal grandparents. Frank's mother, Lotte (short for Charlotte), went to work in her brother's factory as secretary. Frank's father, Norbert, kept house. Never able to recoup his former standing, Norbert, an early Zionist, was always playing with the idea of emigrating to Palestine. In 1933 after the loss of his business, he was on the verge of making *aliyah*, the Hebrew for immigrating to Palestine. Lotte vetoed the move. The family stayed.

The Meissner household was bilingual. Norbert spoke mostly German; Lotte and her parents spoke Czech together. Frank and his older brother, Leo, grew up bilingual, often unaware of their mixing the two languages when they spoke. He had, as he reported, his first official exposure to cultural differentiation and pluralism when his first-grade teacher unscrambled his linguistic mix-ups, making him aware of the differences between German and Czech.

Frank's second cross-cultural exposure arose when youngsters taunted him with anti-Semitic barbs. In a small town where everybody knew everybody else, he was known to be Jewish because his father was the president of the Jewish religious community, the third generation of Meissners in the post. Discrimination in Třešť was mostly subtle, although he was occasionally roughed up because of his religion.

In 1934 his parents sent 11-year-old Frank to Jihlava, the county seat, to attend the gymnasium. No secondary school in Trest offered a good enough education to enable graduates to enter a university. In Jihlava he boarded in the house of a poor Jewish family, sleeping on a pullout bed in the living room and sharing the room with his brother, with whom he did not get along. Frank was not particularly bothered by the sleeping arrangement. Six people in two rooms; that was just the way it was. He went home to Třešť every weekend, arduously traveling the 12 kilometers that took two hours on the train and required two changes.

Feeling unloved at home, Frank was not a happy teenager. Because it was too regimented and autocratic, he hated school. An avid reader, he felt he should be a good student, but he did not want to put in the effort. Other interests were more important to him, primarily soccer. Leo, who was two years older, was the good boy and the good student, not as smart as Frank but a hard worker. His parents and teachers always admonished Frank, "Why can't you be like your brother?" to which Frank replied, "I am not my brother." Some of his rebellion at school was showing everybody that he was different from Leo. Living away from his family had made him quite independent.

Following the German annexation of Austria in March 1938, the family again considered moving to Palestine. Once again, his mother vetoed the idea, saying, "This could not happen here in democratic Czechoslovakia." Frank decided to act on his own. He joined the Zionist Youth Movement in Jihlava in preparation for emigrating to Palestine alone if he had to. The thought of leaving his family did not preoccupy him. He felt misunderstood and unappreciated at home anyway.

In October 1938, now beyond mandatory school age, Frank arranged to flunk out of school to spite his father. He asked his uncle to take him into his machine factory as an apprentice lathe operator, figuring that a practical trade would be a better base for making a living in Palestine.

When Germany invaded Czechoslovakia in March 1939, Frank took the next step and signed up for a special training course in Prague for youth who were preparing to go to Palestine. His parents agreed to pay for it. There he met Hardy Berger, who became a lifelong friend. In September 1939, after Hitler invaded Poland and the war started, plans changed. Instead of going directly to Palestine, the youth group would first go to Denmark to learn about agriculture. With more applicants than slots, participants for this program were selected by lottery. On the afternoon of October 3, 1939, about 15 eager young Czech boys and girls, including Frank and Hardy, said a tearful goodbye to their families in the main Prague railroad station. By nightfall the youth arrived in Copenhagen. Most of them were never to see their parents again.

The Danish Chapter of the Women's International League for Peace and Freedom sponsored the youth *aliyah* group, preparing the youngsters to become pioneers in Palestine. A liberal organization founded in 1915 in The Hague, WILPF had contacted Zionist organizations in Central Europe to help save Austrian, German and Czech children from the clutches of Hitler. When Frank arrived in Copenhagen, the organizers sent him to a farm about 100 kilometers south of Copenhagen; there he was known as "the Jewish child." The farmers spoke only Danish; as his languages were German and Czech, he had no one to talk to. He arrived in the fall, the harvest season for fodder beets. Pulling beets out of the muddy ground was dirty, hard, cold, backbreaking work. After supper when he turned off his oil lamp in the unheated loft above the barn, the boy who had so wanted to get away from his family felt miserably alone.

He often wrote to his parents in Třešť, who attempted in their frequent letters to cheer up the unhappy lad. He also tried to obtain Danish visas for the family but did not succeed. In any case, his parents were not eager to leave, not believing the rumors of deportation that circulated. Frank's mother could also not face the thought of leaving her parents' graves behind.

After a few months, Frank graduated to a better farm, where the work was not as hard and he was not so isolated. Several of the other youngsters he had met lived nearby. By then he had learned some Danish and could communicate with the farm family. The spring departure to Palestine was looming until April 1940, when the Germans invaded Denmark. The departure was first delayed, then became impossible. Frank started to do some long-range planning. Still working as a farmhand, he obtained a scholarship to a regional agricultural school for the winter months. The Jewish youth group threatened to expel him if he went to that school, since he would not be connected to any Jewish group there. He considered the trade-offs and went to school.

At the end of the winter, he contracted for a one-year job as a foreman for the school's herd of thirty milk cows. He would need the money if he was to be able to study as his parents exhorted him to in every letter they wrote. He had to get up at 3 a.m. during the summer and at 2 a.m. during the winter to set the milk on the road in time for the truck pick-up at 6 a.m. The school was running a state-supervised hog-feeding experimental station with sixty purebred animals. Weighing all the feed daily to see how much the animals were gaining, he then reported the results to the state inspector who came to check on him every month.

Frank had altogether too much responsibility and too much work for a growing boy already burdened with worries about his family and his future. The Danish Farmers' Union added to his tribulations by chiding the school director for letting an undomiciled immigrant deprive Danish farmers of salaried work. The school director retorted that Frank was helping out only temporarily while fulfilling his three-year on-farm work requirement for agricultural college admission in 1943.

The news from home hinting at impending deportation became increasingly upsetting. Finally, in a letter of May 13, 1942, his father wrote the following:

"On the last day before our departure our thoughts are with you. This morning Mother and I went to the cemetery to take leave of our departed ones. In spite of being upset, we found reassurance in their peace. That's all I can say today. Hopefully we will be able to write soon."

When his parents learned that the authorities would deport them, they kept reassuring Frank not to worry because they were in God's hands and God would take care of them. The family—including Leo, his new wife and Frank's grandfather—was moved to the ghetto in Teresienstadt (Terezín), Bohemia. From there they were allowed to write or receive postcards of no more than twenty words. They wrote only that they were well and were working and thanked Frank for the parcels that he managed to send occasionally. In August 1944, after two years in the ghetto, the family was deported to the extermination camp in Auschwitz and was never heard from again. Fortunately, like many ghetto inhabitants they had no idea what their fate would be when they were transported east.

In September 1943, with enough work credentials, Frank registered at the Royal Agricultural College. He found getting back to full-time study tough. Classes were big and impersonal and the subjects difficult. Furthermore, he worried because his savings would not last much beyond Christmas. Would he be able to get a scholarship? Mundane freshmen concerns became as irrelevant as last year's snow.

On Monday morning, October 4, 1943, Frank went to his freshmen chemistry class. He sat in the back, close to the last row in the largest auditorium of the college. Suddenly the janitor walked in and whispered something to the professor, who happened to be the college president. He turned to the class and asked, "Is Mr. Meissner here?" Frank raised his hand. "Could you please come down, I have an urgent message for you." Those 25 seconds getting down from his seat were among the longest in his life as he wondered, "What did I do wrong now?"

The professor took him by the arm, accompanied him into the hallway, closed the door to the auditorium and said, "Your landlady just called. The Gestapo came to pick you up a few minutes after you left this morning. The Germans are rounding up the Jews. Don't go back home. Try to get to Sweden. Do you know anybody who could help you?" The professor added, "Let me know if you don't succeed in a day or two."

Frank was stunned for a second or two. Then a thought flashed through his mind. He remembered that the pastor of a Lutheran church, the father of a fellow student, had always said to call him if he needed help. He would go there. Taking along his two chemistry books, he rode his bicycle to see the Lutheran pastor. The pastor was not surprised by Frank's predicament but scolded him. "Did you not know that for a couple of days now the Germans have been trying to pick up our Jewish fellow citizens?" Frank had not heard, because he was not part of the Jewish community. The pastor made a couple of phone calls. Within a half-hour he gave Frank instructions to arrive at 9 p.m. at a certain fishing village in the Dragör port. Then he offered, "Now let's have lunch. You can spend the afternoon in the bedroom upstairs. Try to leave here by 5 p.m."

Frank arrived in the fishing village near the Copenhagen airport at 8:30 p.m. In the darkness, the fisherman's wife showed him the way to the landing, where a small cutter was moored. Frank left his bike with her. A dozen men, women and children piled into the hull. After covering the passengers with nets, the fisherman turned on his diesel motor a little after 9 p.m. and slowly eased the boat out into the dark harbor and onto the Öresund, the narrow strait separating Denmark from Sweden. The autumn sea was rough and people were seasick. Little was said; people prayed. Within an hour, the lights of Malmö, Sweden, came into view. The boat landed at about 11 p.m. A waiting police van took the passengers to a temporary refugee center in a school. By midnight, Frank was fast asleep on a straw mat in the gym of a school in neutral Sweden. A miraculous rescue!

The next morning, the Swedes registered and debriefed Frank and gave him pocket money and clothing. Two days later, he found his Czech friend Hardy from the Jewish Youth Group in Denmark, and together they decided to sign up for harvesting sugar beets. The money was attractive but the work was hard. The second day, Hardy had a brilliant idea. "Let's write to the agricultural college in Uppsala to see whether we can get a job there." Frank was skeptical but thought it would be worth the postage. A couple of weeks later a reply came. "Yes, come on up. We'll find something."

The work there consisted of testing the cookability of peas by measuring their hardness under boiling conditions—a lesson in boredom. A few days later, Frank received a letter from the Danish Refugee Office in Sweden, a quasi government in exile, offering him a scholarship to study at the University of Uppsala, just as if he had been a Danish student.

Shortly afterward, the Czechoslovak Government in Exile in London informed Frank that if he wanted to retain his Czech citizenship, he must present himself for the draft. He reported for duty but thought it was preposterous. How were the Czechs going to get him to England in the middle of the war? Just in case, he took courses to learn more English. In September 1944 the call-up from the Czechoslovak army came. He was to fly on a civilian Brett Airlines plane from Stockholm to England. After 12 trips to the airport to find that something always prevented the plane from leaving, on the 13th try, exactly a year after arriving in Sweden, he took off for northern Scotland.

The Czech army assigned him to an infantry unit in the south of England where he had nothing to do. His Czech commander was an ex-major in the French Foreign Legion, a roughneck SOB, anti-Semitic and anti-intellectual. After several run-ins with his hateful superior, Frank spent much of his free time "confined to barracks." Fortunately, he was able to transfer to the Czechoslovak wing of the Royal Air Force. In the RAF he became a weather forecaster but again had little to do. One of the commanding officers suggested that he sign up for a high school diploma correspondence course offered by the Czechoslovak State School in Wales. So the "original high school dropout" found his own way to get the diploma that had mattered so much to his father. He graduated in July 1945, when the army was just about to demobilize him. He chose to be demobilized in Denmark because he saw no reason to go back to Czechoslovakia. By now the concentration camps were empty and Frank still had no word from his parents. None of the Jews from Třešť had returned.

Once he sadly accepted that his entire family had perished, he stayed in Denmark, where the government treated him like a Danish victim of Nazism and gave him a scholarship to study at the Danish Agricultural University. His appreciation of the Danes knew no bounds. He got his undergraduate degree in 1948, the year Czechoslovakia elected a Communist government. Another reason not to return to Czechoslovakia.

With the help of an American minister he met while guiding a group of American church people on a city tour of Copenhagen, Frank obtained a scholarship to Iowa State College in Ames. In January 1949, after emerging from a maze of difficulties with both the Czech and the American authorities, he was able to come to the United States.

So this was the man who wanted to marry me.

Major Decision

Upon coming home, I canceled the plans for the next evening with a man I was dating. Instead I sat down on the couch in my living room and started listing in my mind all the advantages I knew marriage to Frank would offer. What I knew about him by now would make for a good life for me. Most important, he seemed to care for me deeply. He was flexible about the details of living, such as when he ate or what he wore. Otmar was rigid about everything. Frank did not expect to have the good things in life handed to him. Having proved that he was willing to work hard to achieve what he wanted, he was self-reliant but not self-indulgent. He was intelligent and well-read, although not in the "cultural" sense that my mother considered important. Frank did not know much about poetry or belles-lettres, because he had been too busy reading about what interested him more: agriculture, land-reform issues, Israel, Jewish history and Czechoslovakia's past and present. An excellent storyteller, he was especially good with jokes. His comments were incisive, though a bit sarcastic at times. Not given to small talk, he was able to remove himself invisibly from a boring conversation. As inquisitive as I, his interests were broad. I was impressed that he seemed completely comfortable with my independence, actually valuing it. I sensed he would be perfectly happy to have me lead my own life and in many ways would be glad to have me make most of the decisions involved in managing our life together without my consulting him. I was sure that Frank, unlike Otmar, would not agonize over trivial everyday issues, such as what to have for dinner or what color drapes to buy. Clear from the life choices he had already made, his approach to money was similar to mine—wanting to have enough to live comfortably but simply; beyond that, the accumulation of wealth did not seem important. Essential for me, he was politically liberal, although he did not share my pacifist convictions. More than anything else, he was a pragmatist interested in solutions, not philosophizing.

As I checked off on my mental list each one of these positive traits, I became increasingly excited. I realized that what I thought life with him would offer me and what I wanted for myself came unbelievably close. In joyful amazement I concluded that I must marry him.

I held back my answer to contemplate it a little because Frank was so totally different from Otmar and the other men I had been seeing. They wanted a pliable woman whom they could control and who would be content to do their bidding. I did not want to be in that role anymore. Unlike the men I had been dating, here was somebody who loved what he was doing, who felt that he had made wise career choices and for whom work satisfaction was not tied only to compensation.

I wrote him that the more I thought about his proposal, the better I liked it and that I would come to San Francisco in a couple of weeks to give him my answer in person. Two weeks later, as he had confidently anticipated, I said "yes." After that romantic weekend we wrote to each other every day. He did not have money for telephoning, and long-distance calling was still quite expensive and not as common then. At times I wrote to Frank that I had doubts about my decision. I worried that he was younger than I. He replied, "Just imagine: when you're 85, I'll only be 84."

I also knew that living with him I would have to come to more reasonable terms with my own Jewishness. I was confident that he would help me. I learned that he, too, had undergone a baptism similar to my conversion to Lutheranism. He had earlier planned to marry the daughter of a Presbyterian minister in Minnesota. After becoming baptized, he could not face the idea of living in a religious Presbyterian milieu. It just did not feel right. So when he received a scholarship to the University of California, he had a convenient excuse to leave. After learning of Frank's baptism I felt freer to talk about my own baptism. I had rarely mentioned it to anybody, feeling ashamed of having acted out of expediency, although at the time I thought I was following my faith. Since then, I have become a convinced atheist.

When I was wavering in my decision to marry him, Frank did not try to influence me. He simply said that I could worry about our getting married if I liked, but he was not going to change his mind, so I should not look to him for a discussion of potential problems.

His attitude toward our life together was like a breath of fresh air. I would be able to preserve the independence I had so painfully acquired, alongside a thoughtful, stimulating, loving and good man. The common background as refugees and speaking the same two languages was a great help. We understood each other instinctively. Because of my negative experience with Otmar, I kept wondering when the major conflicts in our relationship would appear. They did not. His infectious sense of humor easily overcame my sometimes pedantic arguments about trivial matters. Anyway he was not interested in arguing with me or in convincing me of the correctness of his point of view. We frequently simply agreed to disagree. When the advantages of our future together became clear to me, I became very, very happy and excited.

At first I was embarrassed to tell any of my friends about Frank. They had supported me loyally during the difficult divorce period and held my hand when things were rough. Imagine hearing that I was going to marry a man I had seen a total of 72 hours! Feeling foolish, I waited until Frank came to L.A. for Christmas and then introduced him to my friends as the man I was going to marry. They liked him instantly.

I called the lawyer and asked when, exactly, my divorce would be final. He said, "You see, I told you you would meet somebody and would want to marry before the mandatory year of wait-time." We decided to get married on January 28, 1953, a few days after the divorce was final.

Mother, to whom I wrote in Austria, was very pleased about my happy description of Frank, though she was too far away to come to the wedding as were my brothers. Paul and his family were in Australia, Bruno and Gwen were in Canada, and Felix and Friedl were living in Spain.

Felix had met his pretty Austrian wife, Friedl, in Vienna. They had married there earlier in 1952 with Uncle Robert and Tante Grete as their witnesses. Together with Mother they had gone to Spain on their honeymoon. On a sightseeing excursion to the island of Ibiza, Felix found his "promised land," a beautiful Mediterranean landscape on an island untouched by the 20th century. There the geese walked on the cobblestoned main street where there had been no visitors since the Moors invaded Spain in the 14th century. The whitewashed houses belonged to illiterate fishermen who fished only when they needed food, who did not sell themselves to anyone; they were proud, with no pretensions, and lived just the kind of life to which Felix aspired. On that one-day trip he bought a piece of land with a white shack on it that was to become his lifelong home.

Getting Married

With my family so far away, I saw no need for other than a simple wedding. We began to act on our plans immediately.

Since Frank was in graduate school at the University of California, we had agreed that I would move to Berkeley. I sold my house in Beverly Hills for $14,000, a lot of money at the time. With the proceeds, we bought a house high in the Berkeley hills with a slightly obstructed but still spectacular view of the Bay, all within a month. I also made myself a wedding dress, which in retrospect looked more like a dress for the mother of the bride than for the bride. I will never know why I chose gray lace over a pink background, with short sleeves, a V neck and a small lace collar. I had so little time that I had to make a quick decision, and the color seemed appropriate to me for a second wedding. I had to give up my job, which I knew would cause problems in the firm. Not wanting to leave Juli in the lurch, I gave her a month's notice. She was sad at my leaving but happy that I had found such a compatible partner.

The daily letters Frank wrote to me were a great source of joy. He had a wonderful way of writing. He knew English well, but he had a unique style, very witty and quite ungrammatical. When I commented on his grammar, he brushed off my criticism with "Did you understand me?" And I had to admit that the grammatical oddities did not interfere with understanding. My instinctive urge to get him to use correct English grammar was thwarted. He simply did not care. Later on when he learned Spanish, he again spoke it fluently and full of errors, but people listened to him just the same. He often wrote articles and book reviews for publication. I curbed my desire to edit what he wrote when I saw that the editors did not mind. His contributions were important, so they accepted almost everything he ever wrote for publication as it was.

A few days before our wedding, I wrote to Otmar to let him know that I was getting married. I was then and continue to be sad that we had to divorce, but I felt a great sense of relief that I was finally free from this neurotic bond of 11 years.

I also wrote to Pista to give him the news. Composing that letter was more painful than writing the letter to Otmar. I knew Pista still had not given me up completely, trusting that we would somehow get back together again. This news would mean for him that all hope about us was now gone; for me, something final had occurred. I hurt for both of us.

We were married in the Hillel Chapel of the Jewish Student Union on the campus of the University of California. The rabbi who married us was the rabbi in whose synagogue Frank had been the *shames*, the janitor. He married us for free. Nobody from my family was there. We invited only about half a dozen of Frank's student friends whom I knew. One of them was Ivo Feierabend, a young Czech man who was not Jewish and who had never been to a Jewish wedding. The rabbi came to shake hands with everybody after the ceremony and said "*mazel tov*," Yiddish for good luck. Ivo, who did not know the expression, thought that in good European tradition, the rabbi was introducing himself. Ivo politely responded, "Feierabend," which made us all laugh. We had a wedding reception for about 12 at the home of the Feigers, the people for whose children Frank had been a babysitter. The informal, happy gathering that day was the beginning of a wonderful life together.

The day before the wedding we had moved into our one-story bungalow above the university. So after the wedding dinner we went back to unpacking books. We had already had our honeymoon by driving slowly up along the California coast for a couple of days from Los Angeles to Berkeley for the wedding. Frank had to study for exams and I needed a job. We still had very little money.

Because the marriage came as such a surprise to everyone, including me, Frank decided to send out the following wedding announcement, reprinted here in toto:

"HOW IT ALL HAPPENED"
by
Frank Meissner
Department of Agricultural Economics
University of California

By the way, how far is Berkeley from Beverly Hills? The sister of my brother-in-law from Australia lives there. Interesting woman. Address: 443 South Elm Drive, Beverly Hills. You might get a chance to look her up some day.[1]

This irrelevant piece of information was systematically salted away in my notebook. Just in case—one can never tell.

On October 3, 1952, a business appointment forced me to plan a weekend trip to Los Angeles. Referring to my notebook, I found—alas—the name of Margit Gyorgy, and promptly dispatched a letter to her, entitled "Dear Madam," announcing my contemplated visit.

Upon calling Mrs. Gyorgy, I found that my introductory letter had not reached her yet. When I referred to our mutual friends in Israel, she invited me to brunch on Sunday, October 4, 1951.

The meal was tolerably unexciting, the conversation excellent. Margit interpreted the fact that my letter had not arrived as yet another one of those poor tricks men use. Thus the first insult was bestowed upon my head. The pleasant afternoon included a sightseeing trip, a Hollywood housewarming party and Margit's acceptance of an invitation to visit San Francisco.

At this time no particular significance was attached to this, subsequently recognized as a "gained weekend."

On October 19, 1952, a letter arrived, stating, "I'm coming to San Francisco for the weekend. I'm very much looking forward to seeing you...it's a real good feeling that we'll have a chance to get acquainted a bit better...P.S. By the way, you DID mail your first letter to me. I'm sorry if I accused you unjustly. I'll make up for it."[2]

---

[1] Communication to the author by Dan H. Yaalon, Jerusalem, Israel, dated 2/28/52

[2] Communication to the author by Margit Gyorgy, Beverly Hills, dated 10/19/52

The latter sentence left me wondering. However, the explanation was granted soon, as witnessed in my engagement book entries:

Friday afternoon: Margit, sightseeing
Saturday noon: Margit, lunch with friends
Saturday afternoon: Margit, visit Stanford
Saturday evening: Margit, dinner and dancing

It seemed very obvious that Margit was enjoying the "making up for it" as much as I did.

On Sunday morning, October 16, 1952, at 10:20 a.m. while Margit was packing her bags in room #801 at the hotel San Franciscan, I innocently suggested that if dear Margit wanted to get married again—to me, in this case—I would consider such a decision favorably. She did not say much at the time, but she sure did not seem disinclined. Two weeks later, she came back to San Francisco and said "yes." So—what could I do but accept.

At Christmas, a picture of Margit and me was used for a Season's Greetings card. We wanted to see what we looked like as Mr. and Mrs. Frank Meissner. We liked it.

We were married in Berkeley on January 28, 1953. We hope to live happily ever after. But to be sure, we'll let you know on January 28, 1978.

Epilogue

Don't ever write anything in your letters that couldn't be quoted in court."

This was the first of our yearly progress reports that we sent to our friends, with two interruptions, as long as Frank lived and that I continue to send, in some fashion, to this date.

10

Berkeley and Palo Alto

S INCE FRANK HAD just about enough money to support himself, I needed to get on quickly with my job search. I called Dita Nemes to tell her that I was now living in Berkeley. She still wanted me to work with her, but I did not have any money to invest in a business and she could not pay me. Soon I found work as a ladies'-sportswear designer in the San Francisco garment district. Though it paid well, I did not like the job from the beginning. I especially did not like my boss, who was very arrogant and nasty with the workers. Dita called me frequently, and I continued to give her whatever general advice I could. Meanwhile, when moaning to Frank about my job he would tell me that I should either stop complaining or go into business with Countess Nemes.

Dress Manufacturer

I was so fed up with my boss one day that when Dita Nemes arrived to have lunch with me and again entreated me to go into business with her, I said OK. How could I imagine doing that with no money? Generously, Uncle Robert came through for me once more and lent me the $3,000 I needed to get started as her partner. We looked for a suitable space in which to set up a factory in an area of San Francisco where it would be safe to walk alone in the dark, knowing that we would frequently work late. Surprisingly, we found a reasonably priced loft in a premier location on Union Square in the building next to I. Magnin's, a fancy address in the center of the city. From my previous job I had good contacts among the suppliers of machinery, fabric and notions who were willing to give us credit. And so we began our business.

A few weeks after we set up the factory with one employee, our forelady, Frank got an offer of a scholarship from Cornell University in Ithaca, New York, that would enable him to get his Ph.D. at no cost to him. The offer was too good to refuse. But how could I now leave a new business? As I had made a commitment and received a loan, I had to remain in San Francisco. We decided to accept being separated for the time it took to get the Ph.D. Frank said we had our whole life to look forward to together, so a year or two apart would not be so bad. Furthermore, he was going to be working day and night, and so was I. We took a cross-country car trip together and sadly parted in New York.

After I returned to Berkeley, Mother came from Europe to live with me. Neither Dita nor I took a salary, so I was pleased that Mother could share living expenses with me. Soon she started working in the factory, also without pay and pleased that she could be useful. She became our conscientious shipping clerk. Since our office was right next to I. Magnin's, she would go down to their basement every morning to retrieve reusable shipping boxes, saving us one expense. Sometimes she was overeager in her thriftiness, but she certainly meant well. We had real arguments about three-quarters-empty thread spools. The sewing machine operators would drop the spools in the trash baskets at a convenient point in their work. They were paid by the piece, and anything that saved time was an advantage. Mother could not believe that it was cheaper for the business to discard the almost empty spools than to save them. With her European upbringing in an economy of scarcity, she had difficulty reconciling herself to the American throwaway economy. I continue to have the same difficulty.

Making a go of our firm, called "Countess Nemes," was quite a challenge. We had a few local customers, but not enough to sustain us. Dita and I went on a sales trip through California with nicely stuffed sample dresses hanging from a rod in the back of my Chevy coupe, spending the night in roadside motels. We felt like real traveling salesmen. A number of new, small shops bought a few of our dresses, but clearly we needed to become better known in the rest of the country. Saks Fifth Avenue liked our dresses because they were refined, the kind that wealthy grandmothers bought for a special occasion, and they were less expensive than the ones from our only competitor. Interested in our survival, Saks persuaded one of the crack children's-wear salesmen to promote and sell our collection. His efforts brought us enough business and enabled us to grow sufficiently so we could begin to make a profit. Gradually we had sizable orders from major retailers like Neiman Marcus and Lord and Taylor.

I learned every aspect of the children's-dress business: making patterns, grading them, spreading cloth, cutting, bundling—the entire production process that I had seen before but never had to execute. In addition I had to learn the financial aspects. Dita did most of the selling and managed our customer relations; she was excellent at public relations, and besides, she liked to see her name in print. We shared the designing. Before Frank left, he had set up our books and made a long-range business plan for us. Each step was new and exciting, and I was very energized.

Although not interested in the children's-dress business as such, I was caught up in the challenge of creating a profitable enterprise. Sometimes I went on selling trips to New York that gave me an opportunity to see Frank. I rented a suite in the Waldorf-Astoria hotel, where all the other children's-wear manufacturers had showings of their collections. Such occasions, when I was dressed in my best, made me chuckle, wondering what buyers who came to these elegant surroundings would say if they could see me in the factory. Working there, I was constantly weighted down by bolts of fabric that were too heavy for me, lifting boxes or carrying out the trash. They would have been surprised to see me in a cutter's apron wielding the tools of the trade. My position may have seemed glamorous from afar, but it was not!

I also learned what it meant to have total responsibility, to be the boss. Whenever something went wrong, which it did frequently, in the last analysis the fault was mine because I had not caught an earlier error. Sometimes I had not ordered enough buttons, checked on the way a sleeve was being set or consulted with our accountant in a timely fashion. Because I was learning so much every day, the time never hung heavily and the long hours did not bother me.

Dr. Frank Meissner Returns

Frank came back a year and a half later with a Ph.D. in agricultural economics. In record time he wrote a thesis on milk marketing that quickly landed him a job with Crown Zellerbach in San Francisco, the large paper manufacturer that produced milk cartons. The company was trying to decide whether to adopt the European pyramidal Tetrapak instead of the customary U.S. rectangular milk containers. As a result of his thesis research, Frank had excellent credentials for the investigation. He recommended against changing the shape of the prevailing milk containers and the company listened. Although he liked his well-paid work, in the back of his mind was a desire to travel abroad and work for an international organization, particularly the U.N. He was eager to use his economics skills working on improving agriculture—and the marketing of agricultural products—in developing countries. He eventually wanted to go into academia.

Luckily, Frank was doing well financially and I did not have to work so hard anymore. We could enjoy being together. The work in the factory was routinized now, and I was trying to become pregnant. After I went through the available medical procedures without luck, we decided—I reluctantly, Frank without reservation—to look into adoption.

Amphytrion 38

Meanwhile, Frank's secretary, who was involved with one of San Francisco's experimental theaters, which was producing Jean Giraudoux's *Amphytrion 38*, was looking for a costume designer. Without asking me, Frank volunteered my services. He said that all I had to do was make costume sketches and give them to our skilled forelady to execute. I agreed, albeit grudgingly. I began researching Greek costumes and found that everything was draped and nothing stitched down. However, for the stage, the actors had to be able to get in and out of the clothes in a hurry. I had to find a way to fasten down all the folds that still had to look loosely draped. Since I did not know how to construct such costumes, I could not tell anybody how to do it. After working hours, I sat in the factory night after night, sewing these costumes. I arrived home at midnight every night dead tired. Needing to be back at work early to finish the children's collection we were designing, I got little sleep.

As challenging and exhausting as the business and costume construction were, I was still eager to become pregnant. To find out my ovulation cycle, and therefore enhance the chances of conceiving, I had started taking my temperature every morning. Suddenly during this period of great stress, my temperature curve looked just like the one on the instruction chart that identifies the temperature changes when a woman is pregnant. Incredulous, I took a urine sample to the doctor, who said I should call back the next Tuesday at 5 p.m.

Tuesdays were my hairdresser afternoons—come what may, a sacred date. When five o'clock arrived, I was sitting under the dryer with my head in a big bonnet. From the pay phone in the hallway I called my doctor. He said I was pregnant! I was so thrilled I started to cry, standing there in my rollers and bonnet. I knew I could not reach Frank at that moment, so I went back under the dryer and finished drying my long hair. Now I had another reason besides the *Amphytrion* costumes to be so tired! We decided to call our baby either Paul Amphytrion or Anne Alkmena after the female character in the play.

Motherhood

Paul Amphytrion Leo (for Frank's deceased brother) was born on April 25, 1957. I had wanted natural childbirth, but the labor was so ghastly at the end that I finally agreed to a little Demerol to stop the pain. But the second I saw the baby, all pain was forgotten. Seeing Paul was the most thrilling, most unforgettable moment of my life to date. Frank was present during the delivery. In typical Frank fashion, he said the birth was just like a cow giving birth to a calf. His flip comment was that Paul's birth was a unique event that had happened millions of times. How like Frank! Because Paul looked like a black-haired little mouse when he was born, we called him "Myšíček" (pronounced Mish-shee-check), a corruption of the Czech word for mouse. Sometimes I still fondly call him that.

With her baby nurse experience, Mother's coming to take care of Paul was welcomed but not always conflict-free. I was scared of the baby and was grateful for her presence. On the other hand, I did not agree with her approach to infant care. She still adhered to a strict feeding schedule and did not believe in holding the baby when he cried. I could not stand to hear Paul cry and so my relationship with Mother was stormy at times, though most of the time I followed her dicta. Frank was the peacemaker and he took over the baby when I was too stressed. He managed Mother skillfully with sometimes caustic humor that she did not always appreciate.

Since I was going to continue with Countess Nemes and Mother had plans to assist at the expected birth of Felix and Friedl's baby in Ibiza, we hired a live-in housekeeper. We were lucky to get Bessie, a heavy-set, dark-skinned African-American woman from Texas. Bessie, a Seventh-Day Adventist with an angelic disposition and endless patience, was wonderful with Paul. Wearing a large apron over her cotton print dresses, she was also a very good cook and introduced us to all sorts of Southern specialties. I had gotten used to the mix of savory and sweet by then. We all loved her and she loved us.

So that I would not have to go to the factory so often, and on the assumption that I could do most of the designing and pattern making at home, I had a workroom built in our basement. While that assumption was technically correct, I could not work out my psychological problems of being a businesswoman while being a mother. When I was at home, I felt that I should be at the factory; when I was at the factory, I sensed that I should be at home with my baby. I was torn, constantly struggling with my mixed feelings.

Housewife

One day, after a lot of soul searching, I decided to give up the business. I told Frank, "I am now 35 years old. I waited so long to have that baby. (At that time, 35 was very old for a first baby.) I may never have another child. I can have a business anytime. I want to be able to enjoy being a mother." Incredulous, Frank said, "You are not going to become a housewife, are you?" I replied, "Yes, I am."

Dita Nemes was beside herself when I informed her of my decision. Although we had been partners now for four years, she still did not know much about managing the whole business. Our partnership contract stipulated that either one of us could quit with six months' notice; we could dissolve the business, with each of us getting half of the assets. She did not want to dissolve the business and begged me not to take out my share. Because I knew that she was completely dependent on the income from the business, I acquiesced. I agreed to keep working part time for pay, but not as a managing partner. By being close by, I could help her learn enough to manage the business on her own.

Frank thought that was a mistake. He said I would lose everything. I did not agree with him. Above all, I could not see myself taking out my share and thus closing the business when Dita needed it so badly. His assessment was right. A few years later the business went broke, so there were no assets left to divide. But I was not sorry that I made that decision. At least my conscience was clear. I felt that I had learned so much by managing the business that I had been amply repaid for my investment.

Working mostly at home reduced my stress level, but I did not feel comfortable about Frank supporting Bessie while I was not employed. Also needing more contact with other adults, I had to find work that would pay for Bessie and at the same time permit me to be with Paul much of the time. After much deliberation, Frank hit on the idea of my becoming an adult education dressmaking teacher. When I said that I knew nothing about teaching, he remarked that I had taught the women in the factory during four years and that was good enough experience. Again he was right. I began researching the adult education scene, quite an eye-opener to see the myriad courses offered to thousands of adults eager to learn.

Adult Education

Eventually I found the adult education program in San Leandro, a small community south of Berkeley, which hired me. The school did not risk anything. If I did not attract enough students, the school would cancel the course and not pay me. With sufficient enrollment I was able to teach a course in advanced dressmaking and pattern making. Most of my students had been sewing for years but had never been satisfied with the results. The dresses they had made looked like creations by "loving hands at home," a term used to designate dresses that did not look professional. The problems came from too much handling, improper pressing, too much ripping—all shortcomings that did not occur in factory-made garments. I taught my students to sew as though they were working in a factory. Handling the fabric less, I had them working with pins, for example, rather than basting seams, which required pulling out threads later. Difficult portions like sewing a collar on a curve I had them practice on bits of fabric rather than letting them learn on their garments. That was very different from home sewing. Most dressmaking teachers were home economics majors who did not know anything about production methods. In that respect I was unique.

Unusual in another way as their instructor, I realized that frequently the reason for the students' disappointment had nothing to do with their sewing skills. They were looking for clothes that they had hoped would change how they looked. Some did not like themselves and hoped that the clothes would turn them into different people, as if the right clothes would make their personalities seem more attractive. We spent a lot of time discussing why they had not achieved the desired result; they began to understand that no matter how well made, clothes can flatter but they cannot make over the wearer. My class became more like a group therapy session than a dressmaking class. The same students kept coming because they did not want to give up the discussions. Starting with one class a week, I ended up teaching four nights.

The schedule I had worked out was satisfactory. I spent most of the day with Paul and then left for school in the evening when Bessie was putting him to bed. The school required that I obtain an adult education credential if I wanted to continue teaching. I enrolled in education courses at the University of California in Berkeley, where I learned some of the educational terminology that was of little use to me then. The courses were geared to teachers of the General Education Degree (GED), the high school equivalency program. I eventually got the adult education credential. At least I had one paper credential to my name, never having completed a course of study before.

When Paul was eight months old, he had a convulsion. Bessie, in whose room he slept, realized that something was terribly wrong with the baby and woke me. I had never seen a convulsion, did not know that convulsions happened. We rushed him to the hospital emergency room. By the time we got there, he was fine but I was terrified. I was told that babies frequently have convulsions following high fevers. In Paul's case, the fever came a day or so after the convulsion, not before, so we could not anticipate the next seizure. Paul had another convulsion a few months later, and the doctor wanted him to have an electroencephalogram. Though I tried to hold him in place, he would not lie still for it and screamed the whole time. After a while, the nurse just took him from me to perform the procedure. I remembered my baby's screams for a long time thereafter! Insecure as I already was about my mothering skills, the possibility of a convulsion coming at any time added to my anxiety.

When I found myself pregnant 15 months after Paul was born, by then feeling somewhat more relaxed, I was thrilled with the prospect of a second child. Anne arrived two years after Paul, three weeks early and much faster, after only one major contraction. Instead of naming her Anne Alkmena, we called her Anne Charlotte, after Frank's mother. We nicknamed her "Mapsička" (pronounced Mup-sich-ka), a Czech-sounding word we made up that seemed appropriate for this adorable, black-haired, wiggly little creature. Both children's nicknames stuck with them for a long time. Anne's birth was again "the unique event" that happens millions of times, again tremendously exciting but not quite so emotionally overwhelming as the birth of a first child. I started to nurse her but contracted a painful infection in my nipples and had to wean her to the bottle very soon.

Luckily, Mother had come back to be with us. Even if we continued to have real conflicts about baby-care methods, such as when to pick her up, how often to weigh her or how to place her in the crib, I appreciated her

232

willingness to be there. Due to Anne's premature birth, I had stopped teaching but had not finished designing the sample dresses for that season's collection. Needing to work with the sample maker, I had to return to the factory only a few days after Anne was born. Every morning, Mother, Anne and I went from Berkeley to San Francisco to the factory, where Mother looked after Anne while I worked close by—not a relaxing time. Bessie stayed home with Paul.

Shortly after Anne's birth, we moved to Palo Alto because Frank was now working at the Stanford Research Institute. I was very sad to leave the house in Berkeley with its beautiful view. With tears in my eyes as I drove down the hill, I felt sorry for myself because I had to give up living in what I considered the world's best spot. I made life miserable for Frank for accepting the new job that necessitated the move. He did not humor me, knowing that eventually I would realize that I could be happy almost anywhere. Palo Alto was not Timbuktu; it had a reasonable climate, lovely surroundings and an interesting intellectual community, attributes that were important to me. We bought a modern wood and glass one-story home in a contemporary subdivision of Palo Alto. This desirable neighborhood had the attractions of a community swimming pool, a nursery school and young families with many children playing in the street. On Paul's first visit to the swimming pool, he ran ahead of all of us and right into the pool with his clothes on. Nobody had told him that one wore bathing suits to go swimming!

Terrible Illness

Though I grew to like our new neighborhood, the children's health continued to be a worry in Palo Alto. I was never relaxed about them. After Anne completed her first year without a convulsion, I became a bit less anxious. But then one evening when she was twenty months old, I saw her have a severe convulsion that was not self-limiting like Paul's episodes. Terrified, I rushed her to the hospital where she received a shot that stopped it. She had to stay in the hospital overnight for tests, and no one could stay with her; Bessie was at home watching Paul, who had had another convulsion; and Mother, who was at our house convalescing from a broken leg, needed me. In addition, I was five months pregnant with a third child. Frank was giving finals that night at San Jose State University, where he was teaching, and could not be reached. It was one of those nights that you wished you could forget but never could.

Not long after we brought Anne home, she developed a terrible disease called Stevens-Johnson syndrome. It usually is the result of an allergic reaction to drugs. The disease inflamed all her mucous membranes—mouth, eyes and vagina. Her skin came off in sheets and she was bloody all over. The doctor said that this acute form of the disease would last ten days and that we should keep her at home, where there was less danger from infection than at the hospital. We kept her home lying flat on her back, her arms tied up so that she could not scratch herself. With a high fever for the whole ten days, Anne wiggled and cried a lot. While I could not pick her up, I read and sang to her and tried to get her to sleep. I never knew that ten days could be that long. Even though the doctor did not say so outright, I knew that her illness was life-threatening. I sat with her every night, praying—I do not know to whom—that she would not die during the night, when I was alone with her. Frank was pretty useless in this crisis, so heartbroken to see Anne in her condition that he could not sit with her. Bessie was there praying continuously and taking care of all of us so that I could focus on Anne. I wished that I had that marvelous faith that sustained her.

During that horrible time I had a miscarriage. In a way I was glad. The thought that I could have a third convulsive child, with the inevitable uncertainty and fear, was more than I could bear.

These awful ten days taught me how lonely the human condition is. Other than being with her, I could not help Anne, who had to fight the disease by herself. But watching that little girl fight for her life was so heartrending that I would gladly have taken her place.

The disease must have had some genetic connection. Later, in Vienna, Mother had a similar illness after a powerful anti-arthritis drug was infused into her arthritic fingers. She nearly died from the side effects, but the treatment did help the arthritis considerably. I also had a similar illness on my first trip to Washington with the children several years later. While it was bad, it was less dramatic and shorter-lived than Anne's illness. I remember sitting in bathtub water that was purple from the gentian violet that was used to disinfect the skin.

Eventually Anne recovered completely, though perhaps not from all of its effects. Life became a bit less stressful. Paul continued to have seizures, but by now we knew how to cope with them. They arrived without warning, always signaling that a fever was coming—except once. I was playing ball with him in our back yard when he temporarily lost his sight. He suddenly said, "Mommy, where are you? I can't see you." Then he fell down, very slowly and gently so he did not hurt himself. We picked him up and put him to bed. By that time the seizure was over, and he slept a couple of hours. When he woke up, he was as good as new, as though nothing had happened. He got over it faster than I did.

In Palo Alto lots of children played in our cul-de-sac. Though it was difficult for me to talk about it, I forced myself to tell the children and their parents about Paul's convulsions so they would not be frightened if they saw one and could come to his aid if needed. By now I knew quite a bit about epilepsy and how to deal with it. I found that if I could discuss the condition factually and without being upset, everybody accepted the explanation without trepidation. The most difficult part for me was remaining matter-of-fact when I was not. I was never really relaxed about my children. After her first major seizure at twenty months, Anne continued having self-limiting seizures, some of them in her sleep, so that the only indication was mucous discharge on her pillow in the morning.

I am aware that society's attitudes about epilepsy have changed greatly since the late 1950s. Today it is common knowledge that people with epilepsy can lead productive and fulfilling lives. At the time, the children's convulsions seemed like the end of the world to me. I knew nothing about support groups, if there were any, and I felt isolated and scared. In retrospect I think that I, who coped so well with so many other facets of my life, coped quite ineffectively with this most important task.

Doing my best to leave my fears for the children behind, I continued to design for Dita Nemes and teach dressmaking and pattern making in the adult education program at Palo Alto High School. Capable of hiding the stress in my life, I was a very popular teacher. On the way to school I frequently had no idea what I would be teaching and how I would fill the three hours of class. But the minute I entered the classroom, I was able to let go of my worries and become totally focused on the students. As prepared as if I had spent hours planning the class, I could switch my attention on and off completely. I realized that I was able to live in compartments that I could open and close at will. I cannot do that anymore; my brain will no longer cooperate.

International Customs and Cookery

Soon after our move to Palo Alto, another project captured my imagination. My neighbor Joanne Goldman and I became involved in the Foreign Scholar Program at Stanford University. The Goldmans lived across the street from us and had two boys the same ages as Paul and Anne. Petite, energetic and intelligent, with many intellectual interests that paralleled mine, Joanne and I became friends almost immediately. Through the work of our husbands we were frequently invited to receptions and teas for the wives of the foreign scholars at Stanford. Both of us were appalled at the negative attitude most of the women had toward the United States. Many came from developing countries. They had never been away from home before and found it difficult to adjust to living far from their mothers and sisters as well as without the customary servants. Furthermore, in Palo Alto they lived in primitive student housing, often in Quonset huts, either without a car or not knowing how to drive the one they had. While the wives were homesick for their usual surroundings, their husbands were thrilled to be at Stanford for their professional enhancement and had little sympathy for their wives' complaints. The women had nothing positive to say about their stay here. Except for invitations to the homes of the professors for the holidays, they had no connection with the community. Embarrassed to reciprocate the American hospitality in such shabby student quarters, the women did not have the necessary wherewithal to entertain.

Joanne and I decided to do something to improve their opinion of the United States. Considering all the money the government had spent on bringing the foreign students and their wives to the United States, we did not want the women to return home spreading negative images about America. We had to come up with an activity that would permit the women to give rather than receive, and so we hit upon the idea of their teaching us how to cook the food of their country. We launched the idea, which was well-received by the university's Women's Committee. Starting with one or two wives, we asked them to come to one of our homes and cook a meal for us. One of the first dinners was South African food from the veldt, which introduced participants to unusual combinations of common foods.

Most of the wives did not have recipes, so we observed them, measuring the ingredients and learning to describe how they cooked. We then knew what ingredients to buy, how much time to allow, what oven temperature to use and more. A few days later, we invited members of the Women's Committee to come and watch the food preparation and taste the food, for which we wrote and distributed recipes. The cooking demonstrations were a great success. The meals were usually delicious and an interesting new experience each time. Joanne and I became expert recipe writers and our husbands willing guinea pigs trying out the dish of the week.

Our cooking classes soon became a bona fide adult education offering where the American women students paid fees to cover the expenses. Eventually we offered ten-session courses, each session featuring a different country. In these courses, foreign as well as American women got to know each other and sample uncommon food. We called it International Customs and Cookery. Although organized around food, we spent half the time discussing the customs of the country and exchanging myriad views.

Joanne and I marveled at the willingness of the women to open up about their cultures and their feelings in a way they never would have if they had thought they were coming there to talk. They would not have agreed to come to a discussion group. But this was a cooking session that only incidentally led to sharing thoughts. As facilitators, we added the necessary equilibrium by intervening when tempers started to flare or the discussion touched a raw nerve. When things got too controversial, we might say, "Maybe we'd better stir the rice now." That always lessened the tension.

The foreign women began to feel more positive about their lives in Palo Alto as they made friends among the participants and learned about America. The newspapers began to write about the program. When Stanford built a new foreign student center, the plans incorporated a demonstration kitchen with mirrors. We did not know it, but we were the precursors of Julia Child! We felt proud of our achievements and were pleased that some of our American participants continued to lead the Customs and Cookery classes for many years after both Joanne and I had left Palo Alto. They even produced a little cookbook that we both treasure.

One summer the Foreign Student Center asked me to coordinate a foreign student day, featuring food from all over the world. I organized food booths from some thirty different countries. Before stringent sanitary rules, we did not have to comply with restrictive health ordinances. With a very small budget, I enlisted dozens of volunteers and was thrilled when over a thousand visitors came to sample the food. At the time these ethnic food festivals were not as commonplace as they are now.

Still willing to live a pressured life, I enjoyed the challenge of the festival, especially once it was over. Again, as with every new project that I ever attempted, I learned a lot—this time about new cultures, about working with people and about organizational management. I was able to put that learning to good use in later community activities. As a special bonus, I became friends with many of the women, whom I later visited on our world travels. These encounters continued to amplify my knowledge about the world that had started with family visitors from abroad when I was a child in Prague.

Leaving Palo Alto

Ever since our move to Palo Alto, Frank had been casting around for a job overseas. He had already told me that he wanted to go abroad when we got married. Now that he had his Ph.D. and the children were no longer in diapers, the time seemed right. In 1963 Frank found a job with the International Labor Office in Geneva, one of the United Nations organizations. The ILO wanted him to go to Argentina to set up a productivity center. He got a year's leave of absence from teaching at San Jose State University.

I had been working with Dita Nemes. As we were getting ready to leave, she moved her business to New York, where the firm went broke. I see her there from time to time. Now retired, she lives in New York and still occasionally sells high-priced real estate.

Renting out our house, we let wonderful, angelic Bessie leave us and go home to Texas. We stayed in touch with her until she died.

Next we prepared to go to Buenos Aires by way of Europe. The ILO asked Frank to travel to Geneva for a month of orientation before going to Buenos Aires. All of us spent the summer in Europe, Frank mostly in Geneva and the children and I in Alt Aussee. I had not been there since 1951, and I was eager to show the children the place that had been so important in my youth. Felix and his family had been spending summers there recently with Mother, who enjoyed being the lady of the manor.

Felix had re-established the house, less elegantly than before but as best he could. Much of the good furniture and other valuables had been stolen or lost. During the war, the German *Gauleiter*, the commandant of the region, had used the house as his guesthouse and had kept it in excellent shape. At the end of the war, in the few days before the U.S. Army arrived, locals helped themselves to whatever their hearts desired. Believing that the villa was Nazi property, Patton's 3rd Army soldiers who occupied the house felt free to ransack it. The remaining Persian rugs became car mats and foot warmers for their jeeps and halftracks. They parked these vehicles on the tennis court, destroying it. After the Americans left, the Austrian government used the house as a refuge for Sudeten German refugees unceremoniously dumped into Austria. At the end of the war, the Czech government had evicted millions from one day to the next, with only the belongings they were able to carry. Even after all that, Felix was still able to turn the house into a peaceful home in a glorious setting.

Mother was now receiving reparations from Germany as compensation for the loss of income during the war. With that money and our contributions, she no longer needed to work. She had left New York and installed herself in a small apartment in Zurich and later in Felix's apartment in Vienna. However, she spent most of the year traveling around the world visiting her far-flung friends and children. She was thrilled to spend summers in Aussee, where she could once again keep house her own way, assisted by local cleaning women and Justina, an excellent cook from Zagreb, Yugoslavia, who came every summer to help her.

A sturdy, efficient, middle-aged woman, Justina was happy to earn extra money in Austria to improve her family's economic situation in Yugoslvavia. Like Bessie, she was a loyal jewel of a woman. We kept in touch with her for many years after Mother died and after she moved to Germany to be with her daughter. To help with my children and my brother's three, we hired a young woman from Sweden as an au pair. She made it possible for me to leave for a few days to go to Warsaw to learn more about Poland.

Poland

My Israeli friend, Avigdor Dagan, who entered the Israeli Foreign Service when he moved there from Czechoslovakia, was now Israeli ambassador to Poland. Avigdor, or Viki as we called him, was my brother Paul's brother-in-law whom I had visited in Israel in 1949. Viki's invitation to show us a bit of Poland was tempting. Since Frank was already on his way to Argentina, I accepted the invitation and traveled alone. Going by train, I saw parts of Austria and Slovakia that I had not visited before. I stopped off in Bratislava to visit Czech and Slovak friends who were having a rough time living under the Communist regime. They were writers by profession but as "politically unreliable elements" were forced to work in menial jobs. They lived with the pervasive threat faced by intellectuals at the time; when the doorbell rang, they never knew whether the police were coming to arrest them.

Arriving in Warsaw, I was met by the ambassador's driver. The driver was a survivor of the concentration camp Majdanek. He insisted on taking me there to show me the remnants of the camp; I was the first American he could take to see the camp. The Communist countries had obliterated as many landmarks of the persecution of the Jews as possible, stressing only the Russian casualties of Nazi cruelty. The Communists did not want to call attention to the frequently willing participation of the local populations in persecuting Jews, because many of those Polish fascists had now become valiant Communists. Left as it was when a camp, Majdanek had been preserved virtually intact. My visit predated the establishment of a museum there.

I was shaken by the experience. The driver pointed to the various barracks where he had lived as a prisoner, to the gas chambers and to the ovens where he had been detailed to shovel out incinerated corpses. I saw a barracks full of shoes, a large container full of hair that had been shorn off prisoners to be used for some war purpose and an exhibit of cooking utensils used in the camp. The immediacy of standing close to these shocking reminders and the explanations of the driver made the horror of camp life become poignantly real.

I wondered why the driver was so eager to show me all this. Was it to remind himself of the terrible experience? But I soon understood that what was most important to him was that the world should know and not forget. I accepted his credo and continue to believe that the world must not forget. The visit will remain one of the most powerful and unforgettable experiences of my life.

Still trying to assimilate the wrenching experience, I returned to Alt Ausee. Felix met me at the station with the news that Paul had had another convulsion. The children's health was a constant worry. They were generally healthy, had no more colds or ear infections than other children, but concern about the unpredictability of their condition was always with me. Paul had also had a convulsion the day we arrived in Alt Aussee. Felix had never seen a convulsion, and I will always remember the horrified look on his face as he stared at Paul.

A few weeks later, on our way from Alt Aussee to Spain before going to Buenos Aires, Anne had a convulsion that did not stop spontaneously. We were staying in a little Italian mountain village far away from any hospital. This episode started us on a trip to a doctor, driving on winding mountain roads in the middle of the night. I felt as if I were living the "Ballad of the Erlkoenig," a song by Schubert with words by Goethe about a father who rides through the wind and fog trying to bring his dying child to safety.

Despite these potentially serious episodes, we were leading a regular family life. My anxiety about the children did not change our lifestyle; it just overshadowed it all the time.

11

ARGENTINA

W E LEFT ALT Aussee at the end of a wonderful summer and drove to Barcelona; from there we could ship our car to Argentina. From Barcelona we flew to Ibiza to visit Felix and his family and admire the extensive establishment he had created out of the one-room cabin purchased 11 years earlier. Felix and Friedl had raised their children amid primitive living conditions. When he had bought the cabin, it had no heat, electricity or plumbing; water was hauled from a nearby well. Now it was a five- or six-bedroom house with a complete kitchen and proper bathrooms. From the two large red-tiled terraces, one could admire the view of the Mediterranean on one side and the Puig, a hill with a church-fortress constructed in 1577, on the other. Like the typical Ibizenco houses, Felix's home was flat-roofed, brilliantly white and set in a well-tended garden with a large swimming pool.

After exploring the island for a couple of weeks, in mid-September 1963 the children and I flew to Buenos Aires via Madrid. During the exhausting flight, Paul again had a scary convulsion. Fortunately, the United Nations had issued us business-class tickets, so there was space for Paul to lie on the floor and sleep off his seizure. He arrived in Buenos Aires as good as new, better than I.

Martinez

We moved into a furnished house that Frank had found us in Martinez, one of the nicest residential districts of Buenos Aires. In getting settled, I found that my Spanish was not very helpful. What I spoke was based mostly on my knowledge of Portuguese and on my experience at the OWI. I could read the editorial in the *Prensa*, the prestigious daily, but I could not make myself understood in the market or the hardware store. Once again I hired a teacher who came to the house twice a week and I started studying Spanish. I took lessons for about three months, long enough to speak fluently but with grammatical errors. I thought that my knowledge was adequate for the time being and that I would take it up again before long. Stopping that soon was a mistake. Much to my chagrin, my Spanish remains riddled with errors.

In a strange environment and without playmates, Paul and Anne at first would not leave my side. In Palo Alto they had played independently outside in the cul-de-sac, but in Buenos Aires they became totally dependent on me. It was not customary for Argentine children to play on the street or for their parents to reach out to newcomers. With houses behind high fences and the streets in the suburbs deserted, meeting our neighbors took a while. Eventually we got to know wonderful neighbors with whom we remained good friends. Anne soon went to an English-speaking nursery school; there, she learned quite a bit of Spanish, which the Argentine children spoke among themselves. Paul stayed home. Though he was now six years old and had been in kindergarten in Palo Alto, in Buenos Aires he had to wait to start classes until February, the beginning of the school year in the Southern Hemisphere.

Adjusting readily alongside his international colleagues, Frank had begun Spanish lessons as soon as he arrived. As the United Nations staff came from all different countries, the official language of the office was English. But he needed to speak Spanish when giving lectures and seminars to the Argentines. He learned enough to make himself understood, without bothering about grammar.

I had learned enough to communicate easily with Edilbes Culver, the competent housekeeper whom we engaged. She was a slight young woman with closely cropped hair. Twenty-three years old, she had two children, ages six and seven, who were living with her parents in the country. She had married at 15, had her first child at 16 and her second child at 17. By that time her husband had taken up with another woman, and her father absolutely forbade her to have anything to do with him. He did not even allow her husband to pay for anything for the children. Instead, Edilbes was to go to Buenos Aires, get a job and send all her earnings home to pay for their upkeep. When she came to us, she said she needed no day off, because she did not have any money with which to go anywhere. She was sure that her life was over, that she had no future. I was appalled to see a well-intentioned and hard-working person have so little hope. What a waste of human potential! Soon I found a solution. I would not hire the second maid. In Buenos Aires, well-off families usually had at least two live-in maids as well as a laundress. After I got to know Edilbes and realized that she was very capable and bright and could do all the work by herself, I doubled her salary. She accepted my offer gratefully because she needed the money badly.

My Argentine acquaintances tried to dissuade me from this domestic arrangement. They said I was going to ruin the wage scale for everybody else if I paid my maid that much. I did not listen to them. I was disturbed at the upper-class mentality. Though Argentina was a much more developed country, the attitude was almost as objectionable as the one I found earlier in Egypt.

Life for the upper classes in Argentina was ideal: the country was beautiful, very rich in natural resources and had a lively cultural life. The wealthy people had lovely houses and good servants. They traveled a lot, though rarely in Argentina, because they saw it as a second-rate country. Instead they went to Europe or the United States for vacations. Considering Spanish a second-class language, they felt that if you wanted to be "educated," you had to know English and French or German. Of the multilingual upper classes, Frank would say in his flip way, "They speak four languages, but they have nothing to say in any one of them."

The upper classes also had no sense of civic responsibility, not a tradition in Latin countries. While charitable, they did not get involved in building the civic society that is so vital to a democracy. We were in Argentina after the time of Peron, the famous dictator who had worsened matters and alienated the upper classes. It was not in the Argentine tradition to exert oneself politically. The upper classes had a dual set of values: helpful, honest, correct with family and friends and shamefully corrupt and lawless vis-à-vis strangers or the state. I found this attitude unacceptable and increased my appreciation for the United States, where people wanted to work for their communities and where the individual as a civic activist was valued.

Without much orientation before leaving Palo Alto, I had expected to come to a Third World country, which is true for most of Argentina but not for the center of Buenos Aires. Though slums surrounded the city, in the *Centro* the best-dressed women in the world attended theaters, concerts and lectures on a high cultural level. Buenos Aires was also a city of ethnic ghettos: the Italian-Argentines, the majority of the population, originally from impoverished Sicily and Southern Italy; the Spanish-Argentines, who had come with little or no education from Galicia, Spain's poorest province; the Anglo-Argentines, who had arrived in the 1800s to build the railroads; the French-Argentines and the German-Argentines, eager to profit from the rapid economic expansion of the country and increase trade relations with their home countries. Many Jews had come at the end of the 19th century sponsored by Baron Hirsch, who created an agricultural colony in the jungles of the Chaco Province; many also came later to escape Hitler. Each of these groups had its own schools and its own civic associations, intermingling little. We belonged to a variety of groups: the Americans, the United Nations international crowd, and the central European Jewish refugees, most of whom had achieved substantial success in this rich country.

We were invited to dinners almost every night. In Argentina, dinner is served at 11 p.m. You were invited for 9:30, but nobody arrived before 10. I would put the children to bed, leaving them with Edilbes, and get dressed to go out. The party was basically over when dinner was finished. Of course I had to reciprocate. Not knowing what to expect in Buenos Aires, we had brought only plastic dishes and basic tableware with us. I saw that what we had to offer was shabby compared with how elegantly the etiquette-conscious Argentine women entertained. It did not faze me. I thought if the guests did not like it, so be it! I also made a point of inviting people from different ethnic groups to the same dinner as an attempt to open the ghetto doors a bit. Departing guests frequently said that they felt very stimulated at our home.

Civic Activist

One of the Central European Jewish ladies told me about the orphanage for girls that she and her friends were supporting. While the Catholic Church offered most social services in Argentina, for needy Jews social services came through the Jewish organizations and the synagogues. In an

Orthodox Jewish community with less interest in girls than in boys, these organizations had had no plans earlier for supporting Jewish girl orphans. The orphanage I heard about filled a real gap.

The girls in the orphanage had an unusual background. Most of them were the daughters of Jewish fathers who had come from Eastern Europe to the Baron Hirsch colony on the border between Argentina and Paraguay. There they married Paraguayan Indian women and tried to recreate the Polish *shtetl* atmosphere in the jungle. The Indian women could not adapt to that community structure and disappeared into the jungle, leaving the children behind. The men brought the girls to Buenos Aires, hoping to find refuge for them; these were the children of fathers who were escaping from Hitler.

The European women who took on the task of looking after these teenagers complained that the girls were not grateful. The walls were full of graffiti, the girls did not clean up after themselves and the ladies did not get the kind of do-gooder satisfaction they had anticipated. The women had tried to recreate in the orphanage the atmosphere of their own middle-class European homes. They did not consider what would have felt like home for the girls, who came from a very different, less affluent and mainly rural environment. Consequently, the girls did not value the orphanage and felt free to misbehave. Twice abandoned, many of the girls were seriously emotionally deprived children who had lived through a lot of trauma. Healing them was complex and would take time.

To get my input about working with such girls, the ladies invited me to one of their executive board meetings. Before attending that meeting, I first observed the girls and talked to some of them. When my turn to speak to the ladies came, I started by saying, "We in the United States…" and got no further. A barrage of objections reminded me that this was Argentina, not the U.S.; that what worked in the U.S. was not applicable here. Lesson number one: Do not bring up the United States as a model. So I said, "OK, maybe I cannot tell you, but maybe I can show you."

I volunteered to give sewing lessons to the girls who were interested in learning. From my Palo Alto days I remembered the therapeutic effects of sewing. Indeed my hunch was correct. I knew that creating a work group where participants could decide how to structure the activities would help their self-esteem as well as potentially enhance their sewing skills. The girls loved it. They came to class regularly and were well-behaved, neither cursing nor fighting. Together we even produced a few wearable items. The girls began to trust me. I tried to tell the sponsors that the girls needed an environment where they were valued and respected as individuals. However, the ladies did not listen. They kept saying, "Yes, but you are very skilled and we do not have such skills." Eventually they came to see that the girls would feel more at home without maids who made their beds and without having to live up to the exacting living standards of the sponsors. I believe, however, that the essence of my demonstration escaped the sponsors.

Meanwhile, with Edilbes's help, our children were adapting to their new lives. Interestingly, for six months the children did not speak a word of Spanish, and then one day out of the clear blue sky they spoke it fluently. Nobody has as yet explained that phenomenon to me! When Paul started school at Colegio Lincoln, the American Community School, I became involved in the school's PTA. The children studied the American curriculum in English in the morning and the Argentine curriculum in Spanish in the afternoon. Most of the children were American or from other international and diplomatic families; only a few were Argentine. Even though the Argentine children learned English, the American children had practically none of the social contact with them that I had been anticipating. Disappointed, but remembering my successful integration of the wives of foreign scholars into the Palo Alto community, I went into action.

Buen Vecino

I enlisted the support of the PTA to start the *Buen Vecino* (Good Neighbor) program to create an integrated school community. Extracurricular activities and outings would enable American and Argentine children and their parents to get to know each other. Frank was a good strategizer and helped me develop an action plan. I found an ally in an Argentine woman who had similar ideals, and together we presented the plan to the PTA. Even with PTA sponsorship and publicity, running what became known as the Buen Vecino club was a lot of work. I did not mind the effort, committed to the idea as I was. As in Palo Alto, I again profited from this activity because I met many interesting people with whom I would never have interacted otherwise. I also gained some insight into the lives of Argentine families. Building on my Palo Alto community-organizing experience and with Frank's help, I enthusiastically learned how to plan and execute a more complex program that worked.

Huge Challenge

One day the Colegio Lincoln principal came to me and asked me whether I would like to teach there. He knew that I had an adult education credential. I laughed and said that I had never taught children and that I had never been a child in an American school. He said, "That does not matter. I have watched you now for several months; you can do anything you set your mind to." He was in desperate straits; a sixth-grade teacher who was to arrive the next month had just become ill, and he needed to find a replacement at once.

I thought the idea was absurd. When I told Frank he said, "Wonderful idea. Of course you can do it." He had such faith in me that he thought there was nothing I could not achieve if I wanted to. Still I told the principal that I could not take on a classroom by myself, but I would be willing to be an aide in another classroom for a semester and then possibly be ready to teach alone the second semester. He agreed. However, two weeks before the beginning of the second semester in September, he came to me and said that I had to take on that sixth-grade class after all; the replacement he had found had also fizzled out. I nearly fainted. My English friend who taught at the school and was a teacher trainer in England promised to help me. I knew nothing about sixth-graders or their curriculum.

With a great deal of trepidation, I borrowed all the textbooks from the well-stocked school library and started preparing myself. Thank heavens all American textbooks had teacher editions. The teacher editions explained exactly how to teach and evaluate a lesson and included ready-made tests with the answers. Essentially, if you knew how to follow the instructions you could teach. What I had learned in Berkeley while obtaining the adult education credential came in handy now. Not included in the teacher edition was training in classroom management, that crucial skill a teacher must possess. Helpfully, my English friend gave me some pointers and a lot of moral support. I pored over books every free hour I had, but I was still a nervous wreck the day school started. I am not sure how I survived the first months. Teaching was the most difficult thing I ever had to do, almost on par with parenting.

My day had structure. I taught, came home from school before the children and studied until they arrived. We ate dinner together, I read to them, put them to bed and continued at my desk until midnight just to stay one step ahead of the class. I told Frank that I would not go to any more parties, though he was free to go, and asked him not to invite anybody to the house. I had to concentrate on becoming a teacher.

What probably saved me was that I was attuned to each of the 23 children in my class. Most of them were sweet, bright and good learners. The few difficult ones I was able to win over somehow. I realized that children are captive learners and need motivation to put out the energy and make the effort to learn. I found out that children give up when they feel they cannot do what is demanded of them. They say to themselves, "Why should I try? I know I cannot do it." Knowing that this attitude was deadly, I prepared different lesson plans for each achievement level in most subjects—grammar, reading, writing, math and science—so that, if at all possible, no child would ever have to wait or be frustrated. I did not know that one could teach any other way. I thought it would be sinful to teach children something they already knew and thus waste their time. Finding enrichment activities, such as creating word games or writing short essays for the advanced students, I linked students up with peer tutors or developed other group activities that suited the slower ones. I was absolutely determined not to leave a single child behind. To hold the children's attention, I tried all the teaching tricks that I could find in the books I consulted.

During this first year, I consider that I put myself through teachers' college. Untrained as I was, I often doubted my ability to be a good teacher, although the children respected me and parents complimented me because I was the first teacher who had individualized instruction for their child. Energized by the effort, I felt that now I was really doing something worthwhile. In contrast, when the Countess Nemes business became successful, I never felt that I was doing something of significance.

I invented my own grading system using three components: effort, correctness and neatness. If a child knew the subject and the work did not require any effort, he or she got a low grade for effort and a high grade for knowledge. Neatness was self-explanatory. I frequently asked the children to assign their own grades. They were much stricter than I. Some really bright boys handed in smeared and almost illegible papers. Trying to motivate them to rewrite their work brought mixed success. On the other hand, if I rewarded a slow learner for the effort made, regardless of errors, the child would continue trying.

I also created my own reward system. When the class had worked particularly hard and attentively, they would have an hour on Friday afternoon to pick whatever activity they wanted. Invariably, they wanted to play baseball. I knew nothing about baseball and I still do not. I would ask a tenth-grader to supervise the game while I just observed, without learning how to play. The game kept the kids happy and motivated them to work hard again the next week.

My lack of knowledge of ball playing, evident in Argentina, came up again years later when we were living in Bethesda. I had an agreement with Paul that I would give him an undivided hour of my time every so often where we would spend the time in whatever way he suggested. He always wanted me to watch baseball or another ballgame with him on television. Attempting to explain the game to me, he was appalled that I never seemed to get it. He finally gave up, saying, "Mom, you're hopeless."

My preparation for class was extremely time-consuming, but I felt I owed the students individualized instruction. In retrospect, I think that nobody could teach this way for any length of time. All that planning was just too demanding. Eventually, a teacher would have to become more realistic about what was possible versus what was ideal.

In Buenos Aires while I was teaching, Paul and Anne were in generally good health but kept having convulsions. Both children had normal electroencephalograms. That diagnosis did not reassure me, because I knew that EEGs were not accurate diagnostic tools. One day, Paul started walking around as though he were drunk and about to lose his balance. His eyes got cloudy and he just did not seem himself. When I picked him up at the school bus stop, I saw him fall down the steps. When he got up, he could not keep himself erect. Frantic, I talked to the pediatrician, who with just a cursory glance thought it could be a brain tumor. What a frightening diagnosis! I tried to recap what possibly could have happened. The thought occurred to me that he was taking the Argentine equivalent of the American anticonvulsant medication that he had been taking for years. Although the pharmacist had earlier insisted that the medication was identical, I became suspicious that it was not. Against the doctor's advice, I took him off the drug at once. I just could not watch this little boy remain in the condition he was in. Paul improved within a day and was back to his old self in two or three days. I never had him checked for a brain tumor and never put him back on anticonvulsant medication. Fortunately, he grew up and has stayed seizure-free to date.

Anne Starts School

The following year, Anne entered first grade. Though she had liked nursery school and kindergarten, after the first few days in school she did not want to go to class and became very difficult at home. I knew something was the matter with her but I did not know what. I talked to the school counselor, who said, "But Mrs. Meissner, how can anything be wrong with a child who has learned such fluent Spanish?" It was not a helpful answer. One day I noticed that Anne came home with her shoelaces torn to tatters. She must have been tearing at them all morning. She had also come home with blank sheets of paper on which she had been told to copy words from the blackboard, which she could not do. Her teacher told me to have her evaluated. That was easier said than done. I had to find a suitable psychologist and make arrangements to have her tested.

Eventually the shattering test results indicated that she was retarded. I knew that she was becoming temperamental, but it never occurred to me that she could be retarded. As I drove home from the psychologist's on the great Avenida Libertador, tears streamed down my face. I tried to assimilate the verdict. Was it true that my sweet little girl was retarded? I was desolate that I could have a retarded child. How could that happen to *me*? My reaction to the word was the typical reaction born of ignorance, fear and shame. I was ashamed of her and of myself for being her mother. I felt that something had been torn out of my sides. When I told Frank, he was silent for a moment and then said reassuringly, "We are going to love her anyway." He was generally much less apprehensive about the children than I and much more optimistic. I needed a long time to overcome the pain and accept that diagnosis.

Although I now had been teaching for quite a while, I did not know anything about educating children with disabilities. The field of learning disabilities that Anne would eventually belong to was in its infancy. In 1959, when she was born, "learning disability" had just become a recognized disability in American education, like blindness or deafness. Yet most teachers and psychologists still knew nothing about it; the condition was first called "brain damage" or "brain dysfunction." No tests for children like Anne existed in 1965 in Argentina. So the Argentine psychologist used the tests for mental retardation because she had nothing else. Of course I did not know that. In reality, Anne had a severe visual-motor perceptual handicap; her brain could not correctly translate what her eyes saw and could not correctly signal information to her hands or feet. All this I found out much later when we returned to the States and I started studying learning disabilities.

Leaving Argentina

While I was preoccupied with the children's health and my teaching, Frank was energized by his success at the United Nations Productivity Center. A well-regarded lecturer, he was becoming an authority on food marketing in Argentina. With his Argentine counterpart, he visited markets throughout the vast country and consulted with entrepreneurs interested in setting up supermarkets. Conscious that the establishment of supermarkets would eliminate precious jobs on which many people depended for a living, he tried to interest investors in creating "intermediate-technology" markets that would automate some but not all of the market's functions, such as using cash registers instead of adding by hand. His two-year leave of absence from San Jose State University was up. Unwilling to extend it, the university asked him to come back. Preferring to stay with the United Nations, Frank resigned his position and became dependent on the U.N. system for employment. After three years in Argentina, the United Nations wanted to assign him to another country. This change came up at the end of the school year. Unsure how many months the decision would take to become final, I stopped teaching so that I would not have to leave in the middle of the semester.

During these few months of waiting, one of my Argentine friends from the Buen Vecino program approached me to help create a day-care center in a slum in Buenos Aires. This task required community organizing: finding allies, letting people make decisions for themselves, trying to reconcile conflicting opinions among the participants, building trust and working toward the possible rather than the ideal. Both my friend and I knew that a less than ideal location, one that would get the children away from playing in the gutters and the garbage-strewn alleys, was better than nothing. From the beginning we had no intention of controlling the project. Working with the local priest, we searched for people interested in helping and willing to take over the planning and decision making. The leaders who eventually emerged were a couple of illiterate but strong women. We obtained a small amount of money from the Salvation Army, no strings attached, with which the leaders hired a director. The center staff would also teach untrained, primitive but loving mothers how to care for their babies. Coming from the harsh climate of the Andes, some of the mothers kept their babies bundled up in heavy wool shawls in subtropical Buenos Aires. Other mothers punished their babies harshly when they cried. Patience and skill were needed to change habits. Above all, the existence of the center would give the dispirited mothers a sense of hope. As organizers, we knew we had to remain in the background so that the community would not perceive the center as being imposed on them by some foreign agent. When projects funded by such donor agencies as the World Bank or the U.S. Agency for International Development did not have sufficient community support, they frequently had minimal results.

Before the center was completed, I left Argentina. The experience taught me a lot about community development, especially about the type of approach that the Peace Corps uses with its emphasis on community leadership. I was pleased that I was able to participate in this grassroots project, which required tact and faith in the ability of people to learn and grow under the right circumstances

Back to the U.S.

In 1968 Frank was faced with deciding on a new U.N. job. The United Nations wanted to post him to Turkey. I objected. In view of Anne's situation, I did not see how we could go to another underdeveloped country with still another language. With conflicted feelings because he loved his job, Frank resigned from the United Nations and accepted a job offer from the W. R. Grace Company in New York, a company with multiple interests in Latin America. The Grace Company needed someone with his background to help it adjust its operations to comply with new land reforms in Peru.

Before leaving, we still had to consider the future of Edibles, our wonderful housekeeper. During her time with us, in addition to running our house and taking care of the children—including her son Eduardo, who came to live with us in Buenos Aires for more than a year—she had gone to school. When we left Argentina after three and a half years, Edilbes was eager to come back to the States with us. We offered to bring her children if she liked it in America and was sure she wanted to remain there. She could not travel with us. It would take time to get her the necessary papers. Because the Grace Company wanted Frank right away, he headed for New York and left me and the children, as with all our relocations, to move by ourselves.

I was sad in some ways to leave Argentina, as I had made good friends and had had fascinating opportunities. Yet I was glad to go back to the U.S.A., where I might find effective help for Anne. Even though I did not know how to go about my search, I was confident that there I would find answers.

Margit and Otmar, 1943,
after Otmar became an Army officer

Bruno, 1943

Otmar Gyorgy

The house in Lawton, Oklahoma, where
Otmar and Margit lived in 1943

Life as an Army couple, 1943

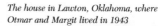

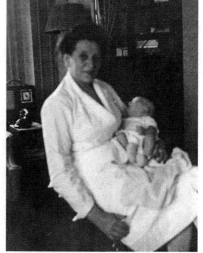

Mother as baby nurse, 1943

Paul Perich, our driver
in Nuremberg, a
displaced person (DP)

Book Day in American Youth Center in Furth near Nuremberg, 1947

Margit trying on donated Czech boots on German children at Youth Center, 1947

Paul in Australia, 1947

Felix in Europe, 1945

Margit at a diplomatic party,
Alexandria, Egypt, 1949

Pista in Budapest, 1948

Margit with partner Countess
Nemes in children's
dress business, 1954

Margit Gyorgy and Frank Meissner married January 1953

Business bloomed after Britain's Princess
Elizabeth was photographed wearing a
Juli Lynne Charlot Skirt

Juli Lynne Charlot felt
skirt for 1948 election,
"I Like Ike"

Frank's grandfather, Bobeš

Frank's brother, Leo, and his wife, Sonia

Frank's family, 1926
Frank is in center front

Family home in Třešt'

Frank as agriculture student in Denmark, 1940

Norbert Meissner, Frank's father

Lotte Meissner, Frank's mother

Frank as soldier in RAF in Great Britain, 1945

257

Margit teaching home economics at EduCage, White Plains, N.Y., 1969

Paul and Anne with Culver family, 1965

Paul and Anne, first school day in Argentina, 1965

First and only family reunion with Mother.
*front row, from left: Paul Meissner, Anne Meissner, Tim Morawetz, Ibi Morand, Tito Morand
second row, from left: Margit, Bruno, Mother, Felix, Paul
top row, from left: Anne Morawetz, Frank Meissner, Susan Morawetz, Gwen Morawetz, Tom Morawetz, Anita Morawetz, David Morawetz, Judy Morawetz, Friedl Morand, Dita Morawetz, Miguel Morand, 1968*

Margit teaching 6th grade at American Community School in Buenos Aires, 1965

PART 4

KALEIDOSCOPIC VIEW OF THE YEARS SINCE 1968

12

WHITE PLAINS

W HEN WE ARRIVED in New York in the fall of 1967, we stayed with friends in Manhattan for a few days so I could orient myself. My main goal was to find appropriate schooling for Anne, who was now eight years old. None of my contacts in New York were able to help me, so I was pretty much on my own. I was so ignorant at the time about the existence of special education programs and how to access them that I marvel at how I ever found anything. After considering various suburban communities around New York City, we moved to Westchester County. I had heard about good special education programs there and knew that Frank's commute to his office in the Wall Street district of Manhattan would not be too arduous for him. With a few pieces of furniture shipped from storage in Palo Alto, we rented a house in White Plains for a year to give us time to find a permanent home.

Arranging for Anne's education was an ordeal that taxed all my inner resources. Arriving in late September, after the beginning of the school year, I knew it would be difficult to find a space for her right away, assuming of course that I could find the right program. Armed with the psychological report from Argentina stating that Anne was retarded, I entered the bureaucratic maze of special education placements. My first encounters with programs for children with disabilities took me to facilities, some of them residential, for severely mentally retarded children. I got more depressed by the day. I still was very upset to think that I had a retarded child.

Frank did not view Anne's situation so tragically. He was more disturbed by my trauma. Wanting to reassure both of us, he kept saying, "Not everybody can be a genius. She is a very cute little girl; what's the problem?" Dejected and hurting, I followed every lead, which only directed me to the wrong programs. Finally, after a couple of desperate weeks of intense searching, I turned the corner. I now knew what to look for and quite fortuitously found an elementary school with a classroom for retarded children close to our rented home.

When I first took Anne to school, my heart broke again. The class consisted of six other children: two black girls who looked much bigger than Anne and who seemed perfectly normal; a blind boy with cerebral palsy who could move around only by propelling himself on his knees; a tiny Mongoloid boy; and a huge, obviously retarded autistic-like boy. I left her there with the greatest misgivings. At the same school, Paul pretended not to know his sister. When he saw her on the playground amid the visibly handicapped children, he was so ashamed of her that he did not greet her. My attitude had rubbed off on him.

As I write this in the year 2002 and reflect on my later twenty years as a special education professional in the Montgomery County Public Schools, I shudder at my own ignorance and prejudice in 1967. However, the painful experience of looking for schooling for Anne and eventually coming to terms with the reality of her situation was effective preparation for my future role as advocate for children with special needs and their parents.

With both children in school, I was free to hunt for secondhand furniture for our rented house. I became the queen of fancy Scarsdale garage sales where, for a song, I bought such high-quality furniture that we still use some of it today. Driving around with a map, the children in the back of the car asking me, "Mummy, are we lost yet?," I learned my way around Westchester County. My other task was to get the immigration papers for Edilbes; her responsibility was to learn to drive before she arrived. She joined us after a few months and we were delighted to be reunited.

Unexpectedly, Anne had a very good year our first year back. The teacher was excellent and, because she had such a diverse group, she had to teach each child individually. Anne learned to read and write there. The two black girls became good friends of hers. Through them I had a chance to visit the housing projects where most of the poor blacks lived, another eye-opening experience that would be useful to me later on.

In mid year, a school psychologist re-evaluated Anne and classified her as learning-disabled. She was assigned to a class for learning-disabled children in another school for the following school year. Though the new class was much more homogeneous, Anne did not make as much progress there, because her teacher was not up to the task of individualizing instruction.

Once we had worked out Anne's schooling, we settled back into life in the United States. Though I was homesick for California, White Plains felt like a good place in which to live and raise children. Both urban and suburban, with beautiful homes and gardens and well-tended public parks and playgrounds, Westchester County offered lots of opportunities for family recreation. We reconnected with old friends from New York City and through them, as well as through Frank's work, we met others with compatible interests. Guests from abroad who visited New York often stayed with us because the commute to Manhattan was convenient for them as well as for me during non-rush hours. I enjoyed being a tourist in New York. After Edilbes came, armed with her driver's license, we bought her a car so that she could drive the children to their various after-school activities. With Edilbes in charge of all household chores, I was able to look into other areas of interest.

Although the children and I were settling in comfortably, Frank was still not thrilled about having given up the United Nations job. He had really seen himself staying in that stimulating work environment. But given Anne's diagnosis, he knew that moving around in the world was not possible and the W. R. Grace job was a temporary placeholder. Frank's thankless responsibility was to liquidate Grace trading companies all over Peru. The new Peruvian land-reform requirements had obliged Grace to give up its vast sugar plantations and now its local general stores. Frank had to close stores in small towns, laying off people in places where no other work opportunities existed. He disliked his assignment, which deprived many long-term employees of the company of a livelihood. Furthermore, his travel schedule was also an irritant. Spending two weeks in Lima and returning to New York for a week before going back again was a stressful way to live, not just for him but for the whole family. In short order he began looking for something less stressful and more rewarding. While I commiserated with him, my concern about Anne still required most of my attention.

Elizabeth Freidus

The one person with whom I discussed Anne's situation was Anita, my brother Paul's Australian daughter, who had known Anne since she was a baby. Anita was studying psychiatric social work in New York that year and told me about Elizabeth Freidus, whom she heard speak during her social work training. Elizabeth became a very important person in my life. She taught a master's-level course about learning disabilities at Teacher's College at Columbia University. At the time, she was one of the outstanding experts on learning disabilities (LD) at both the national and the local levels. Her innovative four-credit-hour summer course was geared to teachers and mental health professionals. To obtain a slot in this highly regarded course for their child, parents had to agree to attend all the lectures. Demonstrating her teaching philosophy, Elizabeth taught a group of LD children on the stage of an auditorium observed by her students. After about 60 or 90 minutes, the children would go to a playground with another teacher, and the adults would discuss what they had seen.

Elizabeth had an unorthodox and controversial approach to children with special needs. Her educational philosophy threatened the more conservative educators. The establishment thought you had to evaluate and label a child a certain way and then place the child in a program according to the label, without understanding the individual. Elizabeth hated bureaucracy and hated labels; she thought that every child could learn if the teacher understood how the particular child learned. Labels did not tell the teacher anything about the child; the teacher had to understand what task the child had difficulty with and then chose the right method for helping the child compensate. That method was basically true for every learner, from the slowest to the fastest. With the mothers in attendance, the graduate students in the course could discuss the behavior of a child with the mothers. Often, children acted very differently in school than at home, and mothers saw them through different lenses. Upsets at home frequently influenced the child's behavior in class; if the teacher did not know about them, she could not adequately help the child. Elizabeth stressed that regular communication between teacher and parents was indispensable.

Anne and I started in Elizabeth's class in the summer of 1967. Observing Anne with Elizabeth's guidance was the most incredible learning experience for me—and for Anne. I discovered that Anne had no depth perception; she could not judge how high or low things were. She could not climb through the obstacle course in the classroom on stage because her eyes did not guide her. I began to understand why Anne as a toddler had always climbed to the top of the slide in the playground in Palo Alto and launched herself fearlessly. She simply did not realize how high it was. The other mothers on the playground would marvel at this courageous child, while I had my heart in my mouth. In addition, the class activities showed that everything that you and I see at a 90 degree angle, Anne saw at a 45 degree angle. Thus, when she got up from her seat to go to the blackboard, she could not find her way back. She saw her pathway at a different angle; for example, she would go three seats over and tell the child who was sitting there to get up, that this was *her* seat. In the ensuing fights, Anne was always the culprit. Also, when she copied from the blackboard, her writing started at the top left of the page and ended up diagonally at the bottom right, a 45 degree angle again. The remedy was easy as soon as one knew her needs. Elizabeth told Anne to count the seats from the end of the row before getting up and then count again before coming back. A similar remedy fixed her inability to copy addition or subtraction columns from the blackboard. She would add the first column and skip to the second column without realizing it. If the teacher first drew a line between the columns, the line helped guide her eyes so she could add correctly. A ruler under a line of words in a text would help in reading and writing sentences. The diagnosis and remedy were a revelation to me: so obvious, except that nobody had identified them before Elizabeth Freidus. Both Anne and I made good friends during these sessions who enriched our lives.

Unfortunately, these insights came late for Anne. By age nine she had already had many failures when learning to read and write. Like others with similar disabilities and with teachers who did not understand them, she often was not able to complete assignments or follow instructions, absorbing only the first part of the direction. Later, and also related to her perceptual disorder, she often had trouble getting along with the other children, misunderstanding the meaning of their gestures and comments. As these painful experiences added up, Anne became convinced that she could not learn and could not get along with others. As a result, she often acted out. I was grateful that by then I understood her difficulties but at the same time saddened that I had not known how to remedy them earlier. How was it that her teacher in White Plains did not know how to help her?

Part-Time Jobs

While I was still attending courses at Teacher's College—without Anne, who was now in her own school in White Plains—I started looking for part-time work. Unsatisfactory as the three and a half years in White Plains were for Frank professionally, they offered me welcome opportunities for growth. I had three interesting jobs: one at a local rehabilitation hospital, another at the Westchester County Mental Health Association and the third at a unique school for high school dropouts.

The rehabilitation hospital hired me as an interviewer on a socio-medical rehab study. My job was to find out which patients achieved the best rehabilitation results in a hospital where great rivalry existed between the nurses and the physical therapists. The study's hypothesis was that those patients who related best to the therapists would recover best. It turned out that the hypothesis was wrong. My own lay hypothesis was that patients who had a good family support system would achieve the best rehabilitation outcomes. That was also wrong. The study showed that what really made the difference was the attitude of the patient toward his or her condition. Patients who accepted the challenge of their condition recovered much better than those who were angry, depressed or unwilling to cooperate with the therapists. This was true regardless of whether the patients had a lot of money, frequent visitors or good family support. Even the loneliest and least affluent patients, who could accept that they might never walk unaided again, achieved good outcomes.

After that research was completed, I worked for the Mental Health Association on a study of the emotional health of children. The association hired me to code responses to questionnaires. The study found that the emotional health of children was most closely correlated with that of the mother and her feelings about herself, rather than her race or her financial situation. If a mother felt good about herself and was comfortable with her own child-rearing practices, even if these methods were often punitive, the children thrived. Children who were the least well adjusted had mothers who were depressed and lacked self-esteem. Of course, to some extent racial and socioeconomic factors were involved because poor mothers rarely felt good about themselves and most of the poor mothers were African-American.

The emotional health study coming to an end, I looked around for what to do next. Always lucky at finding interesting part-time work, I met Les Fernandez while attending a lecture by him on high school problems. Les was the director of Edu-Cage, an unusual, new, private alternative program for high school dropouts. Before creating Edu-Cage, Les had been in his spare time the volunteer boxing coach in a walk-in program for boys hanging out on the streets. The program was located in a seedy downtown White Plains basement pool hall called the Cage. Because the boys identified with the name, the new school took the name Edu-Cage.

Les was a teacher and school administrator, tall, burly and good-looking, with an irresistible twinkle in his eyes. When we got to know each other better, he invited me to become the Edu-Cage home economics teacher. The students were almost exclusively African-Americans from "the projects," low-income housing developments with the attendant crime and violence of such places. Most of the students had been expelled from school and were in trouble with the law. They had to be out of school at least two years before Edu-Cage accepted them; the only youngsters eligible for the program were those who had had a hard time on the street and had realized that they needed more education to survive in the world. Frequently rougher than the boys, some of the girls had been expelled from school for threatening or assaulting a male staff member.

Working with this difficult group, I again tried a sewing project, which I knew had therapeutic value. Both boys and girls wanted dashikis, the then-popular poncho-like, African-print garment. The girls were interested in sewing because they had no money and wanted something new to wear. I knew that they would be proud if they could wear something that they had made, even if they contributed only a little bit to the completed garment. The novelty attracted the boys. I had no trouble recruiting students of both sexes. Sewing was an elective subject, unlike the mandatory math or science.

Teaching them was rigorous and taxing. The students of both sexes were the most impatient, most impulsive group I had ever seen. Each one needed my full attention all the time, and waiting one's turn was an unknown concept. I had to be the best, most skilled sewing teacher ever to keep the demanding students involved.

Eager to build on my experience in the orphanage in Buenos Aires, I was most interested in getting to know the girls. I had never come across a group like this. Having just returned from nearly four years in Argentina, I knew nothing about the "underclass" or current "ghetto culture" in the United States. The girls looked at me with as much wonderment as I at them; they had never come across someone like me either, an upper-middle-class, now middle-aged white woman who listened to them and cared about their learning.

During the sewing lessons, the students began to talk and tell each other their life stories. I was appalled when I heard how they lived amid poverty, cruelty, abuse and ignorance. What troubled me the most was their attitude about babies. They thought that having a baby would be fun, believing that if they gave birth their family and friends would be proud of them. They expected to be able to leave the baby in the care of a mother or other relative and go about their lives as though they had no responsibility for that child. Those who already had babies knew nothing about infant care. Without hesitation, they would give the baby some whiskey on a cotton wad to get her to stop crying or wake her up whenever it suited them just to braid her hair or show her off.

Because the sewing sessions lent themselves to talking about topics of importance to them, I wondered what they knew about contraception. They knew none of the facts, and what they knew was mainly inaccurate. I was again appalled and determined that someone ought to keep these girls from having babies. When I spoke in a staff meeting about preventing pregnancies, the staff of Edu-Cage was not interested in doing anything about it. They said to me, "What more do you want us to do? At least the students are in school. We are teaching them to read and write, isn't that enough?" My response to this narrow-minded attitude was not exactly friendly. I thought that teaching the students about life and preventing unwanted teen births was much more important than helping them to pass a math test.

Without much support from my colleagues, I took the girls in small groups to Planned Parenthood. The eye-opening experience demonstrated how vulnerable they were. Some of these really tough girls—the same girls who walked around with bravado in their voices and a switchblade in their purses, who threatened their boyfriends—would not let go of my hand. They wanted me to go in with them to see the nurse and were trembling, so fearful were they of the visit. I was totally unprepared to witness how needy they were, so scared under that tough exterior, so unready to be adults.

Disturbed by the students' ignorance about nutrition, I added cooking to the sewing classes. Though most of the students were poor, when we went to the supermarket to buy the food needed for the cooking sessions, they picked out the brand they knew without regard to price. Comparing prices was an unknown concept. I once lent a girl money because she had none and wanted a drink of milk. She returned to class with a quart of milk, poured herself a glass and drank it. Then to my horror she poured the rest of the quart into the sink. She had had her drink; the present was all that mattered. To her there was no future.

My friends thought that I was foolish to have gotten involved with that program. The students were all African-Americans from the ghetto, and on top of it they were dangerous. What did I want with them? I did not buy the idea that a white person could not teach African-American students effectively. I found that my background was immaterial to the students; what mattered was that I showed respect for them and they in turn respected me. Some stealing was the norm at the Cage; except for one time, I never missed anything. Always interested in broadening the students' horizon, I was pleased when one day they wanted to go to the big city to buy African fabric for the dashikis. They had never been to Manhattan, giving me an opportunity to teach a bit of history and show them something new. My friends warned that I was endangering myself with this volatile group. I went with six boys and girls in one car and felt perfectly safe. Contrary to my friends' fears, in the city the students insisted on being solicitous and taking my arm as I stepped off the curb. So toughened at a young age, they eagerly proved that they knew how to behave like young ladies and gentlemen when they were away from their normal environment.

To my utter dismay, and despite all the birth control information, some of my girls became pregnant. I agonized over the babies of such ignorant young mothers and naively asked my pediatrician where one could learn parenting. I found that parenting was taught nowhere, because girls were supposed to learn mothering from the example of their mother. The mothers of these girls were often absent, on drugs or in jail. Some example! I was so determined to make sure that the girls learned to become good mothers that I spared no effort and somehow managed to convince my colleagues to let me start a baby-care program. They realized that I was obsessed, so they did not try to stop me.

When I began investigating the possibilities for starting a new program, I found nothing but obstacles: building codes, health codes, fire codes, social service regulations. The skepticism from social workers, nurses and my colleagues seemed overwhelming. Eventually my determination overcame them all. In 1969, with a small federal grant, I set up a "teaching" day-care center patterned on a teaching hospital. The church where the Edu-Cage program was located gave us the necessary space. I managed to interest the local Head Start agency in being part of it; we hired a pediatrician and a pediatric nurse—both African-American—to provide the expertise, because I certainly did not know enough about infants to do the teaching. The young mothers brought their babies to school in the morning and spent at least one hour a day plus breaks between classes in the Infant Care Center watching the nurse care for the babies. We asked the young fathers to come in as well. I wish we had had a motion picture camera—video cameras had not been invented at that time—to record the rough young fathers learning to handle their babies gently.

When calamities happened, the girls called me rather than the African-American women who worked in the day-care center. They knew they could rely on my problem-solving energy and my empathy. I will never forget the night when one of the girls called at 2 a.m. to tell me she and her boyfriend were fighting. He was dangling the baby out of the sixth-floor window threatening to drop it. I must have successfully encouraged her to make up with him. When another girl called in the middle of the night saying that she was going to kill her boyfriend with a switchblade, I asked to speak with him and calmed them both down. With so many unexpected crises, I worked day and night. After the center had been open for a while, the staff and I realized that we had made a mistake in accepting only the neediest, most hard-core girls. They fed on one anothers' pathology. We then invited a few less needy, still poor girls who were not so traumatized into the center. Their presence created a better, more stabilizing balance.

Slowly the Infant Care Center was becoming well-established. When I finally left White Plains a few months later, the center continued under the leadership of the Head Start agency. As a model program, the center attracted lots of publicity. I fretted over leaving, but I was so exhausted emotionally from the day-and-night challenges that I was willing to let someone else continue. I kept in touch with the new director.

To the best of my knowledge, no one ever carried out a meaningful evaluation of the program, although many school districts subsequently started similar programs in high schools. When I later moved to Montgomery County, I tried to interest our local school system in the idea. I was met with the same objections: "Margit, what else do you want us to take on? Are we not doing enough?" I did not pursue the idea, because by that time I had entered the field of disability.

Paul's Bar Mitzvah

Busy as I was at Edu-Cage, I found time to find a rabbi who would prepare Paul for his upcoming bar mitzvah. Paul went along with Frank's insistence that he prepare for it, initially strongly against my wishes. For myself I had and still have no feeling for any kind of religious observance, but this milestone was important to Frank. Religious in his own way, Frank had an individualistic approach to his Jewishness. He clearly identified himself as a Jew even without attending services in a synagogue. He still remembered the aggravations of his youth in Třešť when his father obliged him to go to the synagogue on cold winter mornings to complete a minyan and his grandfather slipped him a coin to sweeten the ordeal. Frank used to say that he communicated with God by himself; he did not need an intermediary. When I realized how important Paul's bar mitzvah was to Frank, I stopped objecting. I told him that if he wanted Paul to have the experience, the two of them would have to arrange it. Paul started going to the nearby synagogue for Hebrew lessons. I went with him for the first couple of lessons, thinking I might like to learn another language. However, Paul was a much better student than I, and I stopped accompanying him when I could not keep up with him.

Proudly, Paul made all the plans for the celebration. The members of the wealthy White Plains community customarily made elaborate preparations, with large numbers of guests. In contrast, Paul invited 12 of his friends, most of whom were not Jewish, and only a couple of our friends with whose children he was friendly. For the menu he selected roast beef sandwiches, soda pop and a cake with blue and white icing. Paul performed very ably in the temple, and Frank gave a truly inspiring speech about his parents. Eloquently he explained what it meant to him to be Jewish and to have a son on whom he could bestow the tradition. Frank's speech moved me to tears. The bar mitzvah took place on a beautiful spring day with the children playing in our yard after the ceremony, and enjoying the simple refreshments. When I said goodnight to Paul at bedtime, he said it had been the best day of his life. He has not been in a synagogue since.

Prague Spring

Paul interrupted his Hebrew lessons in the summer of 1968 when we went to Alt Aussee to be with Mother and Felix and his family. With Mother looking after our children and their Spanish cousins, Frank and I acceded to the wish of my Australian nephew, David, to guide him through Czechoslovakia. Nineteen sixty-eight was the year of the exhilarating Prague Spring, when a courageous prime minister, Alexander Dubček, had begun to modify the oppressive Communist practices, trying to show that communism could have a human face. After years of censorship, articles opposing the government appeared in the press and people stopped being afraid that a knock on their door at 2 a.m. meant imprisonment without cause or recourse. We were glad to show David an upbeat and optimistic Czechoslovakia. The vision of unpainted, unkempt houses, the neglected public spaces, the monotony of the food stores and the uniform, state-imposed menus in eating places could not conceal the infectious feeling of freedom in the air.

We drove around the countryside to satisfy Frank's curiosity about the development of collectivized agriculture there. Once when we stopped on an open road to photograph the ubiquitous Stalin-sponsored housing developments in the distance, I suddenly faced a Czech soldier with a sub-machine gun staring into my face through the windshield of the car. Unaware we had stopped in a forbidden zone near a military establishment, where the only and immediate security response was a threat to shoot, we were lucky to escape unharmed. The political situation was not as rosy as it had seemed. In fact two weeks later the Soviet Union invaded Czechoslovakia, unleashing not only more repression than before but also installing what was considered the most oppressive Communist regime of all the satellites until the fall of the Iron Curtain twenty years later.

Observing the rape of his country saddened all of us but especially Frank, who was such a Czech patriot. He had had high hopes for the Prague Spring, and its failure left him disillusioned about the possibility of humanizing communism forever after. Even the "Velvet Revolution," the peaceful end of the Communist regime and the takeover by democratic forces in 1989, a year before his death, did not sway him. People with his professional skills could have helped the new government greatly, but he wanted no part of it.

To Washington

When an official from the Inter-American Development Bank (IDB) in Washington approached Frank with an assignment to go to Paraguay on a six-week mission, Frank thought that this offer could be the change for which he had been looking. I agreed that he should go. At the end of this mission, the IDB offered him a job in Washington as an agricultural econ-omist. All such jobs were probationary for the first year and made perma-nent thereafter if the employee had proved effective. He wanted to accept the offer, but I was adamantly against it. First of all, I was not about to give up life in White Plains, where we had barely settled in, and move to Wash-ington. Second, I did not think that Frank with his unconventional approach to problem solving and his irreverent manner could survive in the bureaucratic environment of what I had been told was a rather staid organization. Against my better judgment, Frank accepted the job. The children and I stayed on in White Plains for a year while he worked in Washington and lived at a hotel during the week. He returned on the train every weekend and went back to D.C. early Monday morning. The job went better than I had expected; he really liked it and they liked him.

A few months before, in the fall of 1969, Edilbes's children, 13-year-old Eduardo and 12-year-old Patricia, arrived in White Plains. They spent a few miserable months attending school without understanding a word of English. I felt responsible for their plight. While I had not made the decision that brought them, I had championed this major change in their lives. That they were good learners helped them acculturate quite quickly. At times the emotional energy needed to sustain the adaptation of that family was exhausting. Not only did the Culvers change culture, they also changed class. Middle-class problem-solving methods did not come naturally to them. At times they needed real mentoring, the kind that assumes responsibility for the advice one gives. Today, Edilbes is a highly respected licensed practical nurse in an old-age home near Boston. She is also a licensed real estate broker. Eduardo, with a master's degree in public administration, is an independent financial advisor, and Patricia, a trained interior decorator, is married and stays home with her little daughter. I am very pleased that Frank and I had the courage to undertake this venture. We all lived together harmoniously in White Plains until we moved to Washington and it was time for the Culvers to find their own home. We are family to each other and are proud of their achievements.

Family Reunion

At Christmas of 1969 we had the one and only reunion of my whole birth family: Mother, her four children with their spouses and her 12 grandchildren all got together for a week at Bruno's farm in Peterborough, Ontario. This truly memorable occasion enabled siblings who had not seen each other in years and cousins who had never met to get to know each other. We enjoyed sleigh rides, skating parties, skiing outings and lots of opportunities for just "hanging out." The children, ages six to 28, organized games and produced skits that enhanced a feeling of family togetherness. We all left enriched by the warmth of good family feeling and the knowledge that even though we lived on four different continents—Australia, Asia, Europe and North America—our common heritage could bridge the distance.

13

BETHESDA

RETURNING TO WHITE Plains from the family reunion in
Canada, I reluctantly went to Washington to look for a house.
Friends in White Plains suggested that I look up the Engelmann
family before I started my search. What a lucky suggestion that was!
Through them I found the house in Bethesda, Maryland, that has been
home ever since. Originally from Germany, gray-eyed Erika Engelmann
was a social worker and mother of two children, slightly older than ours.
Exquisitely and conservatively dressed, an unparalleled hostess and faithful
walking partner, she became my best friend in Carderock Springs, the community in Bethesda to which we moved at the end of the school year. Over
the years, we spent many birthdays and holidays together with the Engel-
manns and became as close as if we had been family.

This time Frank was around for the move. Still certain that I would hate
Bethesda, we moved on the first day of July 1970. Unexpectedly, I loved it
from the day we moved in! The neighborhood was beautiful, the house
very comfortable, the environment invigorating and the international
neighbors stimulating. The kids had a pool, in which they practically lived,
and I found the peace and quiet exactly what I needed after the emotionally draining year at the Cage.

With Edilbes and her children back in White Plains, I no longer had nor
needed a live-in housekeeper. The children were older now; Paul was 13,
Anne 11. Before we moved, I had found a special education class for Anne

that happened to be in our neighborhood elementary school. Paul went to junior high. Both children took the bus to school, since our community has no sidewalks. I was fairly free and decided to stay home, furnish our house and give myself a rest.

Anne's Development

Although Paul seemed fine by then, I continued to feel uneasy about the children's health. Anne continued to take anticonvulsant medication that controlled her seizures to a large extent. Physically she was thriving, but emotionally she was sometimes troubled. In her teen years, friendships and peer relations became a stumbling block. Counseling did not help much because, I now believe, psychologists did not yet have much experience with learning-disabled adolescents. In Anne's later school years, she continued in some special education classes. As her visual-perceptual deficits had improved with maturation, she was able to attend some regular classes.

Though I always knew how to help her, in retrospect I believe I should have stayed out of her school learning. I discovered too late that my help set Anne back; she had internalized from my tutoring that she could not learn on her own—a destructive concept that carried over into adulthood. Her learning problems related to reading, writing and counting are all gone. Ever since graduating from high school, she has performed normally in academic areas while still having some trouble perceiving abstract concepts. And much human interaction is responding to abstractions. Nonverbal cues such as head nodding or lack of eye contact at times elude her. Without catching these cues she may react inappropriately. In such instances, communication becomes jagged. This perceptual misconnection is one of the causes of her difficulty in maintaining relationships, even clouding our relationship at times.

Nowadays much more is known about brain functioning, but unfortunately, most of the knowledge is still diagnostic with little that has led to cures. But there is hope! One thing is certain: today, the deficits of children like Anne are picked up in nursery school and treated immediately so that the children do not have to feel the frustration and sense of failure that she experienced.

My leisure time did not last long. One of my neighbors urged me to become involved in the Parent Teacher Association of Anne's school. I became the assistant to the PTA newsletter editor. As I became known in the PTA, parents would stop me to ask why Anne was in the special education class. She looked perfectly normal, and they wondered why she had been removed from the regular program. Very few people understood what learning disabilities were, including the kind principal of the school. This administrator trusted that if one just kept these nice little kids in their own class and wing, all would be fine. Yet, the principal's bias emerged every time trouble erupted. When the fire alarm was activated or a fight broke out, she came looking for the culprit in the special education class.

Her attitude galvanized me into action. I started speaking publicly about learning disabilities, even though I still struggled with the stigma associated with being a parent of a child in special education. Remembering only too well my own pain before I learned to accept Anne as she was, I felt that such advocacy was my calling. After finding allies among the faculty, together we organized lectures for parents about different learners and how parents and classmates could help them.

PTA President

The next year, I became PTA president. I took that office very seriously and became increasingly involved in the Carderock school community. We created a Special Needs Committee in the PTA because most of the parents of the special education students did not feel comfortable in our school. Special education classes were—and generally still are—made up of children from all over the region who thus do not benefit from the advantages of a traditional "neighborhood school" environment. Also, these parents felt ostracized because of the stigma associated with special education. Many parents preferred to hide, feeling embarrassed or ashamed of having a child with special needs.

How well I knew that feeling! The Special Needs Committee gave the parents a place where they felt welcome and where they could discuss their common concerns. After some initial hesitation, when they realized the benefits, the parents of the children in the special class became enthusiastic committee supporters. Together we organized programs to inform the community about the needs of special learners and the issues surrounding special education. To improve the overall climate in the school, we also organized workshops on raising self-esteem and eliminating put-downs. I was thrilled that many teachers saw the relevance of these activities for all children and became active in the committee, although traditionally PTA is a parent organization with little teacher participation.

Special Needs Committee

As PTA president I belonged to MCCPTA, the Montgomery County Council of Parent Teacher Associations of the nearly 200 public schools in the county. The activities of the Carderock PTA came to the attention of other community activists and several administrators of the school system. Montgomery County probably has more citizen involvement in its governing activities than any other place in the world, and the school system had dozens of citizen commissions and committees that advised the school board and the superintendent. Various leaders asked me to join some of these, and I was pleased to have been selected. For example, one committee was drafting educational goals, another was studying whether to change junior high schools into middle schools. I became incredibly busy, going to meetings, drafting position papers, consulting with others and organizing presentations. Assisted by my growing reputation as a forceful advocate, before long I built a wide network for my cause: spreading knowledge about learning disabilities and eliminating the stigma that faced children with handicapping conditions.

Other parents of special education students found out about the Carderock PTA Special Needs Committee and asked me to help them set up their own. Eventually I influenced MCCPTA to create a countywide special needs committee that I would head. MCCPTA had a small budget, something like $600 a year for all its committees. My first year on MCCPTA's board, the new Special Needs Committee developed a budget and requested $300. The Executive Committee collectively gasped when I made the request; they eventually acquiesced when I pointed out that the other committees had not requested any money because they were not very active. I felt no compunction about using chutzpah to request the money, because the cause was good and I was willing to fight to get what we needed. In subsequent years we did not have to defend the budget request. It became a given that Special Needs was the most active committee.

Reconciling motherhood and volunteerism was a constant balancing act. Busy as I was, I made a point of being home every day from 3 p.m. to 6 p.m. When the children were little, I had felt that letting somebody else wipe their noses or change their diapers was all right; but only I, or someone like me, could answer the existential questions that emerged as they became older. And since I could not hire anybody like me, I had to be there when the children got home from school. Additionally, I was interested in their moral development. One of my goals as a mother was to raise children who would not become gullible and fall under the spell of some demagogue. More important to me than their academic achievement, I wanted them to become decent human beings, aware of their privileged setting yet willing to assume a constructive role in the life of the community, not just seeking financial gain. I hoped that my extensive involvement in volunteer activities would demonstrate to them that the individual counts and that "Let Johnny do it!" was not an acceptable attitude. Many discussions about relationships, right and wrong, and might versus right took place the car. Having turned into a part-time chauffeur driving the kids to their various after-school activities, I cheered when Paul got his driver's license.

I was out four nights a week. When I stayed home after dinner, Frank and the children would say, "What's the matter, Mom? How come you don't have to go to another meeting?" They made fun of me, but they were proud of me. Soon I received requests to represent the entire special education program in various countywide activities. Known for being inquisitive, outspoken and assertive, I think I was well-respected. Without making enemies I was able to stand my ground as an advocate. I liked what I was doing better than anything I had ever done before and felt fulfilled by my efforts.

Mother in Bethesda

During that period, Mother, who was now 81 years old and ailing, came to live with us. She had been staying in Felix's apartment in Vienna to safeguard it for him, as the city could have reclaimed it without a family member living there. Felix was able to keep the apartment as long as he did not rent it out. After Mother had a heart attack and could no longer live by herself, Felix put her into an assisted-living facility in Vienna, where she was so unhappy that she refused to eat. When I found that out, I went to see her and urged her to come and live with us. She agreed. I thought that she might have another six to eight months to live. Her health improved once she settled here, and she lived another eight years in our house.

The house was well-suited to her needs because she had the run of the lower floor. Unfortunately, she was not happy here either. She felt as if she were in a golden cage, because without a car she could not leave the neighborhood. Mother could easily have afforded to use a taxi, but she was too tightfisted for that. She missed Vienna, with the stores just downstairs where she could go shopping every day, and her coterie of admiring elderly ladies, whom she regaled with her travel stories. But most significantly, she missed being in charge. She resented living in my house and not in her own.

She had been in control of her life—except for interruptions by Hitler and the war—ever since Father had died in 1932, when she was 39 years old. And although I made all kinds of concessions for her, she still had to conform to our way of life, which was not always her way. Liking her meat marbled, she objected to my almost fat-free cooking. I tried to pick out special cuts for her. Also, our flexible lifestyle, with spur-of-the-moment changes in schedules, irritated her. She hated Frank's casual custom of lying on the living room sofa with his papers scattered on the floor and then leaving the living room without picking them up. I disliked that habit as well but had learned it was easier to pick up the papers than argue about it. While she tried to fit in, having to adapt rankled her and increased her sense of frustration. We included her in our extensive and interesting social life, entertaining Frank's visitors from abroad and like-minded friends whom I met through my volunteer activities, but it was not enough.

Mother got along well with Paul, who said, "Yes, Grannie," to whatever she wanted and then did exactly as he pleased. Anne, on the other hand, argued with her, and the two of them were frequently at loggerheads with me in the middle. Yet they enjoyed playing Scrabble, at which they both excelled. Frank and Mother got along all right, although she objected to his generally nonchalant manner. She was always saying, "How can such an intelligent man be so messy?" He used humor with her that she did not comprehend. I was grateful that he did not question her living with us, even though at times her presence really bothered him. As a defense, he tended to use unwelcome sarcasm against her critical attitude. When we disagreed over some substantial matter concerning Mother, he would say, "Leave me out of it; you'll do it your way anyway!" To some extent that was true, although at times I would have preferred his being more involved in family decisions.

I sensed that I was the one who disappointed Mother the most. She did not agree with the way I dealt with the children, saying I was much too permissive, not insisting on proper manners like certain greetings or removing elbows from the dinner table. Besides not liking my cooking, she resented that I did not have enough "quality" time for her. After a while, she learned to keep her criticism unspoken, but one look at her face told me exactly how she felt. My friend Erika named her "the walking reproach."

Truthfully, we did not get along well enough for me to enjoy being with her. The informality of the way we lived typified the United States, of which she was so critical. She still felt she was living in an uncouth and uncultured county and everything in Europe was better. I heard, however, that when she was in Europe she praised the U.S. to all her friends. While I tried to avoid arguments with her, she wanted me to listen to her complaints. Limiting our time together was a compromise. Most of the time she was basically in good health and was able to care for herself. As her eyes became weaker and reading became too strenuous, we found helpers to read to her. Some of them became her friends and took her out for visits. She also enjoyed listening to talking books. Since her weak eyes did not keep her from typing, she was able to carry on her still voluminous correspondence. When we had guests, she usually was the belle of the ball. They all admired her greatly for her worldly ways and her cultural knowledge. She loved being in the spotlight, but such moments were not enough to ward off depression. I was sad that she felt that her life no longer had any value; Frank and the children and I felt that, in her own way, her presence contributed an extra dimension to our family.

We never had a dull moment at our house. My brothers and their families visited as often as they could. Friends from near and far came to stay with us, attracted partly by Mother's presence or by the proximity to the sights of Washington, D.C. We enjoyed having continual houseguests at Hotel Meissner. At one point my brother Felix's daughter Ibi spent a school year here, followed by her brother Tito. Mother delighted in them, as they were European children with good European manners. Both were very sweet young people whom I happily introduced to the United States. The extra work did not bother me.

What I did resent was Mother's discontent, although I knew she could not help feeling it. She felt guilty because she knew she should be grateful that she had almost everything that she could want and still was not satisfied. Often I was quite despondent because I wanted her to feel comfortable. Yet I was not willing to give her much of what she craved the most: my attention. Maybe she also wanted me to be more openly affectionate, but the relationship between us had never been that way so we both found it hard to change.

Although I often tried to explain it to her, Mother never grasped how important my volunteer work was to me. Throughout my many and diverse volunteer activities, starting in Palo Alto, I had attempted tasks that I would never have dared to undertake if I had been paid for my time. I would have felt that I had insufficient training or experience for the job. But as a volunteer I could try out the assignment. If the organizers felt that I did not measure up, they could easily tell me that they no longer needed me. No hard feelings. Yet, in fact, every one of these volunteer activities prepared me for the next one so that eventually I would feel sufficiently competent to accept a paid position. In addition, I was proud to contribute my ideas and some of myself to my community. I welcomed being able to energize others and be a model for my children. These activities were major building blocks in my life.

Working in MCPS

One day shortly after Mother had settled in at our house, I received an unexpected call from an administrator in the Montgomery County Public School system who knew me as a volunteer on a special education planning task force. He wanted to know whether I would be interested in a job with MCPS. A new, liberal superintendent had recently initiated a study of the special and alternative education programs with a view toward reorganizing them, and the administrator in charge of the study was asking me to be the community voice on this study. He said that I had shown myself as being assertive but not aggressive, meaning that I could make my points effectively without offending people with different points of view. The job would entail working three hours a day for three months at six dollars per hour. I hesitated, fearing that I was not qualified. First I called Frank, who predictably said, "You know more about this than all the professionals. If they want to pay you, take it." I told Mother of the job offer, knowing she would not be overjoyed. My being gone from home more frequently meant that she would be home alone more often. I pacified her somewhat by saying I would be working for only three months.

The children were no longer as dependent on me as before. Paul had graduated from high school the year before. He had been so fed up with school, tired of sitting in a classroom all day, that he managed to obtain permission to graduate after three years instead of the customary four. Before going on to college, he went abroad for a year. For the first few months he lived on a kibbutz in Israel, then he spent the winter in the French part of Switzerland skiing and learning more French, and finally he stayed a few months in Felix's apartment in Vienna learning more German. Anne was in high school by then. I only had to drive her to school in the morning. I thought I could manage a job for three hours a day for three months. As it turned out, I stayed for 18 years.

As I began working on this comprehensive analysis of the existing programs for children with various special needs, I felt intimidated because my colleagues were highly credentialed and very experienced. Still apprehensive about my own competence, I soon found out that Frank was right. Indeed, I brought a different perspective to the study because I represented the children. The professionals always thought to protect their professional groups. Every time a suggestion came up, they would speculate how the recommendation would affect them, whereas I would ask, "And how will it affect the kids?" Embarrassed silence frequently followed. I became very bold, not caring whether I was popular or if they fired me. Fortunately not dependent on the salary, I became a significant member of the study team.

Continuum Education

In the end, by happenstance, Elaine Lessenco—another low-level colleague—and I ended up presenting the study results to the Board of Education. Controversial as our findings were, the school board adopted the recommendations of the "Continuum Education" report and set about reorganizing special and alternative education. The "Continuum" in the title was meant to indicate that the recommendations would improve educational outcomes for all children along a continuum from the slowest to the fastest learners. The new organization had the potential for leaving no child behind. Unfortunately, soon thereafter a reactionary school board majority was elected that dismissed the superintendent, reversed many of his innovations and largely declined to follow our recommendations. Interestingly, because MCPS has little institutional memory, a reorganization begun 25 years later recommended many similar approaches to improving the school system. Another case of *déjà vu!*

When I started working for MCPS, Frank was extremely helpful to me. Though frequently traveling on IDB missions and immersed in his position as agricultural marketing specialist in Latin America, he took me on as an apprentice author of official reports and position papers. Willing to critique my drafts, he did so savagely sometimes, but always constructively. To satisfy him, I had to know exactly what I wanted to say so that I could communicate my ideas clearly and concisely. In addition, he urged me to focus on the average reader and eliminate jargon. Without his help I might not have learned to write professionally. Eventually, even though I was the only non-native American in my office, I became the chief editor of all important reports.

The superintendent who had requested the study appointed an administrator to head the new office. The new leader asked me to stay on to write the policies and procedures for the new office, as well as job descriptions for newly created positions. We were now responsible for supplementary services for all children who needed more than what the regular program offered. In addition to special education for handicapped students, included were the Head Start and Title One programs for economically disadvantaged children as well as the instruction in English for Speakers of Other Languages. These programs together affected some 20 percent of the school population. Soon I became sufficiently confident in my ability to carry out the assignment, but I still wanted Frank to look over my final copy.

Special and Alternative Education

The three months of the study had long since elapsed. Mother had found that she could get along all right without me because we had managed to find people to come in and read to her, take her out or just keep her company. My new boss, whose job description I had written, depended on me to assist him in making the organization work. I was now working full time with a decent salary, although I had no contract. I did not mind. Thrilled with what I was doing, I brought enormous energy to the task. If I had gone through the normal personnel channels in MCPS to apply for my position, I would never have been hired. With no academic credentials, my application would not have made it past the screener in the personnel department.

In addition to developing policies and procedures for the special and alternative education program, I frequently represented MCPS in efforts of other agencies concerned with vulnerable children. I staffed the school system's mental health advisory committee and served on the countywide commission to prevent teenage births. When the state of Maryland first mandated that school personnel report child-abuse suspicions to the police, my task was to write the appropriate procedures; together with the appropriate county agencies, I helped develop staff training programs so that workers would know how and when to report concern.

As though I needed another challenge, the Maryland State Department of Education asked me to write and record on videotape a segment in a series on educating teenagers with disabilities. I had never considered going before the cameras, but the idea appealed to me. For many weeks I trudged bravely for the taping to the Maryland Public Television station that disseminated the program nationwide to special educators.

Master's Degree

Because my employment situation was so odd, my boss suggested that I get some credentials. I located a master's degree program in special education offered in collaboration with MCPS at Trinity College in Washington that seemed the right program for me. I had to con my way into this program because I had neither a high school diploma nor a bachelor's degree. But as my application came highly recommended by my supervisors, Trinity admitted me conditionally. After the first year, when I had proved that I was up to the task, Trinity admitted me fully. My supervisor gave me special permission to study and continue working part time. As a reward for working what seemed like 24 hours a day, I graduated with all A's. My master's thesis on teaching career education to children with emotional and learning disabilities was directly related to my work, so integrating study with work responsibilities was not difficult.

More difficult was finding time for family activities. I put everything on hold except the absolute minimum, just as I had in Buenos Aires when I started to teach. At the time I entered college, Paul had just graduated from the University of Maryland, where he had been the manager of the lacrosse team.

Paul and Anne After High School

Not sure what to do next and speculating that he might be interested in becoming a sports journalist, Paul found a number of related jobs, ending up as assistant to the head of the sports department at Virginia Commonwealth University. Not really fulfilled by what he was doing, he cast around for other opportunities and eventually applied to the Peace Corps. The application process was lengthy and arduous, including several tests and interviews. At first, the Peace Corps had no openings and Paul had to wait.

Anne also went on to college. After graduating from high school, she left for Providence, Rhode Island, to attend the well-regarded Johnson & Wales Culinary Institute. After two years at the institute, she followed in Paul's footsteps and went to the same kibbutz where he had lived in Israel. Originally thinking she might remain in Israel, she began to attend an ulpan, the intensive Hebrew course that Israel offers to all immigrants. But after a few months of intensive living, she was eager to come back home. Fortunately, by that time her seizures were well-controlled so that she was able to obtain a driver's license. She then worked for a couple of years as office assistant in the Center of Unique Learners, which offered tutoring and counseling for learning-disabled youngsters. In addition to volunteering in a senior center, she held several food service jobs. For a while she became interested in photography, but nothing really caught her fancy. When a friend of ours came to visit and invited Anne to return to Ecuador with her, Anne eagerly accepted the initiation. Our friend divided her time between her farm outside of Quito and her Center for the Development of the Individual. With nearly perfect Spanish, building on her stay in Argentina and our speaking Spanish at home with the Culver family, Anne learned about the cultivation of avocados and bananas as well as meditation.

She came home after half a year and moved into our small apartment in downtown Washington that we had been renting out. There she became an expert crossword-puzzle solver and an avid follower of the daily news. As I was attempting to organize my snapshots, her excellent memory frequently helped me identify people and place events in their proper time frame. Her wide-ranging interests in the culinary arts and pottery demonstrated that she had a real talent in both fields.

More Challenges

After completing my master's degree in 1982, at age sixty, I was looking forward to a slightly less demanding work schedule when Montgomery College staff approached me about teaching a course on learning disabilities for teachers. I could not refuse this offer, because I still found that many teachers were unaware of the type of perceptual handicaps from which Anne had suffered. After a couple of years the preparation for the course became too demanding, and I was glad to find among my former students a teacher who was willing to take over my teaching load.

Keeping up with federal initiatives for the education of children with special needs, I was very pleased when in the mid-1980s the federal government established a new grant program to improve the transition from school to work for students with disabilities. The initiative addressed the same issues I had focused on in my master's thesis. Since the U.S. Constitution leaves the power over education policy to the states, the only way the federal government can legally promote education initiatives is by offering grants to educators who are willing to try new approaches. The new grant program was basically the extension of Public Law 94-142, the Education of All Handicapped Children Act of 1975. The implementation of that law had been my first major assignment in MCPS.

Transition from School to Work

Committed to the fulfillment of 1975 law, I was eager to obtain the newly announced federal grant for MCPS. As an advocate, and now a professional, I knew that the tremendous cost of special education was a much-debated political issue, both locally and nationally. Many taxpayers believed the expense was not justified if the schools could do no better for special education students than graduate them to the TV set in their living rooms. I shared that view. I was convinced that public education owed the students more effective preparation for work while they were still in school.

I did not get much support from my boss for applying for that grant; he did not want me to add anything to my already overloaded schedule but I was adamant about seizing the opportunity. When my boss's boss, the superintendent of schools, finally gave me the go-ahead, he said, "Margit, we should do it. It makes sense. And if we don't get funded, we'll do it anyway. We'll find money on our own." I was thrilled. With the help of community advocates, I wrote the grant proposal. Learning the specifically prescribed intricacies required by the federal regulations, a novel experience for me, proved most enlightening.

Before I started writing the proposal, the Montgomery County Government staff inquired whether they could collaborate on the grant with the school system. The county wanted to improve its record in the employment of people with disabilities. But proposal guidelines did not permit such collaboration. Searching for the required endorsements for the grant proposal, I found business and industry people who also were interested in a better-prepared work force. By now adept at building coalitions, I came to know state and county agencies that worked with adults with disabilities and became acquainted with wider employment and work-force issues. Another new world! I again worked night and day and loved it.

The grant proposal outlined new programs for students, teaching them work ethics and work skills in school, as well as arranging for internships in community work sites, supervised by their teachers. These innovations meant developing new curricula in living and self-advocacy skills and the corresponding training for teachers. What an exciting prospect! After submitting the proposal, we had to endure the customary long wait to hear whether we would be funded.

We did not wait. Before learning whether we would win the grant—we did not—my boss agreed to let me start laying the groundwork for the implementation of these activities. While writing the proposal, I had acquired valuable allies who facilitated our progress. Eventually the school system created the new Transition Unit, and I became its head.

TransCen

As we were establishing the MCPS program, we continued discussions with the county government staff members who had been so eager to participate. We suggested that they help create an independent, private non-profit agency that would coordinate all the players involved in the school-to-work transition process: the school system; the post-secondary education system; the adult service system, which included the Division of Vocational Rehabilitation; the county's health and human services system; employers; employment services; and, of course, the parents and families of the students. All these players had to collaborate in a synchronized fashion to ensure that the students would enter the world of work successfully. In 1985 with initial funding from the county government, TransCen—the coordinating agency—was born. Today, TransCen is a nationally recognized and highly valued leader in the field of employment of people with disabilities. Thousands of such people are in the work force today as a result of TransCen's activities; and thousands of employers have learned how to hire, employ and support those with disabilities in a businesslike and profitable manner. TransCen has influenced the whole school-to-work initiative of the federal government. I consider the creation of TransCen the most significant accomplishment in my career, and I am very proud of having been influential in its success.

Shortly after TransCen was up and running, the Marriott family became interested in issues concerning employment of people with disabilities. For six months I consulted with Marriott staff on developing the Bridges to Work initiative. Once the program was ready, the Marriott family created a family foundation and designated Bridges to Work the recipient of its national giving program. Bridges still provides internships in local businesses for students with disabilities during their last year in school. School and employer staff collaborated on making the internship successful for both intern and employer. The MCPS–Marriott–TransCen partnership lasted for many successful years.

Although we had a mandate to prepare all students with disabilities effectively for work, we still had to overcome significant obstacles. Not everyone in the school system or the community was convinced that the school system should be responsible for transition training. These critics feared that the new initiative would siphon funds from other programs they considered more important. Principals had to free up teachers for training; the MCPS transportation department had to change some bus routes and train new bus aides; and teachers had to learn how to teach students on the job site or in the community instead of the classroom. Helpful community support was essential before we could induce individuals and agencies to collaborate with us. Among the major barriers were the prejudice and the fear born of ignorance about disabilities that prevailed among the population. It was not easy to change these lifelong attitudes. But even if we could not change people's thinking, we could ask them to change their behavior.

So that students in wheelchairs could ride the bus to work, the county transportation programs began to provide wheelchair access to buses. With more people with disabilities working in public places, we helped the Police Department train police officers. They were glad to learn to recognize symptoms of mental retardation and to respond appropriately when the need arose. They became aware that some people might not be able to understand the policeman's questions and therefore not answer immediately or appropriately. For a long time we had to battle our own MCPS personnel department because it was reluctant to hire our well-prepared graduates until a new assistant took on the hiring responsibility.

I had learned thirty years earlier in the Office of War Information that if you were willing to assume responsibility, higher-ups would grant you authority. And I was interested in being in a position of authority, since I liked holding the strings in my hand and orchestrating the activities.

In my new position I attended many workshops, mainly as a learner but also as a presenter at conferences around the country. Frank frequently joined me when I spoke. He was proud to be introduced as "Margit's husband." I became well-known in special education circles; the state of Maryland and even the federal Department of Education frequently asked me to consult. I thought I had the best job in the world and I loved every minute of it. I was paid for what I would gladly have done for free. No money under the sun could match the pleasure I got from my activities.

During all this time, I never wavered in my aim: Every graduate from an MCPS special education program would be well-prepared for employment and would have learned to plan for the future. I am happy to say that when I last checked, that vision was close to becoming reality.

Impact on the Family

Re-reading what I just wrote about my commitment to work and my many simultaneous projects, I am beginning to understand why Anne felt neglected. She now says that nobody had enough time for her when she was a child, which was probably true. That was also Mother's well-founded complaint for herself. Both wanted me around more. With the children I was primarily interested in their learning, but I was not always sufficiently tuned in to their emotional needs. Children, some say, also have great spiritual needs. As I probably have not much of a spiritual side, I may not have been able to respond to such needs. Paul would likely say that his parents concentrated on the intellectual, that learning was uppermost on their minds and that he was satisfied with this kind of family life. He seemed strong enough to thrive under our stewardship. Anne was not, and I did not pick up on what she was missing. She also feels that Frank was remote, that he did not show his feelings enough and was not sufficiently available to her as a father. Yet I always thought that Frank was much more giving than I. He did not press them about academic achievement in school, whereas I wanted both children to do as well as they could. With disappointment, Anne says that her father was willing to pay for her wishes—such as travel—to make up for his lack of emotional involvement. While I did not see Frank's treatment of Anne that way, her perceptions became her truth.

She sought approval from both of us and felt any criticism keenly. Having been wired as a different learner either by birth or as an effect of convulsions, she has needed more understanding than she received about the considerable amount of disability she has overcome. As a family we were loyal to each other, with unspoken love underlying the relationship. We were not a demonstrative family. With the greatest sorrow, I regret that I was not able to give Anne enough of the kind of loving support that she remembers needing in her youth.

We are still working out a somewhat bumpy adult relationship. I am glad that we share approaches to politics and react similarly to world events. Most important, beneath all the conflict we know that we can rely on each other when the need arises. I recognize that both of us ought to try harder to manage our conflicts more creatively as they emerge and not allow vexing issues to fester. Together, we have been through many significant moments in our lives.

Frank and I also did not have much time together, but we were comfortable with the stimulating way our lives were going. From the very beginning we had built our marriage on the basis that each one of us had our own life, of which the other shared a piece.

Frank's Interests

Frank was greatly involved in his work and his other interests. A frustrated journalist, he submitted many articles on agricultural and agriculture economics topics to professional as well as lay publications, most of which were glad to publish them. An avid reader with a fertile and creative mind, he wrote a review of every book he ever read. He converted his considerable knowledge of Central European history into articles for journals such as the *Jewish Genealogical Review*. He also wrote papers and presented them at various conferences, such as the Czech Society of Art and Sciences. One of his special interests was the growth of the state of Israel and the development aid Israel provided to other developing nations. With a missionary zeal about his field of work, Frank believed that the world produces enough food to feel its entire people. He wanted to fix the faulty distribution and marketing system that he considered to be a major cause of world hunger. He co-wrote two books on food marketing and contributed many articles to marketing publications. Frequently, he acted as judge of manuscripts submitted by other authors.

Frank was happiest when surrounded by paper: books to read and paper to write on. The one place in our house where he was absolutely king was his study. We had the most serious row of our marriage when I tried to clean it up while he was away. I had never seen him so angry before. Thereafter, I never tried to tidy up again. Miraculously, however, if one asked him for a certain reference, he was always able to fish it out from the piles of accumulated papers; whereas I had an excellent filing system and no retrieval ability whatsoever!

As my career was evolving, so was Frank's. His colleagues at the Inter-American Development Bank and others with whom he worked held him in high regard. They recognized him as a well-intentioned, effective iconoclast whose optimism was infectious. He was impatient with colleagues who dwelt only on problems instead of seeking solutions. Well-known for his humorous approach to problem solving, he believed in the power of positive thinking.

We liked traveling. In the beginning, Mother was able to spend summers in Aussee or Spain with Felix and his family, freeing Frank and me to travel by ourselves while the children were at camp. Later we had to make arrangements to have someone look after Mother while we were gone. We went to the Soviet Union and Outer Mongolia, then to South Africa and Kenya and many other places in Europe. Frank was a wonderful travel guide. Tremendously interested in all our destinations, his fascinating comments enriched our travels. Sometimes my brother Paul would join us, adding a special interest to our trips. Paul had established his own unique lifestyle, dividing his time between Australia, Vienna and Israel, and playing in bridge tournaments around the globe. We tried to catch up with each other wherever possible.

Mother's Death

We were home when Mother died in her sleep on February 1, 1981. She was 87 years old and tired of living. The night before she died, Paul had received word that he had been accepted into the Peace Corps. We went out for a quick dinner to celebrate, but Mother did not feel well enough to join us. She had a heart condition that fortunately did not cause her pain. Because I was not comfortable with the way she had looked when I went to sleep, I checked on her early that Sunday morning and found her dead in her bed. I kissed her and sat by her side awhile to say goodbye to her before calling the family. I was sad, but a feeling of relief overshadowed my grief. As she had wished, she had been able to die at home without any of the medical interventions she had dreaded and that I had promised to avoid. She had wanted relief from the burden of living and often said to me, "If you were really a good daughter, you would help me die." Though knowing she meant it, I could not carry out her wish.

I called Paul in Australia, Felix in Spain and Bruno in Canada to let them know. Since Mother had wanted no funeral and no memorial service, they did not need to come. She had made arrangements to donate her body to the anatomy department of the Georgetown University Hospital. Two hours after I found her dead, her body was gone. Frank, Paul, age 22, and Anne, age 20, were with me when the hospital men arrived with a gurney to pick up her body.

The family and I sat and talked about Grannie and wondered how we could inform her many friends around the globe of her death. She had traveled around the world three times by herself so that she could act as baby nurse to her grandchildren in Australia, Canada, Spain and the United States. She knew people from visiting us in Argentina, and her best friend in South Africa. On each of these trips, she made friends with whom she kept up a voluminous correspondence.

In view of the many time zones involved, we decided to light a candle in her memory at 3 p.m. Eastern Standard Time on Sunday, March 1, 1981. We sent out a hundred notices around the world so that those who wanted to remember her could join us in honoring her memory at the same time, a comforting thought. The woman who was Grilly to her Australian grandchildren, Grandma to the Spaniards and Grannie to the North Americans— the lady who was born Lilly Tritsch in Vienna, had become Lilly Morawetz in Prague and then the anglicized Lilly Morand in the United States in 1941—would be remembered simultaneously in many different places.

Our local friends felt the need to say goodbye and celebrate her life. Our son Paul, who was close to Grannie, thought she would have been happy with our planting trees in her honor. In early May we invited her friends and admirers to our garden to a party in her memory. A lovely occasion, the sun shone brightly; the sky was a cloudless blue, the azaleas were in full bloom and dozens of friends stood watching Frank plant the trees. Many spoke about her keen mind, which explored lively interests to the end. They mentioned her typical battery of intelligent, searching questions on subjects dear to her visitor so that she could become better informed. Our friends remembered her as the unceasing learner who read books on tape because of her failing eyesight; they knew that she looked up and noted on a little pad on her night table every word she did not know. Others marveled at the energy she had and how at age eighty she still dove into the swimming pool head first. What a woman she was!

While Felix decided to remember her from his home in Spain, Paul and Bruno came for the event. The three of us stood together, each one thinking of the influence Mother had had on us and acknowledging the strong family ties that she had engendered in her offspring across the oceans. When I spoke, I recognized more fully how much she had influenced me throughout my life, how many of my characteristics were similar to hers, both positive and negative.

Mother continues to be a vital presence in my life. Almost daily, I imagine her coming up the stairs in our house. I hear her various dicta still embedded in my consciousness. Even at age eighty, I have not quite resolved my feelings about our relationship.

14

FRANK'S LAST YEARS AND DEATH

THE YEARS BEFORE Frank's illness were good years for us. Paul returned from three years in Ecuador. He had spent two years in the Peace Corps helping villagers in remote areas build wells and sanitary installations and one year working for CARE in the Ecuadorian province of Loja establishing water supply systems.

Before returning to the States, Paul—by now no stranger to riding on local buses along with *campesinos* taking their animals and other wares to market—took himself with a knapsack on a grand tour of Latin America. In addition to teaching him a great deal about water supply issues and about his own ability to endure primitive living conditions, the Peace Corps experience led him to a mission in life. Paul was going to study public health administration and improve sanitation in the developing world.

Enrolled in a master's degree program in public health administration at the University of North Carolina in Chapel Hill, he met Jennifer Ringstad, recently returned from two years in the Peace Corps. Jennifer had spent her stint in Northern Thailand in a malaria control program and was now studying medicine in Chapel Hill. She shared Paul's commitment to improving health care and sanitation in the Third Word. While they were studying, they had to content themselves with being advocates, joining student groups that railed against U.S. support for repressive governments in Central America.

Meanwhile, Anne, settled in her cozy apartment near Dupont Circle, had taken up pottery at a pottery studio at Eastern Market in downtown Washington. She was making colorfully glazed, interestingly shaped bowls and mugs that we all admired. Very generously, she shared her creations with family and friends, who to this day remark that they still use Anne's deep blue mugs daily. Anne also became the purveyor of pretty crocheted baby blankets, eliminating the perennial puzzle of what kind of present to give to a newborn. After attending the culinary school in Rhode Island and spending several summers working in Uncle Felix's Snoopy bar on Ibiza, where she served simple foods, Anne had become an excellent cook and baker. Her chocolate chip cookies are renowned, requested by all children when they visit.

Bruno

We took the cookies along on our frequent Christmas holiday trips to Bruno and his family in Peterborough, Ontario, where he had bought a farm. After getting his degree in philosophy from the University of Toronto, Bruno had become a lecturer there but did not feel fulfilled in that position. Over the years, with much labor, determination and enthusiasm, he had turned Camp Ponacka into one of the most desirable summer camps for boys in Canada. After a few years at the university and with a family of four children, Bruno decided to leave Toronto and lead a simpler life on the farm. He loved the farm, but it was too small to support the family. Finances were tight for many years because the camp did not make much money either. His wife, Gwen, had become a librarian, and when the children were older she worked full time as librarian in a prestigious private boys' school. In addition to farming, Bruno started a great-books group and lectured on existential topics at various venues around Ontario.

Bruno was enamored of the theater. He volunteered in the local amateur theater as prop hand, stage manager, even actor and singer. When we visited, we could hear him sing "Hello, Dolly" with great gusto in the shower. Eventually, when the camp started producing a reasonable income, Bruno and Gwen were able to travel more. We visited back and forth frequently, especially as long as Mother was alive.

Felix

Felix, now the father of two sons and a daughter, also had come to visit Mother quite often, although he disliked leaving his beloved island. After so many years in the countryside, he found big cities in America perplexing, especially the department stores with so much bewildering choice. He did, however, remain faithful to his boyhood pastime of tinkering; he could spend hours here in hardware stores, marveling at the selection of gadgets he had never seen before. As when he was a boy, he still bought them.

When we had visited Felix and family on our way to Argentina, we had admired Can Bufi, the grandiose home he had built for the family from a small shack in Santa Eulalia, a small town on Ibiza. Felix had acquired several other properties, including a hilltop restaurant run by a Belgian chef and a small kiosk-like bar/restaurant in town that the family ran. That was where Anne spent summers, working alongside her Aunt Friedl and cousins Ibi and Tito, learning to make the Viennese potato salad that the mainly German tourists liked.

At that time, Ibiza had become the choice destination for many of Europe's hippies. They all seemed to find Felix, who was always willing to listen to their tales of woe and counsel them on how to live on Ibiza with no money and without going to jail.

Much to Felix's dismay, Ibiza did not remain the idyllic island he had found so attractive. With the tourist boom in Spain, investors started building large hotels and high-rise apartment houses, spoiling the vistas and the scenery. One day a British travel agent approached Felix, asking him whether he would consider renting his property to a British association of homosexuals who were seeking a restful recreation home. Felix agreed and moved his family into a smaller house he owned in the village. Thus Can Bufi was featured for a while in many Spanish vacation catalogues until the AIDS epidemic interfered with travel and the British travel agency could no longer afford to rent it.

Not wanting to move back into the big house, Felix tried to turn Can Bufi into a hotel, but it was not large enough to be profitable; the house could provide some income if the family were to perform the labor associated with running a family *pension*. That worked for a while until his now-grown children wanted to leave.

Felix had bought several pieces of real estate and was trying to make money selling them, but many deals fell through. Spain was different now. Before Spain joined the European Community, tax collection was lax and good connections could overcome bureaucratic impediments. Spain's entry into the EU changed all that, and Felix found it hard to adjust to the new conditions.

Felix's Death

Furthermore, Felix's health had deteriorated. He had a heart condition but was adamantly opposed to the bypass surgery that could have saved his life. In Vienna, where he went to escape the summer heat of Ibiza, the doctors could not persuade him to agree to the surgery. When I visited him there in the fall of 1985, he knew he had not long to live. He told me that having reached age seventy, he had lived long enough and did not want to interfere with the natural course of things. Also, he was discouraged because life on Ibiza had become economically very difficult and he no longer wanted to struggle. He died in Vienna on October 28, 1985.

Frank's Final Illness

Just about a year later, during Frank's mandatory medical checkup in September 1986, the doctor found a suspicious mole on his back. As usual, Frank did not mention to me that she had suggested he see a dermatologist. A few weeks later he told me that a dermatologist had removed a mole on his back and sent the tissue to pathology. The diagnosis came back as malignant melanoma. The seriousness of the diagnosis did not sink in with either one of us. I knew that melanoma could be cured if it was caught early enough and had not penetrated too deeply. When Frank postponed the recommended surgery to go on a planned bank mission, I did not think the delay was wise, but he was his own man. One of the doctors had said that a few weeks would not make any difference, a pronouncement that we did not verify and that fitted our ignorant state of mind. Certainly cancer was not anything that could happen to us! Frank was not eager to talk about the diagnosis except to the children and did not want anybody to know. We were in exquisite denial.

When the surgery finally took place in December 1986, the melanoma was already two centimeters deep. That was the first time that the awfulness of it all sank in. The surgery was painful and on top of it, Frank had to have unrelated prostate surgery the next day. During tests for the prostate surgery, doctors found spots on his lungs that they were going to monitor. At first they suggested no therapy. Frank recovered rather readily from both surgeries, but nobody was willing to give us a prognosis. They said that people in his condition could live three months or six months or three years or six years. Outwardly at least, Frank disregarded the dire prognosis and carried on as usual. The sword of Damocles was hanging over our heads, but we managed to ignore it.

The next checkup a few weeks later showed that the spots on the lungs had increased imperceptibly, and the doctors now advised chemotherapy. Frank tolerated the chemotherapy without major side effects, going after work to the hospital, where I joined him for supper. Overnight the nurses connected him to the intravenous infusion, and in the morning he went back to work. An unspoken and denied sense of doom penetrated our lives, but on the surface nothing changed. We entertained, we worked and we traveled as before.

In the spring of 1988 Frank had what seemed to be a heart attack. Paul and Jennifer, who happened to be here to prepare for their wedding, rushed him to the hospital. While Frank had not had a heart attack, the doctors could not diagnose what he had had. He was desperately ill for a few days with a high fever and in great pain. I stopped work and stayed at the hospital most of the day, going home at night. Seeing how he suffered was ghastly; he could not breathe and all I could do was watch helplessly. The doctors gave him morphine to sedate him but offered no explanations or other therapy. Panicked, I thought he was dying.

I remember driving home from the hospital in tears, scared and despondent. During these desperate days I started coming to terms with Frank's dying. I tried to analyze why I was in such a panic. I knew that I could manage on my own; God knows, I had been alone often enough during Frank's many absences, taking care of the necessities of life by myself. I also knew I would not be destitute. Because the doctors could keep Frank comfortable, I no longer had to fear his suffering. In these lucid moments when I was not crying, I realized that the panic I was feeling was not justified rationally but that I was starting to sense a tremendous loss. I dreaded losing the wonderful life we had together, of uncoupling the unit, of tearing apart the bond. An overwhelming feeling of sadness remained that is still with me today. Time has mellowed the pain, but it is still very much a part of my life.

Without ascertaining the cause of his illness, the doctors pumped Frank full of drugs and sent him home after about a week, very weak and tired. His recovery took a long time.

At the time of this hospitalization Frank was six months away from mandatory retirement from the IDB at age 65. The chief of personnel at the IDB, whom I knew well, suggested to me that Frank retire right away because I would be better off financially if he retired before he died. Frank was too ill to contemplate options. Tough as it was, I took it upon myself to make the recommended decision. Tougher still for me was to tell him what I had done a few days later. I knew what a blow retirement would be for him. Fortunately, he took the decision in good spirits. He had a special attitude toward his own death. Frank kept saying that he would, of course, like to live longer but was not upset if he had to die now. He had had a wonderful life, fifty years longer than his brother, who had died in the Holocaust, and he had a lot to be grateful for. He really meant all that.

After Frank recovered from this scary episode, he finalized his retirement. Though he was now getting very tiring radiation treatments, he still managed to work for the bank as a consultant. Also as a consultant, he joined a mission of the Food and Agricultural Organization of the United Nations that involved travel to the Dominican Republic and to Rome. I took vacation time and went along. We enjoyed the trips and treasured our togetherness. The IDB then commissioned him to write a book about its agricultural lending history. He was delighted with this project and tackled it with his customary zeal.

We celebrated Paul and Jennifer's wedding in North Carolina in June 1988, and their daughter Lynn Emily's birth in July 1989. While visiting them in Chapel Hill, Frank had a convulsion, a sign that the cancer had spread to the brain. We knew that that was the beginning of his end. In our frequent discussions about death, he again insisted that he wanted no life-prolonging measures, although he was looking forward to many still unrealized projects.

Sometimes I was angry with him for having cancer. How could he do that to me? At times, when I became frantic, I reminded myself of my earlier internal conversations when I determined that I had nothing to fear about the future. The fear then always melted into pervasive sadness.

During his last months, Frank worked feverishly on his book. This effort seemed to keep him alive. Suffering from neuropathy, a byproduct of the chemotherapy, he had trouble holding a pen, and numbness in his toe kept him from walking properly. Undeterred, he kept writing his book on yellow pads in a hand that was now almost illegible. Luckily, his devoted secretary was able to decipher his scrawl.

The day after he turned in the first draft of the book, *Seeds of Peace*, he fell into a coma. A week later, on January 19, 1990, he died peacefully at home with the help of the hospice and with all of us around him. I had never been present at somebody's death. I was grateful that we were at home, where his friends had come to say goodbye and where we felt none of the atmosphere of doom typical of a hospital ward. The children and I were relieved at how peacefully he passed away. Six-month-old Lynn diverted our attention from dying to living. According to Frank's wishes, his body was cremated and we planned no funeral.

His colleagues at the IDB held a memorial service. Many of them talked with great affection about this freethinker who was so passionate about solving the world's huger problems. They recognized that Frank's legendary energy and optimism had led to a series of successes in improving the lives of the people of Latin America through better food distribution. They acknowledged his rare ability to look at failures as opportunities for learning, stressing that he was never too jaded to stop trying to fix problems. Witnessing the outpouring of appreciation and affection was heartwarming for us. A couple of years later, the IDB published and the Johns Hopkins Press distributed bound copies of *Seeds of Change*. I was immensely sad that he was not able to be present at the unveiling of his most cherished project.

A few months after his death, the children and I held another memorial get-together at our house for our friends who felt that they needed this last rite. Some reminded us of Frank's jokes and his ability to monopolize a dinner party conversation with his stories. Others commented that those who did not know Frank well might have thought of him as shy and retiring; he was able to be quiet all evening if he felt he had nothing to contribute. They all agreed that he was a unique person one would never forget. That is how I felt about Frank. I did not need to say goodbye to him in a formal way. Comforting memories of Frank continue to be part of my life.

15

ANOTHER BEGINNING

I WENT BACK TO work a couple of days after Frank died. The children and Ibi and Ramon, her husband-to-be, had come to be with us when Frank was dying. Now they had left and I knew that returning to work would be the best therapy for me. The distraction made it easier to stop thinking of the loss. I was fortunate that Beatriz was in the house and I did not come home to an empty house every evening.

Beatriz

Beatriz was a young woman from Argentina who came to live with us two days before Frank died. Several months earlier, Edilbes's daughter Patricia had asked us to help her friend get a job in Washington. With little forethought, Beatriz had arrived in the United States without money and without a work visa. When Patricia came to Washington to introduce her to us, we liked Beatriz and agreed to help her. She was hoping to become a bilingual secretary in one of the international organizations where she would not need a work visa. We had expected her back much earlier. She finally arrived at a most difficult moment. However, she was very helpful during these last days before Frank died. She graciously helped host Frank's Latino friends who came to say goodbye to him. After his death I was glad to have her in the house. Her situation was complicated, and I used a good bit of energy helping her. She did not have the necessary clerical skills to become a secretary, and after a number of attempts she finally found other work. She lived with me for more than two years as a member of the family. We got along well and she was very thankful for my help. In turn I was grateful to her for smoothing my transition to living alone.

When her father became ill in Argentina, she returned home to take care of him. To ease the homecoming financially, she took Frank's car along, having convinced me that she could sell it for twice as much as I could sell it for here. The profitable sale of the car proved an illusion and caused much wrangling and heartache for both of us. Fortunately, the rest of her life is turning out well. She is now happily married in Buenos Aires and has a good job in an Argentine public relations outfit. She remains a member of our family.

Aside from my pervasive sadness at having lost Frank, I adapted to single life surprisingly easily. My friends loyally included me in their social activities as before. That love and intimacy would no longer be part of my life I accepted without too much grumbling. Sometimes I hungered for a hug but overcame the absence of it, knowing that I had had my share.

More Travels

Shortly after Frank died, my friend Uli in London invited me to spend a couple of weeks with her in Grundlsee, near Alt Aussee, where she had rented a house. Uli and I had been friends ever since we had met in Alt Aussee in 1936. We had stayed in touch throughout the years and visited back and forth frequently. Her English actor husband had died several years before Frank, and Frank and I had comforted her during that difficult moment in London. I was very fond of Uli and was happy to accept her invitation.

In Grundlsee we realized that we would make excellent travel companions. Different as we were from each other, we were compatible and able to adapt to each other's idiosyncrasies easily. We were both energetic, eager to see new places and learn about different cultures. Ready to travel as vagabonds, we refrained from too much prearrangement. Sometimes my brother Paul or Bruno and his wife or Uli's friends joined us. Between 1991 and 1996 we took many adventurous trips together, several in France and Italy as well as Austria, Scotland, Czechoslovakia and Turkey. We always rented a car and followed our mood, laden with guidebooks and maps, accepting the mishaps that inevitably accompanied this kind of unstructured travel. We might end up in an unsavory hotel or on a narrow, curvy one-way road without exit in Italy. Backing down the road, I swore I would never again rent a car in Italy. We enjoyed sharing impressions of the out-of-the-way places we often discovered. Sadly, Uli passed away quite unexpectedly in 2000, after only a brief illness. Her death is a great loss for me.

I also traveled quite a lot on my own. After meeting Czech educators at an international education conference in Washington, the Prague school board invited me to lecture in Czech about the education of children with handicaps. Proud to be invited, I accepted without hesitation. I should have known that my Czech was not good enough to lecture about a topic I had neither researched nor heard discussed in Czech. Instead of being fun, the experience was traumatic. Luckily, many in the audience knew English and helped me as I struggled to find the right expressions.

Because of my interest in how the Vietnam War caused such an upheaval in the United States, I visited Vietnam and Cambodia with a small group led by an authority on Buddhism. I came back more convinced than ever before that we had had no business being involved in a war there, because the premise of the "domino effect" was wrong. I did not believe that if one country in Southeast Asia went Communist the rest would follow.

All during the trip I worried about my closest friend in Carderock, Erika Engelmann, who was dying of lymphoma. At every hotel, I found faxes about her condition from her son Martin, until I heard that she had died a few days before I was coming home. I could not quite imagine Carderock without Erika. I think of her every day and I miss her.

Retirement

Much of my travel occurred after I had retired at age seventy in 1992. My memory for names had started faltering, and I did not want to find myself in a position where I was unable to remember the names of the panel members whom I was introducing. This failing seemed to signal to me that I should give up my job and do something else where I could avoid potentially embarrassing situations. I prepared for my retirement quite carefully. Most important, I had groomed a successor to take over the Transition Program. By the time of my departure, I felt certain that my successor could carry on effectively without me. Without that assurance I might have found it hard to leave the program that was so dear to my heart.

Despite my strenuous objections—I do not like retirement parties—my colleagues insisted on hosting one for me. I must admit that I felt validated by the kind words and compliments I received from the many local and state officials as well as from MCPS administrators and colleagues.

After my retirement, MCPS asked me to serve as a consultant to develop the procedures for the school system's implementation of the ADA, the Americans with Disabilities Act of 1992. The project would involve establishing the steps that would make all school programs fully accessible, such as where to build wheelchair ramps or place signs in Braille, when to hire interpreters for the hearing impaired and how to accommodate a person's handicap on the job. Although I had decided that I would leave the field of disability completely, the opportunity was too tempting to ignore. As part of this project I had the chance to develop a videotape informing all school system staff of the requirements of the new law. This exhilarating experience opened a new horizon for me. My producer and I were both pleased and surprised when we received the 1994 Annual Award of Merit from the International Television-Video Festival.

Finally really leaving the field of disability, I began investigating other career directions. My longtime concern about the lack of civility in our classrooms and the inability of children to settle their disputes in a nonviolent manner led me to the field of conflict management. Few teachers were trained to model creative conflict-resolution behavior. I thought I would become an innovator and develop new courses for teachers. But as soon as I started to investigate the field, I found many courses, workshops and a number of organizations already engaged in such activities. They were not waiting for me! My research pointed me toward George Mason University in Fairfax, Virginia, which offered a doctoral program in conflict management. I started taking courses there and became completely absorbed in this newly found pursuit.

Violence Prevention

Unable to let much time pass without engaging in an activity where I would make a difference, I joined the Mental Health Association in Montgomery County and helped initiate Voices Versus Violence. VVV's mission was to coordinate the many public and private anti-violence activities in the county. Program volunteers also taught conflict-resolution strategies to youth and adults in such diverse places as schools, homeless shelters and churches. I attended conferences and workshops as a learner and speaker in this new endeavor. In addition to learning much, I made valuable new friends. My vast contacts in the Montgomery County school, government and business communities from my days in the school system proved helpful. People who knew me were willing to listen and support our cause. The groundswell against violence in the media mirrored public concern about the increasing level of violence in our communities. Children are not born violent. Violence is a learned behavior. Researchers had found that children who are bullies or are victims of bullying tend to become violent adults, contributing to the huge increase in spouse abuse, child abuse and crime. Clearly, the time had come to address this growing concern and raise public awareness about how to prevent further escalation of violence.

The same interest in reducing violence steered me to another organization. I became closely associated with the Youth Workers Training Committee of Montgomery County. This 25-year-old, all-volunteer public–private collaboration brings high-quality, low-cost training to the professionals who work with youth and their families. I helped organize conferences on such topics as "Young and Female," "Young and Male," or "How to Help Youth Build Resilience," always with violence reduction as a goal.

While I was involved with these activities, I did not neglect my physical well-being. I went to exercise classes twice a week, led by a skilled teacher from Colombia, South America. One day a man appeared in her class, a very unusual occurrence. I realized that the man and the teacher were somehow related, but I did not pay much attention until I heard the man say something and immediately recognized his Hungarian accent. My attention was tweaked when the teacher called him Papi, Spanish for dad. How could this Colombian woman have a Hungarian father who looked of an age to be her brother, but certainly not her father? I became intrigued and we started talking. This is how I met Ervin.

Ervin

Though our first meeting in the exercise class was two years earlier, I was 75 and Ervin almost 86 when we fell in love. We were both widowers. I was completely baffled by the onslaught of feelings that engulfed me, since I had not considered the possibility of another man in my life after Frank died. Even though I missed Frank, I had managed to have a full life. Unlike many women who lose a mate, I felt I was still a "whole" person, even without a man at my side. With loyal old friends and new friends whom I met through new activities, I kept as busy as I had been before I retired. I barely had time for the reading, gardening or listening to music to which I had looked forward. Yet I was lonely at times and so was Ervin. We grew close for many reasons that started with sharing our European origins.

Ervin Bognar grew up in Sopron, a small town in Hungary at the Austrian–Hungarian border. The region had previously belonged to Austria, and the inhabitants spoke both German and Hungarian. After Ervin's mother died when he was eight, he and his two older brothers remained under the care of their paternal grandmother. His father was a traveling watch and typewriter repairman who barely earned enough to support his family. The family lived in very modest circumstances in a cramped apartment with no bathroom, the toilet downstairs in a corner of the courtyard. The family was Jewish but observed Jewish customs only during the major Jewish holidays. As Ervin was musical, he sang in the synagogue choir before his voice changed.

By the time his grandmother died when he was in his early teens, the older brothers were already working in other towns. His father had married a non-Jewish Austrian woman and had moved to Austria. Ervin stayed by himself in the family apartment, where he was left to his own devices. A servant cooked his meals. He does not remember feeling lonely; he was busy studying and accepted the situation unquestioningly.

Always an excellent student, Ervin's goal was to become a textile engineer. The field sounded interesting and the employment outlook was good. After finishing high school, he was determined to go to the Textile University in Brno (Bruenn), Czechoslovakia; Hungary had no university-level school of textile engineering. His father objected strenuously because he could not afford to help him financially, but Ervin persevered. He went to work in a textile factory for a year both to save money and to fulfill a condition of enrollment in Brno. The university awarded him a full scholarship after the first few months.

The four years in Brno at a German-speaking university in a Czech town were good years for Ervin. He improved his German but never learned Czech. In addition to enjoying his studies, he found a compatible group of comrades among the Jewish students. The students were Zionists who met weekly to discuss Zionism and Jewish history. They also collected money for the Jewish National Fund to buy land in Palestine for Jewish settlers.

In 1934 after obtaining his degree, Ervin returned to Hungary. The textile factory where he had worked during the pre-university year was glad to have him back now as a full-fledged textile engineer. After a couple of years he had to fulfill his obligatory draft requirements by spending a year in the Hungarian army. He was assigned to a general maintenance battalion, where technicians tested weapons and repaired hardware and other military equipment. Ervin assisted the lieutenant in charge in managing the repair activities. Since he was able to spend frequent furloughs either at a lakeside resort or in Budapest, he returned to his job with fond memories of the year in uniform. Resuming his duties in the textile factory, he advanced rapidly in his career.

But life in Hungary was tenuous for a Jew. Hitler's anti-Semitic ravings fell on fertile ground in Hungary, with its long history of latent anti-Semitism. Ervin realized that his future there was circumscribed. Yet he was the only one in his family who was thinking of emigrating. Like the majority of the Hungarian Jews, the others played ostrich and denied the danger. They thought that Ervin was foolish to give up the good position he had.

But Ervin was undeterred, especially after 1938, when his father and his non-Jewish stepmother were harassed and expelled from their small town in Austria. Forced to leave everything behind to avoid arrest, they arrived back in Sopron with one suitcase. Ervin increased efforts to find a country that would give him asylum. Fortunately, his then fiancée had a sister in Colombia who was able to send them entry visas. His uncle loaned him enough money for the trip. So Ervin, now married, with his new wife, Dusi (pronounced Duh-she), and her mother, set out for Genoa, from there to sail to Colombia. His father and one of his brothers who came to Genoa to say goodbye to them were not interested in leaving Hungary.

All sorts of cliffhanger experiences held back their departure, including canceled sailings, lost ship-passage deposits in scarce U.S. currency, inadequate funds and scary threats. Finally, on the day France declared war against Germany in August 1939, Ervin and the two women boarded a ship bound for Colombia.

Ervin's father survived the war in Hungary with the help of his non-Jewish wife; one of Ervin's brothers eventually perished in Auschwitz and the other brother died during the war while fighting on the Russian front. The Hungarian pro-Nazi government had coerced Hungarian Jewish men into serving in forced-labor battalions. As a contribution to the German war effort, the battalion to which Ervin's brother belonged was sent to Germany's Eastern front to stem a Russian attack. Not one returned.

Ervin and his new family arrived safely in Colombia and began a new life. Colombia, just then beginning to build its now important textile industry, welcomed his professional experience. He worked for one textile enterprise for 27 years managing factories with more than 2,000 employees. Especially valued because he was eager to keep up with new worldwide developments in textile manufacturing, he brought innovative methods to Colombia.

Life in Colombia was good for the Bognars. They had a daughter, Alicia, born soon after their arrival and a son, Fredi, four years later. Dusi, an excellent seamstress, sewed most of the children's clothing, while her mother took care of the children and used her considerable culinary skills to prepare renowned Hungarian delicacies. Sunday lunches at the Bognars became a treat for the Hungarian refugee community in Bogota.

At that time Colombia had a stable government, and economic development was proceeding at an encouraging rate. Cultural life in Bogota was just beginning to flourish. The new immigrants brought some of their own cultural interests with them, but compared with the more developed intellectual communities, little was going on to stimulate the mind. Ervin was interested in music and attended whatever performances were given. He even once sang in a production of *Die Fledermaus*. By and large, Ervin lived the life of the South American gentleman who earned a good living for his family in a management position and who left home repair and household chores to the hired help; well-to-do South American men never dirtied their hands. Ervin and his family led privileged lives there.

After the war, he brought his father and stepmother to Colombia. He helped his father set up a watch sales and repairs business that his father kept going until his death in 1950.

In 1966, when Ervin was 55, an American company bought the factory where he was working. The new owners were not willing to match the salary he had been receiving. Since the political situation in Colombia had started to deteriorate, Ervin decided to leave both the country and the firm rather than put up with changed working conditions and political instability. Immediately he found satisfactory work in a large textile factory in Maracai, Venezuela, an industrial city not far from the capital, Caracas. He retired at age seventy in 1981, shortly after his son died unexpectedly and tragically. His daughter, Alicia, with her husband and two children, had earlier moved to Washington, where her husband worked for the World Bank. Ready to make a new life for themselves in retirement, Dusi and Ervin decided to follow Alicia to Washington.

The Bognars bought an apartment in the building where Alicia lived and led a quiet existence close to Alicia's Spanish-speaking family. Though they had little need to speak English, they attended ESOL (English for Speakers of Other Languages) classes. Dusi, herself an excellent cook, was busy at home preparing food for the whole family. Ervin took a job in the accounting department of the Sears Company. Unfortunately, Dusi soon started having persistent health problems. She eventually succumbed unexpectedly in 1993 during heart surgery. After her mother's death, Alicia—who had meanwhile become a successful exercise teacher—urged her father to attend her exercise classes. She wanted him to remain healthy and get out among people to attenuate the loneliness.

We came to know each other casually through the exercise classes. Sometimes, because he was good company, I invited Ervin for lunch or to join me when I had a spare concert ticket. Since he did not drive at night, he was always eager to find someone who would act as chauffeur. During these occasional get-togethers I found out a lot about him by using my often-maligned yet effective "district attorney" questioning habits. Assisted by knowledge gained during my stay in Argentina, I was able to picture the South American environment in which he had lived. Understanding his Hungarian background from my time in Hungary also helped me to size him up. My knowledge of Spanish and Hungarian eased our communication, because Ervin was and still is much more articulate in Hungarian than in English. Though not so inquisitive as I, he had his own way of figuring me out. Despite these many commonalities, I did not envision more than a friendship, and frankly, I did not much like being his night driver! And then two years later something changed.

The attraction became intense and mutual. I thought long and hard about the future of our relationship, wondering whether it could become permanent. My heart said to take the risk, while my head warned me about taking up with a man of 86, even if he did not look and act his age. Ervin kept warning me, questioning whether I was really aware of the chance that he could become ill or incapacitated. Was I sure that I understood what such a commitment meant? When my daughter-in-law Jennifer heard that Ervin was going to move to my house, she wrote us a note saying, "A woman needs a man like a fish needs a bicycle," a new expression to us that made us laugh. She was right that I did not need another man, but my feelings led me to the conclusion that I needed this one.

My decision to marry Frank in 1953 had been primarily an intellectual one. Deciding to link up with Ervin in 1996 flowed mainly from listening to my heart. I was puzzled by my own readiness to respond positively to this unexpected development. I knew him well enough to know that certain of his habits would disturb me but that I could cope with them. I was willing to make compromises. He is cautious, very slow-moving and deliberate, whereas I tend to be quick and act on the spur of the moment. I am always in a hurry and he is incapable of rushing. The difference in tempo or life rhythm is real and requires both of us to adapt to each other. We were prepared to make the adjustments because we felt so close to each other.

My brothers first suggested our being friends but not living together, afraid that merging our lives would be too stressful. But once we had committed ourselves, Ervin and I found it a strain to live apart. Aware of our ages, how long could either of us expect to live? I believed that even if we had only a year or two together we would be richer for the experience. I cut back considerably on my activities because I wanted to have time for our life together. Furthermore, after five years of single life, I gave up my free-roaming bachelor habits and got used to preparing real meals again every night!

Paul and Anne were surprised but pleased that I was no longer going to live alone. Paul was living in Yonkers, close to the Hudson River and Riverdale, not far from Manhattan. He has been working as a planner in the family medicine division of the Montefiore Hospital in the Bronx since 1991. Initially he was responsible for writing grants to obtain funding for drop-in health clinics in the Bronx, one of the most medically underserved communities in the United States. Subsequently, the hospital charged him with all the planning for the construction and staffing of the centers before turning them over to clinical staff. In addition, he coordinates the network of service providers to AIDS patients in the Bronx. His wife, Jennifer, has been a family physician in a community health center not far from their home. On visits there, Ervin and I enjoy watching the development of their two daughters—Lynn, born in 1989, and Rita, born in 1993. We delight in seeing the devotion with which Paul and Jennifer treat their children.

Living by herself in her lovely house in Silver Spring, a few miles east of Bethesda, and only about twenty minutes away from me, Anne continues to produce beautiful pots and bowls. Some of our friends encourage her to sell her pottery, but she says she is not interested. Having expanded her culinary repertoire, Anne frequently caters my dinner parties and guests often ask her for her recipes. Usually she replies she does not use any, cooking instead by instinct. Generally very helpful to me, she takes on chores, runs errands and sleuths out hard-to-find items, such as a particular brand of tea that I could not find anywhere. When her nieces come to visit, she takes them to the fun places around Washington. They much prefer outings with Anne to the stodgy sightseeing to which I expose them.

Anne is very protective of Ervin. She was amazed that I have been able to be so patient with him and so willing to accept him uncritically. She has become good friends with Ervin's grandson, Ricardo, and his wife, Cecile, who live not far from us with their two children, Gabriel and Maelys. When she is in town, Anne also sees Ervin's granddaughter, Monica, who lives in San Diego with her Navy officer husband and their three little girls. I am pleased to see Anne enjoying the new family birthday celebrations, which occur quite frequently. When the party is at our house, Anne caters the entire party most efficiently. We all appreciate her home-made contributions.

Ervin was surprised to discover the many museums, theaters, concerts and lecture opportunities that he had missed all the years here before we met. I have been constantly amazed at his openness to new experiences, always prepared to go with me to odd happenings that I find interesting, outlandish plays or even county council meetings that have no relevance for him. He was and continues to be willing to attend dinner parties even where he finds it difficult to understand the conversation. Though much improved, his English is still not up to the intellectual conversations across the table, especially about American topics that are totally new to him. He goes to lectures at the Jewish Community Center twice a week and comes home eager to share what he has learned. I enjoy listening to him when he recounts interesting details about music, Jewish history and the Jewish experience in America.

Both of us have been eager to travel. We have taken many interesting trips around the United States, to Europe and Mexico; most of them were as members of a tour group, because the kind of vagabond travel I had been used to was becoming too strenuous. On our own we went to Hungary to visit the places of Ervin's youth. I learned more about his background when we visited places that had been important to him, such as the field where he played soccer or the synagogue, though merely a shell of its former self. We tried to find the factories where he worked, but they are all gone now. These visits underscored for us how his life had changed because he had had the courage to leave when he did and how much better off he has been since.

I was pleased to show him the patrician house in Budapest where I had lived in 1948 with Otmar as the wife of an American diplomat. The elegant mansion was barely recognizable. The police station and the porte cochere were unrecognizable, converted like the rest of the building into small apartments. The former stately mansion looked as shabby as all state-owned houses that had not been repainted or maintained during the Communist regime.

We also visited my beloved Alt Aussee. What fun it was to introduce Ervin to the places of my childhood that still have special meaning for me! Fortunately, the weather was good and the sunshine made the lake sparkle. The meadows were full of bright yellow wild daffodils, and he was dazzled by the splendor of the view from our former home. Every time I revisit Alt Aussee I am again struck by the beauty of the setting, which I still consider the epitome of mountain scenery. When we returned to Bethesda from that trip that had included a barge trip through Holland and Belgium and a music tour of Scandinavia, I was thrilled when Ervin said that he had liked being in Alt Aussee best of all.

Another time we went to East and West Germany, with a stopover in Prague. I showed him the various places where I had lived as a child, especially our former villa. Although everything in Prague seemed smaller to me than I had remembered, the villa still seemed impressively large. We also visited my father's grave and found to our astonishment that the cemetery now uses computers to identify gravesites. When I was there in the 1960s, the cemetery was such an overgrown jungle that it was not possible to find the grave. Since the fall of the Communist government, the Czech Jewish community with help from Czech Jews living abroad has restored the cemetery very nicely. In Prague I also visited friends with whom I had not been in contact for years and shared with Ervin the joy of renewing old ties.

Although we both feel the encroaching years—Ervin walks with a cane and I have trouble with my knee—we feel blessed that we have such a loving and harmonious relationship at this stage in life, when so many of our contemporaries face their end. This feeling was brought poignantly home to us when Ervin, Anne and I visited Bruno in Ontario as he was dying of cancer. Brother Paul, who was in Europe at the time, also came to be with him.

Bruno's Death

Bruno died as he had lived, in control of the situation. He showed us the wooden box for his ashes that he had carved himself and explained all the funeral plans in detail, assuring us that he felt at peace and was unafraid of dying.

When Paul and I were together in Canada before Bruno died, Paul launched the idea of an all-family get-together to celebrate my 80th birthday in February 2002. He liked to plan years ahead. The get-together would also honor Ervin, who would reach ninety in June 2001, and Paul, who would be 87 in November 2001. The only time the whole Morawetz family—Mother, her four children, their spouses and offspring—had been together was in 1967 in Canada, almost 35 years earlier. Since then, Mother's grandchildren had grown up and married, and many have children of their own who do not know each other, dispersed as they are in Australia, Spain, the United States and Canada. Both Paul and I thought it was important to enable the younger generation to forge family ties in the hope that they will want to maintain family cohesion from generation to generation. We decided to schedule the big reunion for late 2001, December being the only time that all children everywhere are out of school. We agreed to look for a resort in relatively easily accessible Mexico with activities for all ages, from six months to ninety. We also agreed to co-host the party and invite the entire family. What better way to celebrate!

Soon after returning from Canada, I started searching for a suitable place. During frequent phone conversations with Paul, who was traveling around the world, I consulted with him about all the details. I carried out the agreed-upon plans because I knew that he was not well. He had had a serious heart condition for many years but had refused to change his lifestyle because of it. He just continued circling the globe, smoking cigars and eating high-cholesterol smoked salmon and soft-boiled eggs for breakfast. Although upset that his memory was getting worse due to a stroke he had had a few years earlier, Paul still played bridge and went to concerts. In the spring of 2001 when he returned to Melbourne, he started fading. His greatest joy was to be with his seven grandchildren, whom he saw frequently. When discussing the plans for our get-together, I told him that I worried about one of us not making it to Mexico. He kept insisting that as long as I could go, the "extravaganza" was on. I listened to him and continued planning our gathering.

Paul's Death

My apprehension was justified. I was not surprised when Judy, Paul's daughter, called on April 28, 2001, from Melbourne to say that Paul had passed away. She told me that Paul had died instantly of a heart attack at home. His son, daughter-in-law and grandson were there to pick him up when he collapsed. I was relieved that he did not die on an airplane somewhere over the Pacific as I had often imagined. He was buried in Melbourne near his daughter Anita, who had died of a brain tumor in 1989, a few months before Frank. A few weeks later, the family held a memorial service for Paul in Melbourne for which I wrote a eulogy. I stressed how close Paul and I had become after we became re-acquainted as adults in Canada in 1946. We shared many characteristics: we took risks; we were extroverts, impatient, eager to see new places and intent on making a difference in the world. He and I were devoted to each other because, in many respects, we were soulmates.

Although Paul, Bruno and I never lived in the same place, we were very close and I mourned them deeply. Ervin was wonderful to me; he understood my pain and his presence was like balm for which I am sincerely grateful.

As the only survivor of my generation in my family, I have been eager to keep the family ties alive. Throughout the eight years that Mother lived with us, I arranged all the family get-togethers and meetings, but she was the center of attraction; I just managed the logistics. She always told me that I would inherit the mantle, and I laughed it off. Now my turn has come to encourage the younger generation to take over from me and continue to nurture our family ties, these bonds that strengthen us all.

EPILOGUE

I HAVE NOW SPENT more than two years thinking and writing about my past and how best to describe it so that it makes sense to the generations that come after me. I also want to understand how I came to be who I am, and what shaped the values I hold so dear.

I am lucky to have lived this life. Born with a silver spoon in my mouth to an exceptionally demanding though loving mother, I was a sheltered child. I lived by the mores of the larger society as well as by Mother's more exacting rules. Living up to her expectations meant practicing self-discipline, loving learning, appreciating the arts and being courageous.

Mother's expectation that I was going to become somebody was deeply embedded in my consciousness before the privileged life evaporated. Thus I found it easy to adapt from rich to poor when I became a refugee. Not having money simply meant that I had no money; it never meant that I was impoverished.

Though recognizing the advantages I derived from it, no longer having that silver spoon became a relief. I had been embarrassed by my privileged position. This awkward feeling helped awaken my later interest in social justice and my liberal political orientation.

I am not quite sure how I became a risk-taker, even before the advent of the circumstances that required it for survival. Beneath my conventional exterior, I must have felt sufficiently self-assured, trusting that I would triumph if I did not shy away from risks. I was always looking for new ways to

317

get to my destination. This sometimes led me into dark alleys but more often to well-lit paths.

By coming to the United States, I was able to break out of the mold for which I was destined. If I had stayed in Prague, my life would have been much more circumscribed, privately as well as professionally. Assuming responsibilities as a volunteer or employee would have been unthinkable without proper credentials. But Americans find it acceptable for people to try and fail, then pick themselves up and try again.

Living in so many different countries and places has contributed to life's lessons. Because I had to cope with varied situations to survive and be successful, I learned to find my way, both physically and metaphorically. I was able to connect with people who helped, and I was fortunate to be able to turn difficult circumstances into opportunities. Many times I was just plain lucky.

Two aspects about my life stand out for me: the frequent change of place and activity; and the ability to make friends and maintain relationships over long periods of time. The variety of activities flowed from the physical moves as well as from my eagerness to accept new challenges. The lasting relationships reflect my loyalty to people who are important in my life.

Throughout the years, many people have commented on my persistent interest in getting to know people I meet. While some people may have considered my inquisitiveness tactless, I believe that most people were glad to tell me about themselves. I have felt and continue to feel that if I want to be friends with someone, I must know who this person is. I do not ask questions of people who are irrelevant to me. My friends come from different walks of life, from different cultures and from different age groups; knowing them has enriched me. I think many feel the same way about me.

I believe that I have lived as fully as one can, and if I have regrets, they are overshadowed by successes. With age beginning to show its effects on me, I still have an unfinished agenda, such as filling some of the academic holes in my education and learning more about gardening. Time seems so precious that I hate to waste it, but Ervin is teaching me that just hanging out is not as sinful as I had thought for eighty years.

This memoir is my legacy. My great hope is that my children's generation will carry the story of this widespread family into the future.

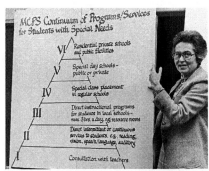

Margit at an MCPS presentation, 1981

*Frank with granddaughter Lynn,
3 weeks before his death, 1990*

Margit and Frank, 1980s

Paul, Felix, Bruno, Margit, Zurich, 1983

Margit and Ervin dancing in kitchen, 2000